MUSIC IN AMERICAN LIFE

Songprints

SONGPRINTS

The Musical Experience of
Five Shoshone Women

JUDITH VANDER

UNIVERSITY OF ILLINOIS PRESS

Urbana and Chicago

Illini Books edition, 1996
© 1988 by the Board of Trustees of the University of Illinois
Manufactured in the United States of America
P 5 4 3 2 1

This book is printed on acid-free paper.

Library of Congress Cataloging-in-Publication Data

Vander, Judith.
Songprints : the musical experience of five Shoshone women /
Judith Vander.
    p.   cm. — (Music in American life)
    Bibliography: p.
    Includes index.
    ISBN 0-252-06545-X (pbk. : alk. paper)
    1. Shoshone Indians—Music—History and criticism. 2. Indians of
North America—Great Plains—Music—History and criticism. 3. Sun-
dance. I. Title. II. Series.
ML3557.V36   1988
784.7'51—dc19   87-24488
                                                                      CIP
                                                                      MN

For Emily, Angelina, Alberta, Helene, and Lenore

To see a World in a Grain of Sand
And a Heaven in a Wild Flower
Hold Infinity in the palm of your hand
And Eternity in an hour

(Blake 1982:490)

Contents

Preface

The purpose of this book is to present the songs and musical experience of five Wind River Shoshone women: Emily Hill, Angelina Wagon, Alberta Roberts, Helene Furlong, and Lenore Shoyo. Each possesses her own song-print—a song repertoire distinctive to her culture, age, and personality, as unique in its configuration as a fingerprint or footprint. Five central chapters focus on the life histories, songs, and musical roles of these five women, allowing them to express in their own words thoughts about songs: issues of meaning, musical process, and musical perception. The principals range in age, almost by decade, from seventy to twenty, and their respective songprints and changing musical roles thus provide historical perspective on many aspects of twentieth-century Wind River Shoshone life. In-depth discussion of individual, cultural, and historical contexts, along with less exhaustive genre analyses and occasional analytical comments, help shed light on the songs and songprints.

The idea for this book and the selection of these five women stem from my first summer field trips on the reservation in 1977 and 1978. At that time I was gathering information on ceremonial music for my master's thesis. Although most of my interviews were with the male musicians who traditionally drum and sing ceremonial songs, I was curious to learn whether there might not be special or separate songs for women. (I knew from readings that women stayed in a small, separate dwelling during menstruation and after childbirth; did they have songs for these occasions?) Older women unanimously said, "No," to special songs in the menstrual hut and "No," to any separate songs for women. But a seed was planted: What sort of involvement did Shoshone women have in music?[1]

Music itself eventually led me to all five women. I observed the two youngest (Helene and Lenore) singing and drumming with their family drum groups during the powwow. Alberta was always part of the group of women singing for the Sun Dance. Angelina introduced herself to me and

1. See Koskoff 1987 for analytical discussions of the cultural identity and musical activity of women in many cultures.

asked for a copy of a Library of Congress tape that she heard I had; her father had been one of the singers on this tape. And I came to know Emily through her younger sister Millie, who proudly confided that her older sibling was a good singer with a large repertoire.

My research methodology for this study has been both pragmatic and eclectic and is based, essentially, on two different models. Adhering to the scientific ideals espoused by ethnomusicologists, I have tried to divest myself of ethnocentric prejudices and to seek an unbiased viewpoint. In traditional fashion I have been a participant observer over a long period of study, beginning in 1977 and 1978 and continuing in the summers of 1979–82, as I gathered material for this book.

During these years I attended the many important communal occasions that occurred during the summer. These included the Shoshone and Arapahoe powwows, Shoshone and Arapahoe Sun Dances, a variety of feasts and Giveaways honoring people for their accomplishments and in memory of dead relatives, and funerals of several Shoshone friends and their relatives. From the start I tried to help in some capacity. During my first summer I simply worked in the kitchen for the feasts that conclude all of the above occasions. This became a habit in the summers to come. I joined in a Handgame after the 1977 Sun Dance; Handgame soon became a yearly pleasure for me. I quickly realized that Shoshones appreciate participation in social events and activities. That I was not an Indian did not seem to matter. By 1978 I had acquired a shawl and moccasins, prerequisites for dancing in the powwow with my friends. I joined in some of the powwow games that year as well, playing on the winning tug-of-war team and the losing Shinny team. I signed up for the Handgame tournament during the 1979 Shoshone powwow and played on Alberta's team. In 1979 I traveled with Emily's sister, Millie Guina, to one of the largest powwows, Crow Fair in Montana, where we camped and enjoyed all the powwow "doings." I also attended the 1979 Ft. Hall Festival in Idaho, camping near Alberta and other Shoshone friends. My extended fieldwork through December 1979 allowed me to attend the Halloween dances and one of the holiday dances between Christmas and New Year's Day. As I became better acquainted with the five women and their families, I followed Shoshone customs concerning the Giveaway ceremony, participating in the dance, receiving gifts, and helping out with financial assistance to the family putting on the ceremony.

While attending the 1977 Shoshone Sun Dance and the three practice sessions and ceremonies that preceded it, I learned many Sun Dance songs. Consequently, I sang with the women in 1978 and every summer after that, gradually enlarging my knowledge of the ceremony and its musical repertoire. I extended my Sun Dance experience by camping on the Sun Dance grounds in 1979 with Emily's sister, and in 1982 with Alberta's family. All in all it was a long, intense, exciting period of my life — a second cultural childhood with growing pains.

Over the years I have taped many songs at some of these occasions. These experiences and songs were my introduction and indoctrination into Shoshone culture, music, and society. The bulk of my work for this book, however, has taken place in private taped sessions with the five women.

Again, following scientific methods, I concerned myself with such things as sample size and representation. Did I record enough songs from each woman? Did the proportion of different song genres in my sample accurately reflect those in the elusive "complete" repertoire? Of necessity, sensitivity and pragmatism tempered these considerations. The actual selection of songs I have recorded follows both the choice and conscience of each woman. Thus, although four of the five know Peyote songs, none felt comfortable to sing them for me.

But it is precisely on the issue of sample size that this study departs from scientific methodology, for my analysis rests on the songs of only one woman in her seventies, one in her sixties, one in her fifties, one in her forties, and one in her twenties. Each woman is unique. In this regard I have followed a second model — that used in Western art and literature. When Cézanne painted a pear or Rembrandt a self-portrait as an old man, the picture depicted one of a kind — a particular pear, a particular old man. And yet at the same time there is an evocation of something larger than the individual; there is something of "pearness," something of old age itself. In like manner, although I have worked intensively with only five individuals, and although I well know how Emily differs from other seventy-year-old women, and Lenore from other twenty-year-old women, their songs and musical lives suggest something larger than themselves. "No man is an *Iland, intire of it selfe; every man is a peece of the Continent, a part of the maine*" (Donne 1952:441). The tension between the individual or the particular and the general or broader abstraction, integral to Western art and literature, is embraced in this study. However, aware of the dangers of oversimplification inherent in this approach, I also point out some of the idiosyncratic characteristics of each woman and how she differs from her peers.

Although I remain sole author of this book, it has been a collaborative effort. The collaboration is very evident in the text itself. As much as possible I allow the women to speak for themselves with the hope of preserving their distinct voices and some of the nuances of meaning that disappear when reshaped and spoken by me.[2] Consistent with this attempt to preserve the distinctive speech of each woman is the choice of all five to use their own names. (All interviews were conducted in English, since even the oldest Shoshones on the reservation today are completely fluent in English.)

My approach to writing this book closely parallels and reflects my method of conducting research. In essence I asked for the performance of songs, which then became a springboard for a great variety of questions: Why did you choose this song? How did you learn it? Where? Why do you like it? What makes it a good song? Did you like the performance of it? Why? My questions ranged from the particularities of a song and its performance to discussions of genre and to broader questions about the particular occasion for which the song is performed. In some places I have stitched together conversations on the same topic that may have actually occurred on different occasions. I also draw on and interpolate passages from my own log notes, always set off by brackets and indicated by a date followed by quotation marks. Although written in a fragmentary style, they often convey both information and feeling-tone of the moment. Finally, I have taken the liberty in a few places to include my own response to and interpretation of events I have witnessed. While not wishing to intrude, I feel that my viewpoint can serve as a foil to the Shoshone perspective.

Angie, Alberta, Helene, and Lenore have all reviewed the final draft of their chapters. Emily received a first draft in 1984. Her health then seriously declined, and she entered a nursing home in 1986. When I visited with her in the summer of 1986, I became painfully aware that her ability to see and hear was failing. I decided not to give her the final draft of her chapter at that time, for it seemed an empty and futile gesture. Emily died on January 14, 1988, after this book had gone to press; her chapter has not been altered, however, to reflect this fact.

My working relationship with the five women is long-standing. I interviewed Emily during the summers of 1977–82. I lived with her in 1982 and visited her in 1983 and 1984. I did not see her in 1985 when I stayed at the reservation because she was in a nursing home in Thermopolis. In 1986 we spent time together in the newly established nursing home on the reservation. My payment to Emily was always food, usually a large pot

---

2. "Is paraphrase possible? . . . Dwight Bollinger has spent most of his career showing that this is virtually impossible and that almost any change in a sentence — whether a change in word order, vocabulary, intonation, or grammatical construction — will alter the sentence's meaning, though often in a subtle way" (Lakoff and Johnson 1980:136).

of homemade stew and side dishes that she and her half-sister Dorothy enjoyed. When I lived with Emily, I bought groceries and paid her rent. I also assumed responsibility for providing her with transportation. Although I met Angie in 1978 and visited her after the death of her husband in 1979, I did not work with her until the summer of 1981, when I stayed at her home. We worked together intensively in 1981 and 1982. I had a long interview with her in 1983, and in 1984 she allowed me to make a copy of a 1952 photograph of her and her late husband. I called on Angie briefly in 1985 and 1986. Angie received payment for all interviews and for rent and food while I lived with her. Alberta and I became friends in 1977 and 1978. Our first interviews took place in 1979 and continued in 1981 and 1982. I resided with Alberta and her family during part of the summer of 1982 and was her guest again in 1984. In 1986 we sat together and sang for the Shoshone Sun Dance. Alberta received payment for all interviews and for rent and food in 1982. Whenever necessary I also provided her with transportation. I met Helene in 1977. A teacher by nature and profession, Helene responded enthusiastically to interviews. We worked on many occasions each summer from 1977 to 1981. I lived with her in 1982 at her home in Crowheart while the Crowheart Powwow was in progress. I paid Helene for rent and food while lodging with her. Initially, Helene and I swapped songs and information. She sang songs and answered questions about Shoshone music, and I gave her guitar lessons and taught her children's songs appropriate for her Head Start students. After I formally began work on the research for this book, I paid Helene for interviews. I visited her in the summers of 1983–85; in 1986 we could only chat by phone since she was living in Nevada. I met Lenore in 1977 and had my first singing lessons around the drum with her and her sisters in early July. I recorded songs from Lenore with various members of the Shoyo family drum group in 1977–81, 1983, and 1984. I interviewed her in 1978, 1979, 1981, and 1983. In 1983 the Shoyo family and I presented a joint lecture-demonstration at the Plains Indian Museum in Cody, Wyoming. I took pictures of Lenore in 1984 and visited with her at her home in 1986. I paid Lenore and her sisters for all interviews and private song recording sessions.

Above and beyond these working arrangements with the women were the personal friendships that developed as the years passed. Our gifts to one another — shawls, beadwork, dress fabric, photographs, books, and music tapes — expressed the growing bonds between us. It is my hope that this book captures some of the enthusiasm for the work we shared together and reflects my deep respect and regard for all five women.

Before plunging into the mosaiclike details of each woman's repertoire and musical life, let me suggest in broad strokes some of the overall findings of this study. First, there are no special song genres for women. I come to this conclusion from my interviews with many Shoshones, not just the five women in this book. While tiny lullaby-ostinato patterns exist, for the most part there are no lullabies. Second, all five women document a strong musical role for women in social, religious, and ceremonial contexts, one that is both differentiated from and complementary to the male musical role. In this century there has been an enlargement of female musical roles, including movement into what were formerly and exclusively male domains. Third, historical perspective reveals a continually evolving balance and synthesis of change and continuity.

Change is very evident in a comparison of the five song repertoires. That the oldest woman sings 147 Ghost Dance songs and 2 War Dance songs, whereas the youngest sings no Ghost Dance songs and 59 War Dance songs, tells us something not only about the demise of the Ghost Dance religion but about the changing musical role of the younger woman: only since the early 1970s have Shoshone women disregarded an older taboo that prohibited them from singing and drumming War Dance songs at the drum. Yet, while there are striking differences in the song repertoires and musical roles of all five women, there is great constancy and continuity in matters of musical process, perception, and meaning — such things as song learning, recall, composition, conceptualization of music in linear-spatial terms, criteria for a "good" song, and notions of the relationship between sacred power and song. The repetition of similar statements by all five women in each chapter documents this.

The balance between change and continuity is not only over time but also within each woman. Each perceives herself as a traditional person, and yet, in one way or another, each has crossed invisible cultural boundaries and participated in cultural change. The recognized traditional status of each woman and her family and, in several instances, the strong support of male family members are important factors in the community acceptance of new musical roles for women. Community acceptance, in turn, buttresses each woman's strong self-identification with traditional mainstream Shoshone life.

Because much of this study rests on the song repertoire of each woman, it is essential to say a few words on the elusiveness of such repertoires in general. Like all natural processes subject to the element of time, song repertoires are continually building up and breaking down. Old songs fall into disuse, erode, and are eventually forgotten. New ones are learned. At the center is a stable core of songs that, for whatever reasons, are learned and retained for a lifetime. There are also varying relationships to songs, including the passive recognition but inability to sing one, the ability to sing one if someone else starts it or it is heard, and the ability to sing with no outside assistance. Forgetting–learning and passive–active are two continua through which songs pass and that place limitations on song collection. One taps into a repertoire at a certain point in someone's life and receives a musical profile for that particular time, but not for a lifetime.

Even within the limitations of tapping into the songs of the five women during several years of work, I have not recorded all the songs that they knew and could sing at that time. Also, the proportion of songs recorded from each repertoire varies. Several factors account for this. I have known and worked with all five women for unequal lengths and amounts of time. Then, too, because we all have different personalities and lives, my relationship and work with each of them has been different. I am part of a variable that I can neither totally control nor standardize. Nevertheless, I do believe the songs recorded and transcribed (213 by Emily, 32 by Angie, 80 by Helene, 93 by Lenore) are reasonable representations of their repertoires.[3] (Alberta's recorded performance of only 14 songs is a special case that I discuss in her chapter.) In each chapter I will present a liberal sampling from this large collection of recordings and transcriptions.

There are fourteen distinct song genres represented in the five repertoires: Ghost Dance, Sun Dance, Peyote, Flag, Honor, War Dance (both the Traditional or Straight War Dance and the Fancy War Dance), Round Dance, Forty-nine, Crow Hop, Handgame, and Shoshone ceremonial songs together with hymns, country-and-western songs, lullabies, and children's songs. I classify the first eleven genres, which are Indian, into three basic categories: songs for social occasions (powwows, community dances, and Handgames), songs for religious occasions (Ghost Dance, Sun Dance, and Native American Church), and songs that accompany ceremonies unique to the Shoshone (Pointing Stick, War Bonnet, Chokecherry, and Giveaway).[4] (There will be no further mention of the Pointing Stick ceremony, last performed in 1968.

3. The issue of repertoire size remains uncharted and needs more data for comparison. See Nettl for a brief discussion of this topic, with specific reference to the repertoire size of Plains Indian singers (Nettl 1983:286, 287).

4. Descriptions of Wind River Shoshone ceremonies with accompanying musical transcriptions and analyses are in Vander's 1978 master's thesis. Willard Rhodes's 1951 recording of the following ceremonial songs is on file at the Archive of Folk Culture in the Library of Congress: three War Bonnet songs, one Giveaway song, AFS 14,618B; and a Pointing Stick song, AFS 14,619A. War Bonnet, Chokecherry, and Giveaway songs are also available on *18 Shoshone Songs,* Indian Records IR 1165. (The latter is also on file at the Archives of Traditional Music, Indiana University.)

In 1985 the sole caretaker with complete knowledge of the ceremony died, leaving behind no inheritors.) These last ceremonies, while religious, do not have the larger scope and structure of a religion per se. For this reason I classify them separately from Ghost Dance, Sun Dance, and Native American Church songs. Actually, religious feelings, associations, and meanings may touch any of the pieces Shoshone sing.

The five women have all felt comfortable talking to me about the Sun Dance and its music and, in varying degrees, the Native American Church and its music. I include this material in each chapter. However, because they and many Shoshones feel sensitive about the actual songs performed at Sun Dances, I have not included in this book musical transcriptions from this religious repertoire, although I have, in fact, recorded all five women singing representative examples. For the same reason I omit two ceremonial songs that I have also recorded. My inclusion of Shoshone Ghost Dance songs that used to accompany this religious dance is a special case. (The last religious performances on the reservation of this dance took place in the 1930s.) Emily, to my knowledge, is the only person on the reservation today who believes in this religion. Between 1977 and 1979 I recorded Emily and the late Dorothy Tappay, Emily's half-sister, singing seventeen Ghost Dance songs. They discussed at great length the meaning of the religion and the songs they sang for me. By 1980 both women found it physically difficult to sing. Unexpectedly, Emily brought out tapes that she and Dorothy had made over the years and allowed me to make copies of them. Thus, in the summers of 1980 and again in 1981, I acquired an additional 130 songs. Emily worked intensively with me in 1981 and 1982, going over the translation and meaning of the song texts. In this way I was entrusted with the preservation of a precious piece of Shoshone cultural history. This book along with an earlier publication (Vander 1986) are part of the fulfillment of my obligation to this material and to Emily.

Today, Shoshones only consider Ghost Dance songs with Shoshone texts, Sun Dance songs, and Shoshone ceremonial songs as indigenous to their culture. The rest are part of a large repertoire shared by many tribes on the Northern Plains. However, the oldest two women remember older Shoshone songs no longer in currency. Their repertoires include Shoshone Wolf Dance songs (the older term for Traditional War Dance songs), Shoshone Women's Dance songs (the older term for Round Dance songs), and Shoshone Handgame songs.

Song genres in and of themselves are not the principal subject of this book. Nevertheless, their profiles emerge and build as we move from woman to woman and songprint to songprint. Therefore, if one wished to focus on a particular genre rather than a particular woman, one could read the book selectively according to song genres (see index). Furthermore this book is not meant to be an anthropological study of women per se. But as with song genres, a wealth of material—in this case the biographical background that surrounds the music and musical experience of each woman—accrues from chapter to chapter and provides much relevant information in this area.

Acknowledgments

This book would not have been possible without the generous friendship of all five women. I thank Emily Hill, Angelina Wagon, Alberta Roberts, Helene Furlong, and Lenore Shoyo for patiently enduring years of interviews and questions. They and their families warmly welcomed me into their homes, introducing me to Shoshone hospitality and humor. I acknowledge my debt of thanks to the five women and, appropriately, have arranged for all book royalties to be paid to them.

I also wish to thank some of my many Shoshone teachers who have taken great pains over the years to school me in Shoshone music, language, and culture: Richard Engavo, Rupert Weeks, Val Norman, Charles Nipwater, Wayland Bonatsie, the Shoyos (Harrison, Ben, Bunny, JoAnn, Coleen, and Linda), Valeria Arkinson, Millie Guina, Dorothy Tappay, Ethel Tillman, Gladys Hill, and Malinda Tidzump. I thank former tribal chairman Bob Harris and the Wind River Shoshone community for their longstanding support and encouragement.

Within the scholarly community I am indebted to ethnomusicologists Judith Becker and William Malm for their guidance and assistance in my earlier research and master's thesis on Shoshone ceremonial music. Anthropologist and Shoshone specialist Demitri Shimkin has been my principal advisor on Shoshone culture throughout the years. I gratefully thank him for all the time and effort he has devoted to critically reviewing every aspect of my work. I thank Charlotte Frisbie for her thoughtful and careful critique of the entire manuscript and William Powers, who reviewed selected sections on powwow music and dance. The early interest and advice of Judith McCulloh at the University of Illinois Press and the superb editing by Aaron Appelstein were invaluable assets.

I could not have sustained and carried out this project without the wholehearted support of my husband, Arthur. His intellectual, psychological, and financial input kept me sane and solvent. The book and I have also richly benefited from his writing and editorial expertise. Personal friendships with the Greeves family and Carolyn Hebb, who live on the Wind

River reservation, also deserve mention here. Their warmth and kindness helped me over rough spots along the way.

Finally, I express my deep gratitude to the National Endowment for the Humanities, which helped make this work possible through a grant from the Division of Research Programs.

I gratefully acknowledge all the many people who helped bring this project to fruition; however, I alone assume responsibility for any of its errors, factual and interpretative.

Note on Orthography

(Correspondence with English vowels are only approximate.)

a		as in f*a*ther
ä (æ)		as in b*a*t
e		as in p*ay*
ĕ (ə)		as in *a*bove
i		as in el*i*te
ï (ι)		as in s*i*t
o		as in n*o*
ò (ɔ)		as in l*a*w
u		as in l*u*te
ü (ω)		as in p*u*t
ai		as in Th*ai*land
oi		as in n*oi*se
E, I		final whispered vowels
~		nasalization
ʔ		glottal stop
ʒ		as in gara*g*e

Accent generally falls on the first syllable and every other syllable after that.

(See Shimkin 1949a and Shimkin 1949b for Wind River Shoshone linguistic analysis.)

xxiii

Key to Musical Transcriptions

B♭ throughout song with no implication of scale or key

↓ or ↑   Pitch lowered or raised by no more than a quarter tone

Slightly accented attack from above and portamento into note

Attack from below and portamento into note

Note released by portamento fading down to an indefinite pitch

Portamento between notes

A partially spoken tone

$\frac{3}{8}$'s   ♪ = one beat, underlying rhythmic organization of threes (or multiples thereof) but not invariable, and with no implied barline/accent pattern

$\frac{2}{4}$'s   ♩ = one beat, underlying rhythmic organization of twos (or multiples thereof) but not invariable, and with no implied barline/accent pattern

$\frac{3}{8}$'s   e - vïn   Notehead slurs: indicate that a word, syllable, or vocable sustains through the music until the next word, syllable, or vocable appears

$\frac{2}{4}$'s   ha wi yo—   Stem slurs: indicate musical phrasing

ö ,   Pulsations on a tone without breaking the tone

xxv

♪♪ ♪♪ ♪♪ x x x	Another representation of pulsation
♩.＿♩. x	One pulse on the first beat of the second note
>	Accent
(>)	Lesser accent
⌐♪	Softer dynamic level for smaller notehead
A, B, C, etc.	Sections of song
A′, B′, etc.	Standardized variant forms of a musical section
≣|	Marks the end of a musical section
,	Brief rest for breath without direct rhythmic significance
(o)	Original starting pitch

Introduction

The approximately 2,400 enrolled Shoshones who today live on the Wind River reservation in west-central Wyoming are but one part of a large group who originated in the Southwest. (Shoshones belong to the Uto-Aztecan linguistic family.) Only the Western Shoshones in California and Nevada remain near their ancestral origins. One group of the original Shoshones moved north into Idaho and are now often referred to as the Northern Shoshones. In contrast, ancestors of the Wind River Shoshone migrated eastward, crossing the Rocky Mountains onto the Plains by at least the early 1500s (Shimkin 1940:20), hence their second name, Eastern Shoshones. In the early eighteenth century the Eastern Shoshones, in turn, split in two and one group moved south, eventually to become known as Comanches (Shimkin 1940:19). For all their disparate settlement and later cultural customs, the Great Basin was a common cradle for all Shoshones. The daily struggle for food and water in the Basin, a dry, harsh environment, left a mark on Shoshone culture. Shoshones name and distinguish different branches of their own people according to diet: Pine Nut Eaters, Salmon Eaters, Mountain Sheep Eaters, and (out on the Plains) Buffalo Eaters (Hoebel 1938:410–12). It is a mindset that endures in this century, as seen in the Wind River Shoshone names for the Native American Church: at first, Peyote Eaters (*Wogwedïka*) and later Medicine Eaters (*Natsïndïka*). We will see the continued concern for food and especially water in the Wind River Shoshone Ghost Dance song texts of the eldest woman.

But Great Basin culture seems as distant and foreign to Wind River Shoshones today as classical Greek and Roman cultures seem to Euro-Americans, and Shoshones now trace their history and traditions to Plains life and culture. They were among the first groups to acquire the horse on the Northern Plains in the early eighteenth century (Shimkin 1986:309). Mounted, the Shoshones successfully hunted the herds of bison that migrated across the Plains, and bison became the new dietary staple. Shoshone movement into the Plains in search of hunting grounds brought both contact

1

and conflict between the different tribes. Men earned prestige and high status through their prowess in hunting, warfare, and horse stealing. Shoshone domination on the Plains was short-lived, for the Blackfeet acquired arms in addition to horses and pushed the Shoshone west of the Rockies (Johnson 1975:26, 27). The Europeans, who introduced the horse and gun to the New World, also brought their families and culture, crossing the indigenous game paths and culture patterns in complex and ultimately destructive ways.

Chief Washakie, who gained prominence in the mid-nineteenth century, foresaw the inevitable decline of hunting grounds and bison herds and concluded that accommodation and friendly relations with the Euro-Americans were the best strategies for Shoshone survival. In 1868 Washakie and other Shoshone leaders signed with the United States government a treaty that set aside a portion of traditional Shoshone territory for their reservation. This treaty also included provisions for farm equipment and seeds, the beginning of the more recent cultural stratum of settled reservation life.

The period 1885-1905 was a cruel time for the Shoshones, an era of privation, sickness, and traumatic change. The buffalo were gone; the government placed the Northern Arapahoes, traditional enemy of the Shoshone, on the reservation; government rations were lowered; agricultural attempts that had at first flourished subsequently failed; and a measles epidemic brought death to many Shoshone children (Shimkin 1942:454, 455). As the old ways and beliefs crumbled, Shoshones looked for new values and traditions. Some were influenced by Mormon proselytizing, whereas others were receptive to the teaching of the Reverend John Roberts (as a result of the latter's long-standing efforts, most Shoshones are baptized Episcopalian). The establishment by the United States government of a boarding school in 1886 brought further inroads of Euro-American cultural domination (Shimkin 1942:455, 456).

During this time Shoshones sought contacts with a variety of other tribes, including the Crow, Comanche, Gros Ventre, and Cree. New religions—the Ghost Dance and Peyote—and new dances—the Women's Dance and Wolf Dance—grew out of the intertribal contacts. The Sun Dance was renewed, combining old beliefs and Christian symbolism, while addressing the grave problems of health and tribal disunity that marked the times. Beliefs forged in the heat of that painful time of cultural flux and physical hardship soon crystallized and cooled. They form the mold for Shoshone beliefs in the twentieth century (Vander 1986:3-5).

Early in this century Shoshones eked out a living through "stock raising, some farming (mostly alfalfa for livestock), some hunting and gathering, lease income, rations, and, for a very few people, some part-time employment" (Jorgensen 1972:96). Beginning in the 1940s an important contribution to Shoshone livelihood has come from the sale of natural resources on the reservation. The allotment of tribal income from natural gas and oil provides critical income in Shoshone households.

Reservation life has taken a particularly heavy toll on men. Hunting and warfare exist in the twentieth century but in reduced and different contexts. Today, hunting occurs in the autumn, to fill the larder with elk or deer, not buffalo. Shoshone men, who have fought in every American conflict in this century, carry forward traces of the older warrior tradition and high status of Plains life. But, clearly, hunting and warfare are no longer primary occupations. The problem in modern times is that farming, ranching, and jobs have become increasingly untenable or unavailable. Farming and ranching have become difficult because with each generation inherited property is divided and fragmented into smaller and smaller parcels. Jorgensen writes, "The distance from markets, poor soil, small and complicated landholdings, and lack of access to credit capital have discouraged Indians and helped sustain their apathy" (Jorgensen 1972:114). The job situation, too, is bleak. In 1977 a booklet at the Shoshone-Arapahoe Tribal Council building reported an unemployment rate that "varies from 45–55% of employable males" (Murray n.d.:31). Unemployment and underemployment are endemic problems on the reservation. There simply are not enough jobs for men.

Shoshone women, on the other hand, continue to fulfill age-old functions of feeding families, maintaining a home, and raising children. They still gather chokecherries, dry game meat, and do beadwork.[1] Beginning in 1947 the distribution of tribal earnings has added a new factor in female contribution to livelihood. Tribal royalties are divided equally among every enrolled tribal member, regardless of gender. Each family pools the per capita payments of its male and female members.

Per capita payment is but one of many social and historical factors influencing the place of women in Shoshone society today. In prereservation days when the nuclear family was the basic economic unit, there was a division of labor (DeRiso 1968:4). The roles of men and women were different

---

1. As regards gender, Shoshone adaptation of reservation life is but one example of a general pattern noted by Lurie: "Indian women seemed to have held up better under the stresses of reservation life than men and were often in the forefront of work in tribal councils and business committees. A possible explanation is that Indian males had suffered greater identity dislocation. The male roles of hunter, warrior and shaman had been destroyed but women still had children to be reared and domestic tasks to attend to" (Lurie 1972:33).

and complementary.[2] In her study of Shoshone female activism of the mid-1960s, DeRiso first quotes and then qualifies Shimkin's assessment that "prestige centered primarily around adult men" (Shimkin 1947b:312). "This is not to say that women were totally subjugated," DeRiso states, "or that they lacked means for gaining social respect but rather that the emphasis was on male activities" (DeRiso 1968:6, 7). Shimkin continued to observe the relative importance of men in Shoshone family and society even in 1937, well after Shoshone settlement on the reservation (Shimkin 1938). In addition to per capita payments, increased car ownership and road construction of the late 1940s contributed to a growing independence and mobility of Shoshone women. DeRiso suggests other factors that have influenced women's lives in recent times.

> The position of women in contemporary [i.e., 1966] Shoshone society has been achieved through the development of new roles derived from the surrounding White society and not through the assumption of male functions by women. [There are exceptions to this in Shoshone musical roles.] The institutional bases for these new roles are essentially non-Shoshone creations such as the public school and the 4-H clubs. . . . However, an important factor associated with female leadership in these areas is the desire to enhance and maintain the reservation as a *separate* community. Thus, what is ostensibly observed as acculturation is actually a mechanism for separatism rather than assimilation. (DeRiso 1968:1)

In an analogous manner we shall see in this study that affirmation of Indian identity helped validate and gain acceptance of new musical roles for Shoshone women. The background is now set for the foregrounds that follow.

2. Marla Powers documents similar findings in her study of another Northern Plains tribe, the Oglala Sioux: "There is an overwhelming agreement that the roles of men and women in traditional Oglala society were complementary" (Powers 1986:5).

Emily Hill

"I want you people to keep your songs, your Indian
songs. . . . Don't lose your songs. Don't lose your
Indian life. Keep up your Indian life. Keep up the
songs and dancing."
— Unidentified Indian man quoted by Emily Hill

Emily Hill has lived virtually her entire life on North Fork of the Little
Wind River, but she remembers her mother saying that she was born
someplace near Trout Creek. The exact location of birth remains unknown,
the date, November 1, 1911. About her birthplace Emily states, "I don't
know, maybe in the willows someplace. In those days Indians didn't go to
the hospital—they just have it out. Old people knows how to take care of
them."

Emily has no remembrance of her real father, for he died when she
was very young. Her mother then remarried, and the family grew, Emily
being the third of nine children. With pride Emily and her younger sister
Millie tell stories of their mother's grandmother, a "warrior woman," whose
bravery in combat and defiance of a famed Shoshone leader mistreating his
wife are part of a family inheritance passed down through the generations.

Interwoven with Emily's Wind River remembrances are details of tribal
history. In prereservation days the Wind River Shoshones were not a unified
tribe but a variety of individual bands who lived separately and had their
own distinctive ways. Emily's mother was a *Doiyai*, "mountain person."
Her father and stepfather were "dirt people who eat roots."[1]

Emily experienced the hard times of early twentieth-century reservation
life when Shoshones lived in tents and small log cabins. She remembers
eating bitterroot soup, whether it pleased her palate or not. And like most

1. Rupert Weeks, Wind River Shoshone author of a book of Shoshone stories, renders
the name of this band as *Hoo Coo Dic Kaw.* He translates it as Dirt Eaters (Weeks 1981:102).
The derivation for this word appears to be from *hukump,* "dust," and *dika,* "eat" (Tidzump
1970:5ES).

5

people of that time who lacked money, her family did not own cows; government rations of meat and other staples issued at the agency supplemented the daily diet. Circumstances schooled Emily to be thrifty; at home her mother taught gardening, religious beliefs, and the love of singing. Emily remained swaddled in an all-Shoshone environment until her sixth year, at which time her attendance at public boarding school on the reservation opened a new world and period in her life. As Emily recalls: "I think I went to school till I was eighteen. Didn't know a thing of white talks. Didn't know what they were talking about when they put me to school. It took me quite a while to learn that, white-man words. You can't even talk Shoshone in school! They're going to punish you. You can't talk Indian."

Indian singing was as forbidden as Indian talking. A 1902 newspaper article gives us a glimpse of the school's music program nine years before Emily was born:

> Closing Exercises of the Wind River Boarding School,
> Shoshone Agency, Wyoming, Wednesday, June 25, 1902

> The girls sang the national anthem in clear loud voices without a discord and the club drill to piano music showed that the youngsters had received the right kind of training. A class recitation by the girls with delsarte movements would have done credit to white pupils and their song "Tenting Tonight on the Old Camp Ground" accompanied by illustrations on the canvass was enthusiastically applauded.[2]

Despite the difficulties she faced, Emily retains many happy memories from her boarding school years. They do not stem from her academic studies but from the work she and other students performed to make the school self-supporting: gardening, canning, cooking, baking, sewing. Basketball, popular today on the reservation, made its debut with Emily's generation. Emily played guard on the school's first girls' team.

Happy school memories counterbalance other serious and life-threatening events of the same period. In 1920, when Emily was nine years old, a measles epidemic swept through the boarding school. Because Emily was among the lucky ones who did not become ill, the attending nurse had Emily accompany her as she made her rounds to the sick children. Emily learned to take temperatures and to perform other small tasks for the nurse. Although Emily later became a traditional medicine woman, she never forgot this early experience and input of Western medicine. In her own life she combines and respects both forms of health care.

A year or two after leaving boarding school, Emily married and even-

2. This article was printed in the *Clipper,* antecedent to the *Wyoming State Journal Newspaper.*

tually had three children. Although all three are now dead, her descendants continue to increase: seven grandchildren and a growing number of great-grandchildren (eight as of 1982). Emily's marriage did not last, and her half-sister Dorothy has been her partner for life.

Emily loves to talk of their hardworking life together before an accident in the early 1950s invalided Dorothy for the rest of her life. "Before day-break," Emily recalls, "we used to go up the mountains, get those great big logs for winter wood." Looking back, Emily calls the two of them "wild ones." Both women broke their own ponies and trained three horse teams. In the haying season they cut and stacked the hay. Emily took care of irrigating their fields.

Besides horses and cows they raised pigs, chickens, and turkeys. They ate their own meat, milk, eggs, homemade butter, garden vegetables, wood-chuck, prairie dog (hair singed, roasted in the oven), chokecherries, and buffalo berries. Emily trapped mink, muskrat, skunk, and beaver for their pelts, which she either sold or tanned and made into work gloves for herself and Dorothy.

The hardworking daily life that Emily and Dorothy shared was, in fact, a man's life. The two women, one a divorcée and the other a widow, stepped into the breach as they logged, hayed, and irrigated to support themselves. There was no question of propriety; it was a necessity. Although the activities were different, Emily's life of hard physical labor echoes and parallels her descriptions of her great-grandmother's life on the Plains. Ac-cording to Emily: "Women do all the work—get up the wood, get water, put up the tepee. And the man sit around out there. Got a fire built and standing around with the kids, and the women doing all the work."

Beyond care for the land and livestock, Emily nursed her sister for close to thirty years. She is a medicine woman, a repository of traditional healing knowledge and practice learned from an old Indian woman. Her medical practice includes traditional medicines, "sticking" throats, and blood-letting procedures. The intellectual underpinnings of her role as a medicine woman include belief in dreams as a source of knowledge and power and the importance of prayer in the restoration of health. We shall encounter these beliefs again in Emily's discussions of Ghost Dance and Sun Dance songs and religions.

These are some of the periods and times and activities of Emily's life— events and experiences that occurred long before my first meeting with her in 1977. Although only sixty-six years old at that time, hard work and sickness had slowed her down. She felt herself a *hivizo*, an "old woman." Many friends, relatives, and all her children were gone. However, loneliness and sickness are not the only harvest of old age. According to traditional Shoshone values, with age comes respect and authority. Gender boundaries blur for the older woman who moves beyond the taboos and danger felt to be inherent in menstruation. As her physical strength ebbs, she gains a new androgynous strength. As an elder Emily speaks out freely to the Shoshone Business Council about injustices that touch her life and for broader issues at the general council meeting of the tribe. People look to her to speak out and call her *degwëhiNI*, which, Emily explains, means she can talk and is brave. (Literally, *degwëhin* means "chief or spokesman," and the suffix *rï* means "person" [Shimkin 1986, personal communication].)

Emily chronicles her own lifetime in two periods, the old times of her youth and the present time of her old age. A sense of continuity with her own past has been broken by too many changes. The rift between the old times and the present runs deep. The Shoshone language itself is a gulf separating the upbringing of the younger generation from Emily's, piercing to the very heart of her own sense of identity. She complains that people no longer teach their children to speak Shoshone: "Now these Indian children, they can't even talk Indian. I tell them, 'What kind of Indians are you? You can't talk Indian.' "

Not only language but matters of politics and dress deepen a cultural estrangement between Emily's past and present. This can be seen in her resentment of young women who, in her view, overstep their bounds at the general council meetings. Emily refers to them by their characteristic dress — "colored pants," a term that captures her disdain for those who symbolically wear men's dress as they move into men's roles. Emily is particularly incensed when the "colored pants" speak in council and try to influence the vote of the older people. Her anger manifests itself at several levels. She feels that older people have adult brains and can decide things for themselves. If anything it is the elders who should influence the younger people and not the other way around. The final rub occurs when these younger women connect their opinions on contemporary issues, perhaps incorrectly, to the words of their elders. Invoking the older generations, they dress in the wisdom of age much in the same way that they wear men's pants — a masquerade in both instances that angers Emily.

Tough independence is only one side of Emily's character. On the other, and in equal proportion, is a direct and earthy sense of humor. [July 19, 1978. "Dorothy and Emily were sleepy. Emily joked that she'd sing 'Pistol-Packing Mama' for me — Dorothy said she'd sing 'Home on the Range.' " (It may be argued that the laugh was on me for missing an unusual recording opportunity!)]

Emily and Dorothy, like most Shoshones, love puns. One time a Shoshone friend visited them and asked if they had any eggs, *noiyo* (an abbreviated form of *gwiyanoiyo*, "chicken egg"). As *noiyo* by itself also means testicle, Emily and Dorothy devilishly took that meaning and assured the friend that they hadn't had those in years! Humor can serve many purposes. [September 30, 1979. "Emily told how she evaded the Mormons—told them that if they baptized her, she wasn't a good swimmer and she might drown. She also said that all churches are the same."] This is Emily, funny and, at heart, deeply religious.

On May 28, 1982, Dorothy died. One month later, as I left the house for the last time and walked to the car, I observed everything that had become very familiar to me over the years. Even with Emily absent from the scene, her house and land express her personality and life: the green grass, the trees planted by her and her mother, the garden to the side (fallow now, a casualty of Emily's old age), a cluster of cats sleeping on the cement in front of her door, chickens by the chicken house, the woodshed filled with tools, and, finally, the gate that links Emily's life with the outside world. Even the gate has a care and meaning to it. It is a wooden gate that fastens to a post with a large link chain. Emily attaches one end of the chain to a nail on the post, slips the chain around the top of the gate and fastens it to the nail, and then wraps the extra length of chain around the gate board. If she finds the gate unfastened or closed in a different way, she knows that someone has been around. The gate stands guard at the border of her own carefully tended and observed environment.

Emily's Songs

"I want you people to keep your songs, your Indian songs. Keep 'em up, get your boys singing. Let them have a drum, make a drum for them. Make certain boys that sing—learn them how to sing. Then you'll have singers here. Don't lose your songs. Don't lose your Indian life. Keep up your Indian life. Keep up the songs and dancing." Emily quotes these words of an Indian man from another tribe who once visited the reservation. (She had recorded his words on what she refers to as the "tape recorder in my throat and mind.") Indian songs and dances and Indian life—the one is equated and identified with the other. To lose one is to lose the other, for music plays an essential role in Shoshone life and always within a communal context. Giveaways, other tribal and religious ceremonies, social dances, and games are performed within this community setting; throughout life—from the blessing of a baby in the Sun Dance to a Memorial Feast in honor of a deceased relative — individuals never cut their bonds to the larger family of the tribe. Singing and often dancing accompany a variety of activities at all these occasions.

Emily attributes much of her extensive repertoire to her mother: "My mother [long-since deceased], she sings good. She's got all kinds of songs. That's where we got our songs." Since our first meeting Emily has sung for me 213 songs, sometimes by herself, often with Dorothy. As their health and ability to sing declined, they played for me and allowed me to make copies of many tapes they had made of themselves over the years. These tapes, some of which date back to 1970, not only provide pleasurable listening for Emily but also serve as an external memory bank. They extend to a twelve-year period my sampling of her songs, the longest span among the five women.

Emily's repertoire is vast. The tapes, both mine and hers, do not exhaust a rich lifetime of singing. Religious songs of the Ghost Dance and Sun Dance form the bulk of her repertoire (147 *Naraya* songs[3] and 48 Sun Dance songs). Women's Dance songs (Round Dance songs), which were very popular at social dances during Emily's youth, are the next largest category (16 songs). Then there are 2 old Shoshone Wolf Dance songs that also date back to social dances of her past (at that time only men sang and danced to these older Wolf Dance or War Dance songs). Because Emily never developed a love for Handgame, a popular team guessing game, she sings no Handgame songs. This is idiosyncratic to her, for Handgame has always been popular with many people, both men and women. In fact, Angie, Emily's junior by ten years, remembers the older generation of women sometimes Hand-gaming on all-female teams and singing their "own" songs. Finally, outside my sample of 213 songs are pieces that Emily recognizes and in some sense knows but does not sing; principally, these are Shoshone ceremonial songs, the Pointing Stick, Giveaway, Chokecherry, and War Bonnet songs. (Again, men traditionally sing and drum these songs. There is a singing role for women in War Bonnet songs, which we shall discuss later.)

The absence in Emily's repertoire of Peyote songs of the Native American Church is noteworthy. It reflects both the incompatible relationship between the *Naraya* (Ghost Dance) religion and the Native American Church and Emily's commitment to the former (Shimkin 1953:467; Vander 1986:67, 68). Also, although Emily's joking offer to sing "Pistol-Packing Mama" reveals

3. The 147 Ghost Dance songs in Emily's repertoire include songs that both she and Dorothy sing. Their solo performances notwithstanding, the songs themselves are part of a shared repertoire between the two women.

a familiarity with the Euro-American pop scene of her youth, non-Indian songs remain beyond the pale of her musical life.

Naraya *(Ghost Dance) Songs*

EMILY: "Well, we said, let's sing those prayer songs, that song that was here long before our fathers and our great-grandmother and fathers, before they're ever born. That song was here, put here on this world for the Indians, for the Shoshones — Shoshones from Nevada and people from Idaho, Wyoming. That song belongs to Shoshones. We got some of those songs, and we'll sing it. They say when you sing those songs it makes berries grow and make grass grow, make water run. Plenty of berries for in the fall, fish, everything. Sing for them, our elk and deer and all them. That's what it's for. It ain't any kind of song. It's for that."

Emily underscores the Shoshone nature and origins of the *Naraya*, passing over the broader Ghost Dance religious movement of the late nineteenth century of which the *Naraya* was a part. In 1896 the United States Bureau of Ethnology published James Mooney's 1892–93 study of the Ghost Dance religion. In addition to visiting many tribes who practiced the religion, Mooney had visited its founder, Wovoka, a Paiute prophet from Nevada. According to Mooney, Ghost Dance doctrine included the performance of a series of Ghost Dances, avoidance of violent conflicts, avoidance of bad relations with Euro-Americans, the promise of plentiful rain, freedom from illness, return of the dead, and the earthshaking arrival of a new world (Mooney [1896] 1965:23). These beliefs, along with the dance and songs, quickly spread among many Indian tribes: Arapahoe, Sioux, Cheyenne, Kiowa, Caddo, Shoshone, and Comanche. The practice and interpretation of the religion varied from tribe to tribe, as did tribal relationships to the non-Indian world. Perceived as a threat by the United States government, the religion was suppressed and hastened to a swift end by the United States Army massacre of a group of Sioux during their performance of a Ghost Dance in 1890.

But the Wind River Shoshones persevered in their *Naraya* beliefs after other tribes had abandoned the Ghost Dance religion. Emily participated in *Naraya* dances, which continued to be held on the reservation through the 1930s.

Mooney had talked with Shoshones on the Wind River reservation during his research and reported that, even then, Shoshones maintained that the *Naraya* revived an older and similar Shoshone religious dance from a half-century earlier (Mooney [1896] 1965:53; Shimkin 1953:433). *Naraya*, the Shoshone name for the religion and dance, does not, in fact, mean Ghost Dance but simply refers to the side-shuffling or dragging step of the dance. Emily grudgingly uses the term *Ghost Dance,* but it remains an annoyingly incorrect convenience.

"That Ghost Dance," Emily expounds, "it belongs here. It's been going on all them years, I don't know how many hundred years they had it. Well, some men, they dream that something's going to be wrong or some kind of sickness or some kind of storm. They know it. Well, we going to dance. It ain't going to happen when we dance. Flu or measles or scarlet fever or a sickness that's some kind of hard cough — one person knows when he's asleep, he knows it's coming. Just like air, it's coming, coming this way. It's coming like a ball of those bees. He can see them at nights asleep. That bad stuff's coming to us. We better be dancing, sending it back, sending it back. We just make it go back. That's the way they dance it. It isn't just a dance."

The *Naraya* stressed the importance of preventive medicine achieved through religious ceremony. There was also a curative side. "Well, it's a song for health," Emily remarks. "When you don't feel good, when you feel sick or something, you dance with them. You feel good then. That's what it's for. It ain't just songs. Some people right today don't know it."

Emily maintains the faith: "We always sing those Ghost Dance songs. Our place looks real good. That's what that means. It makes seeds grow. That's the kind of song it is; it ain't just a song. It's a religious song that you sing to God." Dorothy added: "In the wintertime we always have that Ghost Dance songs on. And when something's [sickness] going through or something going around, we always have that thing on, Ghost Dance song on."

Naraya performances took place close to the river near Emily's home on North Fork. Emily's remembrances of them go back to at least the early 1920s when she was barely ten years old. "They're going to dance maybe four or five nights," she recalls. "They dance nighttime, in the evening when it kind of gets a little dark. Then dance then, maybe till midnight. There's a song that's going to start off. They walk around and sing that song, walk around and then stop. When they dance, they stand after they stop. They go like this. [*Emily patted her body with her hands and then raised and blew across her open palms.*] That means take the sickness away." People also stamped the ground after completing a dance, to wake up the earth so that the roots people ate would grow.

Only the stars, moon, and a large campfire lit the circle of dancers (many of them singing) who moved side by side in a clockwise rotation, unaccompanied by any instruments. The dancer steps sideways on the left foot and then drags the right foot into position next to the left. A man might dance with a woman on each side. After the song ended, the women moved back a step or two and waited for the next song to begin before moving up again and joining hands with the men. In all other regards the dance step was the same for men and women.

EMILY: "When men dancing all together they don't hold hands. Women, too. Just a woman holds hands with a man when she's going to dance with him.

"They sing and they dance around and they stop over there. Then sing another song, different songs. The leader [always a man], maybe two, and some others help in singing. The rest just dance. The leader's going to sing about two, three songs, and he's going to tell somebody else. See, that's how it is. [Other men and women who knew the song could join in.] You learn it. Somebody else sings it and you learn it. There's a lot of them, a lot of different kinds. There's a lot of different kinds of Ghost Dance songs.

"And when they're going to quit, too, they got a song for that. I don't remember them things. I know them, but I can't remember them. When they're going to quit, they're going to dance in the daytime. They're going to have something to eat.

"It isn't just makeup song. They dream it. They dream it someplace way off, someplace in the mountains or hills someplace. Indians dream their songs. They dream it and they're going to sing it."

JUDY: "Did you ever get a *Naraya* song in your dream?"

EMILY: "No, just the men, not the women."

As we shall presently see, this rule was not hard and fast, neither for the Shoshones nor for other tribes who performed the Ghost Dance. Mooney attributes 20 of his 161 published Ghost Dance songs to women of various tribes (Mooney [1896] 1965:214, 251, 253, 258, 275–76, 278, 291, 300, 304–5, 308–9, 317, 319, 326–28).

The issue of gender touched two other aspects of the *Naraya,* affecting who would lead it and who could attend.

JUDY: "Did women ever dream or know that it was time to dance?"

EMILY: "Just men, certain men. Not young people, but old people."

Beliefs and perceptions concerning menstruation imposed another limitation on women. [July 21, 1982. "Saw Emily — she said Shoshones say women have a gun — danger of their menstruation."] Shoshones do not view menstruation as a bad thing per se, but rather it is a power with all the danger inherent therein. If not handled properly and with great care, it can endanger the physical well-being of family members and drive away sacred power and vision. For this reason (both in the past and present), menstruating women are forbidden to come near the Sun Dance Lodge. As to participation of menstruating women in the *Naraya,* Emily comments: "Not in the old times, but in the young times they do anything."[4]

Emily sings one *Naraya* song received by a Wind River Shoshone woman.

EMILY: "That was a woman, she sang that song for them. That's Virginia [Grant] Bonatsie's song. She dreamt that song—just like Sun Dance or religious songs—she dreamt it. When they had a dance she sang that song for them when she was a young woman. She was born in 1890 and died in 1960. She passed away a few years ago." (See plate 4 following page 46.)

Naraya Song no. 1

Singers: Emily Hill and Dorothy Tappay
Note: Almost every *Naraya* song carries a host of small pitch and rhythmic variants that crop up in successive repetitions of the song. For example, the beginning of the third phrase above appears in a later verse as

One finds this throughout Shoshone music (Vander 1978:8, 9).

Evï-n		*denüpi*	*evï-n*		*denüpi,*
Yellow-white	clay	man	yellow-white	clay	man,

Evï-n		*denüpi*	*evï-n*		*denüpi.*
Yellow-white	clay	man	yellow-white	clay	man.

Hupin		*denüpi*	*yòrino,*
Wood,	stick	man	keep flying on [together],

Hupin		*denüpi*	*yòrino.*
Wood,	stick	man	keep flying on [together].

4. According to Shoshone mythology, Coyote, the trickster-hero, is the origin of menstruation and menstrual taboos (Lowie 1909:239). During menstruation and for one month

EMILY: *"Evi,* means that white chalk. It's under ground; you use it. They get it someplace at South Pass, way at the other side. It's mud, the dough, they take it. They bring it out to dry. That's for dressing, putting on your buckskin. It's something like chalk. It's for the Sun Dance — white, smells good. [In religious contexts *evi* is associated with purification (Weeks 1981:100; Shimkin 1953:422).] That man's made of that kind, and man made of wood. *Yorino* — get up, up, flying on."   Emily's explanation stops short. Here, as with many *Naraya* songs, only the person who received the song understood all of its meanings. That it has meanings, Emily has no doubt: "It's something. We don't know what it is. She knows, but that's all I know."

The musical style and texts of Emily's *Naraya* songs differ from the rest of her repertoire.[5] *Naraya* songs, like the Ghost Dance songs of other tribes, bear the stamp of Great Basin musical style. Wovoka, the Paiute prophet who set the religion in motion, sang songs in the style of his people. Although each tribe generated its own Ghost Dance songs, Great Basin musical style survived, as with the Wind River Shoshones, even in areas of very different musical traditions (Herzog 1935a:403, 415, 417). Herzog and Nettl have pointed out some of the distinctive features of this style: undulating melodic contours that move within a narrow range (often a fifth), phrase endings on the tonic, and, most typically, paired patterns through the repetition of every phrase (Herzog 1935a:403, 415; Nettl 1954:14, 15).[6]

---

after childbirth, women used to remove themselves from their family and home and live in a small, separate shelter, *hunagähl.* There are also dietary and sexual restrictions that some women continue to observe. "For menstrual blood . . . would enrage the supernatural power; the consequences were unforeseeable. At the very least, all supernatural power would disappear. At worst, death would come to the entire family" (Shimkin 1947b:290). Shoshone notions and prohibitions about menstruation are similar to those of many other tribes. For example, Marla Powers reports that menstruating Oglala Sioux women cannot enter a Sweat Lodge or a ritual Yuwipi meeting (Powers 1986:194, 200). For an interesting discussion of the positive aspects of Oglala Sioux menstrual beliefs with broader reference to Native North America, see Powers 1980:117–28.

5. Elsewhere I have traced the history of the Shoshone Ghost Dance, described its performance in this century, and analyzed in great detail the music and text of Shoshone Ghost Dance songs (Vander 1986). *Naraya* songs 2–5 and 9–11 first appeared in this publication. Correspondences between song numbers in *Songprints* and the 1986 publication are as follows: 2=1 (p. 38), 3=11 (p. 41), 4=6 (pp. 39–40), 5=12 (p. 42), 9=15 (p. 49), 10=3 (p. 52), and 11=2 (pp. 54–55).

6. Paiute conversational form, like musical form, also moved in paired patterns. Mooney observed and reported that the Paiute listener invariably and immediately repeated every sentence of the speaker throughout a conversation (Mooney [1896] 1965:13).

Naraya song no. 1 conforms with the above description of Great Basin musical style. The absence of a drum accompaniment in Emily's performance followed specifically *Naraya* Ghost Dance traditions (Mooney [1896] 1965:186; Herzog 1935a:403). Emily's singing and vocal quality, however, correspond to Plains rather than Great Basin musical style, as in her utilization of vocal tension and pulsation (surges of volume on an unbroken tone), both important characteristics of Plains vocal style but significantly absent in Great Basin performance (Nettl 1954:14, 24). Although these qualities are somewhat less prominent in Emily's performance of *Naraya* songs than in the rest of her repertoire, they are present nevertheless.[7]

While Emily makes no comments on the form of *Naraya* songs, she clearly has preferences and criteria for evaluating performers and performances. "Dorothy, she's got a good voice. She's got that high voice. Mother, she's a good singer, too. She's got good voice, too, her voice way up. She's got a pretty voice. But me, I got the ugly voice. I had a good voice until I got that asthma. I used to not sound like a man. I used to sing high. Now I can't."

Tempo, too, is an important factor for Emily. "When you're singing [*Naraya* songs] you're supposed to kind of drag your song. Make that song pretty." [August 18, 1977. "Dorothy and Emily sang another Ghost Dance song. Also told me not to sing the Ghost Dance songs too fast." October 8, 1979. "Emily and I listened to part of Library of Congress Ghost Dance tape. She really enjoyed it. She said the tempo of the songs seemed fast. She said Shoshone *Naraya* had slow and fast songs."] Once, after listening to a *Naraya* song on her own tapes, Emily expressed particular pleasure in a song: "I like that song—slow."

To Emily and Dorothy songs are animate. On one occasion when Emily and I listened to her *Naraya* tapes for a couple of hours, she started to sing one of the songs, but her voice gave out. She commented: "I can't sing it. Can't make them songs go. Can't do. I got 'em all taped up, that's why. It's all taped up. It's out of my throat." It's almost as though the song has a single existence, either in Emily's throat or on tape, but not both. Emily's statement also reveals her ambivalence toward the tape recorder itself. She values her self-reliance, depending on the "tape recorder" in her mind and throat. Although she has made and enjoyed many tapes of Dorothy and herself singing and has also recorded singing during the Sun Dance, the tape recorder casts a hostile modern shadow.

7. Herzog's study of Plains Ghost Dance music omitted discussion of singing style because his data was limited to old cylinder recordings and transcriptions by other scholars who did not comment on or notate aspects of vocal style (Herzog 1935a:404).

Songs, being animate, can also be capricious. One time Dorothy started a song, got confused, stopped, giggled about it, and finally declared, "That song ran away from me."

Because Emily and Dorothy know many *Naraya* songs, recalling a specific song can be very difficult at times. Once, when Emily couldn't sing a song, she explained: "I can't think it. Dorothy knows it well. She's the leader of that." Another time Emily related her notion of song leader to differences in musical ability. "Some people don't sing. Some people kind of out of tune, too. Some people make the song tune good. Or out of tune — some people like that. Some of them don't start off a song, they just sing, help sing. Good singers, they lead." Both Emily and Dorothy are capable lead singers.

Unlike the other songs in Emily's repertoire, *Naraya* songs have Shoshone texts, which provide rich information on *Naraya* beliefs and concerns. For Emily they are all prayer songs. *Naraya* texts touch on two topics: the world of nature and the progress of the soul after death. A preponderance of texts refer to the creatures, plants, rocks, mountains, stars, sun, and water that surround and sustain the Wind River Shoshones. Within this *Naraya* world of nature, water is the most important element, and many texts abound with images of water in every form — fog, snow, melting snow, rain, and running water.

Naraya Song no. 2

Singers: Emily Hill and Dorothy Tappay

> *Damĕn doiya-   vaig-e vagïna havenȯrĕ,*
> Our   mountain- above fog   lying while moving,
>
> *Damĕn doiya-   vaig-e vagïna havenȯrĕ.*
> Our   mountain- above fog   lying while moving.

Vagïna vagïna vagïna havenòrë,
Fog   fog   fog   lying while moving,

Vagïna vagïna vagïna havenòrë.
Fog   fog   fog   lying while moving.

EMILY: "Fog, you see it on the side of the mountains. *Havïn*, you see
it moving towards this way or that way. It just keeps saying that fog, fog."

Note that the text identifies the mountains, *our* mountains, reference
to the foothills of the Wind River Mountains, a familiar presence to Emily
and the Shoshones. It is a backdrop for their lives today and their myths
of the past (Shimkin 1947c:332).

Naraya Song no. 3

Sa - i - wai__ doi-ya - vi sa - i - wai__ doi-ya - vi, Sa-i-wai__ doi-ya - vi

sa - i - wai__ doi-ya - vi. Doi-ya dïmp-ün dïmp-vang-zin-go ò - ra dïmp-vang-zin-go ò - ra

e - në, Doi-ya dïmp-ün dïmp-vang-zin-go ò - ra dïmp-vang-zin-go ò - ra   e - në.

Singers: Emily Hill and Dorothy Tappay

Saiwai   doiyavi   saiwai   doiyavi,
Snow melting mountain range snow melting mountain range,

Saiwai   doiyavi   saiwai   doiyavi.
Snow melting mountain range snow melting mountain range.

Doiya   dïmp-ün dïmpvangzingo òra dïmpvangzino òra enë,
Mountain rocky   rock slide   rock slide   (ending vocable),

Doiya   dïmp-ün dïmpvangzingo òra dïmpvangzingo òra enë.
Mountain rocky   rock slide   rock slide   (ending vocable).

EMILY: "*Saiwai doiyav,* it's kind of wet. It's something like the snow
going away from the mountains, melting on those rocks that slide . . . clifflike,
they're underground. They show like this."

Often with a mountain setting, as in the above songs, water images link with images of green plants and animal life. The tiny poetic lines of *Naraya* song no. 4 suggest the larger ecosystem.

Naraya Song no. 4

(1st verse)

Gwi - nan gas___ du - gum - bai - yu, Gwi - nan gas___ du - gum - bai - yu. Bu - hi ba roan - zi ma - ru - kan - du ha - ve - nó - rĕ, Bu - hi ba roan - zi ma - ru - kan-du ha - ve - no - rĕ.

Singers: Emily Hill and Dorothy Tappay

> *Gwinan gas   dugumbaiyu,*
> Eagle's   wing is skying,
>
> *Gwinan gas   dugumbaiyu.*
> Eagle's   wing is skying.
>
> *Buhi   ba   roanzi marukandu havenòrĕ,*
> Green water shiny   under   lying while moving,
>
> *Buhi   ba   roanzi marukandu havenòrĕ.*
> Green water shiny   under   lying while moving.

EMILY: "That eagle's flying, his wings way up there in the sky, looking down to the earth, and seeing the water shining and the grass on the earth green."

There is a haikulike quality to many *Naraya* texts, an evocation of the natural world in a tightly compressed, telegraphic form. The absence of connecting and qualifying words and phrases allows for a rich ambiguity of meanings.

Naraya Song no. 5

(1st verse)

Bu - yŭ - na du - ru - a bu - yŭ - na du - ru - a - gin,   Bu - yŭ-na du - ru-a bu - yŭ-na du - ru - a - gin.

Tsa   pa - ran bang-wa-vi - nó - ra,   Tsa   pa - ran bang-wa-vi - nòr.

Singer: Emily Hill

> *Buyü-na durua   buyü-na durua-   gin,*
> Duck's ducklings duck's   ducklings, very small,
>
> *Buyü-na durua   buyü-na durua-   gin.*
> Duck's ducklings duck's   .ducklings, very small.
>
> *Tsa   paran bangwavinòra,*
> Good in water swimming,
>
> *Tsa   paran bangwavinòr.*
> Good in water swimming.

EMILY: "They're wild ducks, little baby ducks, going along following each other. They're swimming in the good water."

Naraya Song no. 6

(3d verse)

Pen-gwi-bai a-no-ga pen-gwi-bai a-no-ga pen-gwi-bai a-no-ga   e - në,

Pen-gwi-bai a-no-ga pen-gwi-bai a-no-ga pen-gwi-bai a-no-ga   e - në.

Bu-hip-bai a-no-ga bu-hip-bai a-no-ga bu-hip-bai a-no-ga   e - në,

Bu-hip-bai a-no-ga bu-hip-bai a-no-ga bu-hip-bai a-no-ga   e - në.

Singers: Emily Hill and Dorothy Tappay

> *Pengwi- bai   anoga pengwi- bai   anoga*
> Fish-   upon waves fish-   upon waves
>
> *pengwi- bai   anoga enë,*
> fish-   upon waves (ending vocable),

Pengwi- bai   anoga pengwi- bai   anoga
Fish-   upon waves fish-   upon waves

   pengwi- bai   anoga enĕ.
   fish-   upon waves (ending vocable).

Buhip- bai   anoga buhip- bai   anoga buhip- bai
Grass- upon waves grass- upon waves grass- upon

   anoga enĕ,
   waves (ending vocable),

Buhip- bai   anoga buhip- bai   anoga buhip- bai
Grass- upon waves grass- upon waves grass- upon

   anoga enĕ.
   waves (ending vocable).

EMILY: "Fish go through the water and make it go like that [*waves*]. And through grass, too, in the water. Fish go through there and make it go like that." (*Emily waved her hand back and forth.*)

One cannot overstate the importance of water as a primary focus in Shoshone thought. In *Naraya* song no. 7, we glimpse a conceptual category that groups a disparate assortment of animals because of their shared associations with water. They are "water people."

Naraya Song no. 7

Singers: Emily Hill and Dorothy Tappay

Ba   nüwï- tsi   ba   nüwï- tsi   ba   nüwĕn,
Water person (affect., water person (affect., water person,
             dimin.   dimin.
             ending)   ending)

Ba	nüwï-	tsi	ba	nüwï-	tsi	ba	nüwĕn.
Water	person	(affect., dimin. ending)	water	person	(affect., dimin. ending)	water	person.

Ba	nüwï-	tsi	nüwü	wïnenga	doih	yïzïgïn,
Water	person	(affect., dimin. ending)	person	standing in front of you	come up	about to rise,

Ba	nüwï-	tsi	nüwü	wïnenga	doih	yïzïgïn.
Water	person	(affect., dimin. ending)	person	standing in front of you	come up	about to rise.

EMILY: "*Ba nüwïtsïd* means beaver, muskrat, and fish, them ducks, weasel — all those water people, and they come out, front of you."

Naraya texts corroborate Emily's statements on the Shoshone interpretation of the religion. Songs affect nature; texts about water ensure water, and an abundance of water ensures plant and animal life. The Shoshone *Naraya* and songs closely resemble those of the Paiute. Anthropologist James Mooney wrote, "I learned that Wovoka has five songs for making it rain, the first of which brings on a mist or clouds, the second a snowfall, the third a shower, and the fourth a hard rain or storm, while he sings the fifth song the weather again becomes clear" (Mooney [1896] 1965:15).

Looking back half a century, Emily remembers the words of people who urged Shoshones to dance: "Old people say, 'Well, we'll dance. We'll make our earth come, grow up and make more water, more water.' *Datevüntĕg* means wake 'em up, wake 'em up. That song is for that. Johnny Dick [a Shoshone man, originally from Nevada, who led Wind River Shoshone *Naraya* dances] and them Nevada Shoshones say, 'Let's have our berries on our earth. Let the water run; let the grass grow again. Let's dance and make our earth and everything — roots when we eat from our ground — let 'em come alive again.' "

The text of *Naraya* song no. 8 makes specific reference to the roots of a plant that Shoshones used for medicinal purposes.

Naraya song no. 8

(2d verse)
♩. = ca. 72

Do - za - roi - yam - bi do - za - roi - yam - bi do - za - roi - yam - bi

na - ru-kŭm-ba - ni na-ru-ru-kŭm-ba - ni.__ Hu - vi - a - rĕ hu - ku -

ha - vi - ti   na - ru - kŭm - ba   -   ni   na - ru - kŭm - ba   -   ni.____

Singers: Emily Hill and Dorothy Tappay

Doza- roi-   *yambi*   *doza- roi-*   *yambi*   *doza- roi-*
White- mountain- root, plant white- mountain- root, plant white- mountain-

yambi   *narukŭmbani*   *narukŭmbani.*
root, plant magico-religious magico-religious
             power to it   power to it.

Huvia-rĕ *hukuhaviti*   *narukŭmbani*   *narukŭmbani.*
Songs   trail of dust   magico-religious magico-religious
            (?reference   power to it   power to it.
            to whirlwind)

EMILY: "*Dozaroiyĕmp,* something white that grows on the mountain. *Doza* means that Indian medicine. It ain't round here. It's put out up there to the mountains someplace, Bull Lake or Dinwoody someplace.[8] You have to pray for it before you dig the root out. It's for sores and everything.

"I like that song. That's a song from Idaho. Idaho people knows it, and people from here know it. Those Idaho people, Nevada [Shoshone], they come up here and dance with them. We catch on to their songs, they catch on to ours. Songs go back and forth, just like Wolf Dance songs, powwow songs."

In another instance of song swapping, we see that Indian singing secretly persevered at the reservation boarding school. Music served as a common ground in a Shoshone-Arapahoe trade. According to Emily: "Dorothy sang an Arapahoe Ghost Dance song in Arapahoe words. I used to laugh at her. She learned it from my mother. My mother learned it from those Arapahoe girls, her age. When they went down to the government school, they say they used to go down in the basement and sing—my mother and them other Arapahoe girls. That's how Mother learned them Arapahoe songs.

8. Both locations have strong cultural associations. Shoshones regard Dinwoody Canyon, which contains many pictographs, as a very sacred place. For this reason some Shoshones go there in their quest for the power to heal (Voget 1984:302). Bull Lake is also a special place, "both fearful and attractive. It is reported to be the home of monsters; those who kill and eat them will change into Water Buffalo and disappear. It is also the place where ghost people play the hand game" (Shimkin 1986:325). The possible textual reference to the whirlwind (*hukuhaviti*) in *Naraya* song no. 8 relates to another aspect of Shoshone belief. After leaving the body, the spirit of a dead person is surrounded by a whirlwind and, as such, becomes one of several types of ghost (Shimkin 1986:325; Vander 1986:53).

Dorothy just learned one. Mother knows the rest. And I think those Arapahoe girls, they sing the Shoshone Ghost Dance songs, too."

The *Naraya* world of nature embraces life-sustaining water, plants, animals, and the sun and stars.

Naraya Song no. 9

* The pitch lowers one whole step during the course of the song.
Singer: Dorothy Tappay
Note: Although this transcription is from a performance by Dorothy Tappay, the song is part of the large repertoire shared by both Emily and Dorothy.

Damĕ navoi   dazimi doih-   ĭn,
Our   Morning Star   coming up,

Damĕ navoi   dazimi doih-   ĭn.
Our   Morning Star   coming up.

Vago dave wogĭn,
Clear sun   rays streaming out,

Vago dave wogĭn.
Clear sun   rays streaming out.

Daziumbe garegĭn,
Star   sitting lightly,

Daziumbe garegĭn.
Star   sitting lightly.

EMILY: "Morning Star, song about Morning Star. When you see the daylight coming up, when it's coming up, the Morning Star coming up with that light. It's sitting up there just before daybreak."

The Morning Star had particular Ghost Dance significance. Many tribes, after a series of dances on consecutive evenings, concluded with a dance that continued throughout the night until morning. A song to the Morning

Star and closing song marked the end of the final dance. Although Emily recalls dancing only until midnight, it is possible that *Naraya* song no. 9 survives as a relic linking Shoshone (*Naraya*) performance practice with that of other tribes.

Naraya song no. 10 describes the soul—its release after death and subsequent journey to God's home.

Naraya Song no. 10

Singers: Emily Hill and Dorothy Tappay

> *Mugua vagïna-ve*   *mugua vagïna-ve,*
> Soul   fog   (personalizing soul   fog   (personalizing
>   nominal suffix)   nominal suffix),
>
> *Mugua vagïna-ve*   *mugua vagïna-ve.*
> Soul   fog   (personalizing soul   fog   (personalizing
>   nominal suffix)   nominal suffix).
>
> *Mugua yïzïkanzi*   *mugua yïzïkanzi,*
> Soul   floating, flying up soul   floating, flying up,
>
> *Mugua yïzïkanzi*   *mugua yïzïkanzi.*
> Soul   floating, flying up soul   floating, flying up.

It seems singularly appropriate that Shoshone imagery for the essence of life itself—the soul—assumes an insubstantial watery form.

EMILY: "The soul is like a fog when it gets out of the body. Well, when a person dies, the soul goes out of the body and flies in the air. It flies away from you. Then they go to God's home when the body's already in the ground.[9]

9. In his 1909 monograph on Northern Shoshone culture, Lowie also documented

"The spirit, when they go to God's home, they still dance it [*Naraya*]. Someday, some Judgment Day you'll see your folks that day."

Thus far we see the soul, a foggy presence, rising to God's home and dancing the *Naraya*. In *Naraya* song no. 11 we come full circle, as the song foretells the return of the dead to life.

Naraya Song no. 11

Singers: Emily Hill and Dorothy Tappay

Damĕn	*biyanï*	*dave-de*	*doih-*	*n-zi*		*havenòrĕ,*
Our	mothers	day/sun	come out	(dimin.,	affect.	lying while
(Inclusive)					ending)	moving,

Damĕn	*biyanï*	*dave-de*	*doih-*	*n-zi*		*havenòrĕ.*
Our	mothers	day/sun	come out	(dimin.,	affect.	lying while
(Inclusive)					ending)	moving.

Buiwai	*damĕ*	*vand-*	*o*	*gemanòrĕ*	*gemanòrĕ,*
Looking	toward us	above,		will keep on	will keep on
around,				coming,	coming,
down					

Buiwai	*damĕ*	*vand-*	*o*	*gemanòrĕ*	*gemanòrĕ.*
Looking	toward us	above,		will keep on	will keep on
around,				coming,	coming.
down					

EMILY: "Our mother comes when the end of the world—coming, looking for her children. Coming down, see, she's above us and looking down and looking for her children. The day, the day, the Judgment Day comes. Everybody's coming back. People's that's dead coming alive. It's that

---

Shoshone belief in the departure and cloudlike form of the soul after death (Lowie 1909:225). One notes the same imagery in Wovoka's speech to Cheyenne and Arapahoe delegates: "Jesus is now upon the earth. He appears like a cloud" (Mooney [1896] 1965:23).

time. The mothers come, looking down, coming, coming, looking for her children."

That the dead never did return to life as predicted was one factor among many that brought about the demise of the *Naraya*. Emily cites two others that led to its abandonment. The first involves youth: "These young people nowadays, they don't know what this Ghost Dance song is. A few years ago they had a dance down there, and these young people just, you know, getting blankets and covering their heads up and doing crazy dancing. They quit right there. They give it up."

Emily, however, feels that the Native American Church bears the major onus for *Naraya* decline.[10] "When that peyote come there were a lot of people — old women, old men, middle-aged people, a lot of children. After they start eating that peyote, they just passed away. They eat peyote, and they get sick." That the partaking of peyote in the Native American Church ceremony brought sickness and death proved to Emily that both ritual and religion were false and dangerous. This is at the nub of her strong disbelief and disapproval of the Native American Church. While it is customary for Shoshones to enjoy comfortably several religious ties and affiliations — Episcopalian and Sun Dance, for example — a person had to choose between the *Naraya* and Native American Church. They were mutually exclusive (Shimkin 1953:467). Emily's disbelief in the latter and, on the other side of the coin, her belief in the *Naraya* set her apart from the other four women in this book.

Sun Dance Songs

Only Shoshone Sun Dance songs, the second largest category in Emily's songprint, form a central shared core of all five women's songprints (see cumulative songprint, pp. 288–89). The Sun Dance religion is, therefore, a linchpin in this study and, by implication, of Shoshone communal life as well.[11]

While Emily and the other four women of this book express their beliefs and thoughts about the Sun Dance religion and ceremony in their own separate chapters, none has ever felt the need to describe the ceremony

10. Stenberg documents the introduction of the Native American Church among the Shoshones around the turn of the twentieth century (Stenberg 1946:106).

11. Shimkin makes this point in his discussion of contemporary Wind River Shoshone life: "The central role of religious activity and the implied premise of personal supernatural power have remained as meaningful forces. In the 1960s and later, both personal motivation and family pressure led to repeated participation in tribal rituals — and in the Sun Dance particularly" (Shimkin 1986:333).

to me, since I have always joined them as either a singer or onlooker. The following brief description is to give the reader a rudimentary orientation to the Sun Dance. After this I include an excerpt from a series of newspaper articles published on the reservation in 1977. Written by and for Wind River Shoshones, the articles describe and explain the Sun Dance ceremony and its origins. (See the Appendix for a reprint of the entire series.)[12]

Today, the Sun Dance ceremony is performed once a year near the end of July. Shoshones always construct a new Sun Dance Lodge for the ceremony. The basic structure is made of a center pole circled by twelve outer posts, with rafter beams connecting each outerpost to the center pole. Brush encloses the outer circle of posts, leaving an open doorway to the east. Only men dance in the Shoshone Sun Dance. Sun Dancers, who seek health for themselves and family members or who seek the power to heal, enter the lodge on a Friday evening and remain in it until the conclusion of the ceremony sometime on Monday. They wear only shawls wrapped around their waists and eagle-bone whistles suspended from their necks. They must not eat or drink for the duration of the ceremony, the bulk of which consists of dancing to and from the center pole, always beginning and returning to each Sun Dancer's own particular place around the outer perimeter of the lodge. Dancing occurs intermittently throughout the day and evening and is accompanied by singing and drumming (as will be described later). A Sunrise ceremony begins each of the three days. This consists of a special Sunrise song and dance and a special set of four Morning Prayer songs, which the Sun Dance Chief sings. The Sunrise ceremony concludes with a spoken prayer by the Sun Dance Chief. After the Sun Dancers leave the lodge on the last day, there is a Giveaway for visitors. A communal feast on the following day concludes the occasion.

> A man was riding alone in the prairie long long ago. As he rode by a white buffalo skull he heard singing. He stopped his horse and listened, but he heard nothing. Turning his horse around he retraced his horse's tracks. Very slowly he rode, until he heard singing again, he stopped his horse and got off. The singing was coming from the white buffalo skull. He got down

12. There is a wealth of scholarly description and analysis of the Wind River Shoshone Sun Dance, beginning with Lowie's brief publication in 1919. Shimkin's 1953 Bureau of American Ethnology publication, based on fieldwork conducted in 1937–38, remains the classic work on the subject. Voget documented Sun Dance trends that developed a decade later. Johnson's 1968 master's thesis adds another perspective, since he himself participated in Sun Dances in 1966 and 1967. Jorgensen's 1972 study of Ute and Shoshone Sun Dances compares five tribal interpretations and performances of the Sun Dance. It also relates the religion to Indian history and status within non-Indian America. Finally, Voget's 1984 book describes and analyzes in detail the transfer of the Shoshone Sun Dance to the Crows and its integration into Crow culture.

on his knees and looked into the buffalo skull, thru the empty eye sockets. There, inside the skull, Indians were dancing the Sun Dance. Now this Indian was told all about the Dance of Thirst and fasting. He was told all about the Sun Dance.

He was told how he must see a vision and telling him all the sacred rituals or ceremonies of the Sun Dance. How he must go without food and water for three days and nights, sometimes it was four days and four nights. The Sun Dance has been handed down from generation to generation or from father to son by lip to ear. It is like a big church for all of the Indians. . . . (St. Clair and St. Clair 1977, issue 1:5)

There are many reasons why the dancers are in this Sun Dance, sometimes for family or personal health. But very often it is for special blessing, but always the dance is sacrificial. (To suffer the hardship of one's thirst and hunger for blessings.)[13]

EMILY: "The leader that's going to give the Sun Dance, he's going to dream that he's giving that dance, so everybody can live out the winter good. The children should grow up good. That's the way they dream things like that."

As in the *Naraya,* special dreams and concern for everyone's health are important themes in Shoshone Sun Dance belief. Emily has witnessed successful Sun Dance cures that strongly validate her belief in the religion, in contrast to her feelings about the Native American Church. Although there are many differences of form and meaning between the *Naraya* and Sun Dance, beneath their surface is a conceptual framework that nourishes both. Beyond the ordinary physical world, Shoshones see a world of power (*boha*) that affects the everyday world. People tap into this otherworld in their dreams and vision. *Naraya* songs thus received help to revitalize nature and promote health. Participants in the Sun Dance seek curing, protection from illness, and, in some cases, acquisition of power for healing. But the world of power holds danger, too, with equal capacity for harm and destruction. Commenting on the dangers involved, Emily states: "You shouldn't say, 'I'm not going over there to the Sun Dance. I don't want to go there.' Something's going to happen to you. Maybe you're going to get sick or something go wrong with you. Or some of your family's going to go wrong. That's the way it is. You've got to be very careful what you're saying."

One sees connections between the *Naraya* and the Sun Dance in their shared notions of power and concern for health. Water is another potent conceptual link. In *Naraya* song texts water was associated with a healthy, fecund world of nature and with the soul — the essence of life itself. The

13. The final paragraph of the above excerpt is taken from an unpublished version of St. Clair's article and does not appear in the serial publication.

Shoshone name for the Sun Dance, *Taguwĕnĕr,* literally, "Standing in Thirst," is equally revealing (Shimkin 1953:418). Sun Dancers abstain from real water and "suffer the hardship of thirst" to receive "blessings" and power, often expressed in visions of water. Visionary water is both a symbol and sign of power.

The center pole for the specially constructed Sun Dance Lodge gathers all these meanings together. Hebard reported: "The center pole, which should always be a cottonwood, was chosen by the originators of the dance because of its superiority over all other trees as a dry-land tree growing with little or no water. This tree represents God" (Hebard 1930:293). Over forty years later Jorgensen commented: "The center pole is the medium through which supernatural power is channeled. The center pole is also believed to have supernatural power of its own. . . . In all instances . . . power is equated with water" (Jorgensen 1972:182).

Even though *Naraya* and Sun Dance songs are a study in musical contrasts, they share some basic notions of meaning and origins. Emily notes that the Sun Dance song "isn't just make-up song. They dream it. All those Sun Dance songs, they're all prayer songs. That's all just like prayers."

Similarities between *Naraya* and Sun Dance songs end here. Whereas in the *Naraya* dancers and singers were one and the same, each Sun Dancer with his eagle-bone whistle adds only one part to a separate musical ensemble. A large rawhide Sun Dance drum sits flat on the ground in the southeast corner of the Sun Dance Lodge, near the large entrance. Male singers encircle the drum, which they beat with padded buckskin-tipped drumsticks. Within and without the lodge—a circular brush enclosure—women sit behind the male singers, holding bunches of tall willow branches, which they shake back and forth throughout each song. (See plate 5 following p. 46.) An instrumental ensemble of drum, eagle-bone whistles, and occasionally a Sun Dance rattle accompanies three vocal parts sung by a lead male singer, male chorus, and female chorus.

In most respects Sun Dance songs and performance conform to Plains musical style. The melody covers a wide range (often a twelfth), beginning high and inscribing a descending, terraced contour (Nettl 1954:24, 25). There are two sections to the song, the second being an incomplete repetition of the first. This particular form is as quintessentially Plains as paired phrases was Great Basin. The lead singer sings an opening phrase (A); the rest of the male singers repeat it (A'); and the entire ensemble, including the women, sings the next phrase or phrases (B), which ends with a cadential segment (C). The second section repeats the first, omitting the opening call and response: AA'BC/BC (Powers 1980:31; Vennum 1980:47–50). This basic song unit, or verse as Shoshones sometimes call it, lasts from one to two minutes. It may be repeated four times for ceremonial reasons or many times according to the discretion of the lead singer. Vocal tension, pulsation, and a nasal quality are part of the performance style. Texts consist of vocables (syllables with no lexical meaning) that are sung in a fixed order for every repetition of the song. *O he* or *he yo* are ending markers.[14]

All of these characteristics are indistinguishable from other Plains song genres. There are, however, several aspects of song and performance unique to the Sun Dance (for an overview of the form of Sun Dance songs and ensemble performance, see chart 1 below). Especially noteworthy is the presence of women in the musical ensemble and their respective role. Although women of different Plains tribes can and do sing behind the drum in other genres (for example, War Dance songs), it is not the practice among the Wind River Shoshones. (As we shall see later, Helene Furlong and Lenore Shoyo opened up new musical roles for Shoshone women in this regard.) The participation of a strong female chorus is, in itself, a special feature of Shoshone Sun Dance performances. Musical parts heighten their presence. Near the end of the last repetition, the men stop singing and drumming. Women thus finish every Sun Dance song by themselves without any rhythmic accompaniment. This differs dramatically from all other genres (excluding *Naraya* songs of the past), which have continuous drum accompaniment.

Sun Dance song performance is distinctive in many other ways. Drum accents on every other beat cue beginning and end for the dancers, who run in toward the center pole and then step-hop back to the perimeter of the lodge. (Other genres have similar accent patterns just before the final cadence, but only Sun Dance songs have drum accents at the beginning.) The punctuating flurry of two or three drumbeats after the women have finished singing is also unique to Sun Dance songs. The Sun Dance rattle and the humerus eagle-bone whistle appear exclusively in the Sun Dance. Both are keyed to the drum part. Sun Dancers blow their whistle in time to the drum and their own dancing, together producing a pulsing rhythmic cluster. Similarly, each whistle, with its own pitch, merges into a high tone cluster.[15]

14. One finds the use of a final *o* sound in many song genres of various tribes. Merriam cites the Flathead ending vocable pattern: *he yo he yo he yo* (Merriam 1967:315). In his analysis of Plains War Dance and Round Dance songs, William Powers notes the "final ending . . . a definite strongly articulated 'yo' " (Powers 1961b:128; Powers 1961a:99).

15. Commenting on the significance of the eagle-bone whistle in relation to the Sun

Before her health and power to sing diminished, Emily used to join the women who sang for the Sun Dance. Today, she attends, watches, and sometimes records the singing. She reflects on her mother's participation and on her own in years past as follows: "They said a long time ago when my mother was a young woman, young girl, they used to have a place for her to sit at the Sun Dance. She's going to sing all the time, her voice way up. The old man told us, too, that they always have her. She's the main one. She got a pretty voice.

"When they're going to put up that Sun Dance Lodge, women used to help them sing. Women, some sing. I used to be one of them singing. A whole bunch of them were there. They start singing that [Fourth Morning Prayer song] they're going to sing. And they put it up straight." (Emily sang the Fourth Morning Prayer song for me in 1981.)[16] To my knowledge women no longer sing with the men as the center pole is raised.

Shoshones learn Sun Dance songs at the event itself. "That's where you learn it," Emily declares. "You got to get up early and go to the morning prayers, then you can know the songs." Once a person has learned a great store of Sun Dance songs, the problem of retrieving a particular song can be very troublesome. On one occasion Emily began to sing a certain song and then broke off in the middle, saying, "I got it all mixed up with another one." On a different occasion Emily sang two Sun Dance songs and afterward commented about the second, "I almost caught it with the other song."

Several factors contribute to the difficulty of retrieving songs and keeping them separate from one another. Emily, like other singers, knows an enormous number of songs, and many within the same genre are very similar. The absence of Shoshone texts for the Sun Dance songs likewise provides no helpful clues for recall. With few exceptions (the Sunrise Ceremony, Flag, and Morning Prayer songs), there are no titles. In place of titles and words, Emily often associates a song with a singer, perhaps a lead singer who liked the song and frequently performed it. Listening to tapes together, she would tell me about some of the singers of the past and present called to mind by the recording. Each song carries its own history of per-

---

Dance, Voget writes: "Eagle is a bearer of messages from spirit to man, and from man to spirit. The eagle-bone whistle is a traditional vehicle for prayer in the Sun Dance" (Voget 1984:308). Shoshones explain the meaning of the whistle and dance as follows: "Now each time the dancer blows his whistle, he is praying for the earth to be clean and free from disease, like the air, up where the eagle flies. The motion of the dancers is also a prayer, it is a prayer for life and action for a dead body does not move" (St. Clair and St. Clair 1977, issue 3:6).

16. A Wind River Shoshone performance of this song is on the Library of Congress Great Basin recording AAFS L38, side B, the second song on band 7.

CHART 1

The Shoshone Sun Dance Musical Ensemble

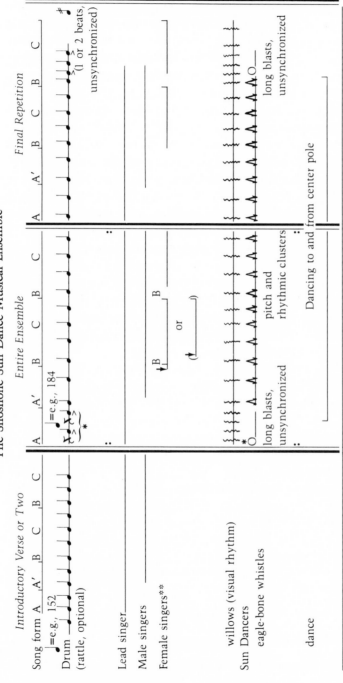

* Drum accents and long eagle-bone whistle blasts occur in the A section only the first time the entire ensemble performs together.
** The vocal entrance of women in Sun Dance songs never coincides precisely with the song form. They enter either at the end of the next phrase to the opening solo call (A') or just after the beginning of the next phrase (B). Likewise, many drop out for the first note or two at the beginning of the incomplete repetition. Throughout Shoshone mu-

sic one finds a counterpoint of strategies, some marking and others obscuring musical boundaries. In the case of Sun Dance songs, female vocal entrances avoid the musical juncture. William Powers notes a similar practice in Round Dance songs: "They [women] usually wait for the first few vocables to go by [of the B section] before they join in" (Powers 1961a:98).

formance and performers. About one Sun Dance song Emily noted that it was actually an old Arapahoe Sun Dance song from the 1930s and 1940s. "The men who sang it," she stated, "are all gone. O. M. sang it. They [Arapahoes] used to help Shoshones sing during their Sun Dance." Once again a song and its performance document the gradual rapprochement between Shoshones and Arapahoes.[17]

Emily is a careful, critical listener and expresses what she admires in singers, songs, and song performance. Her mother typified the good female singer: high voice and a large repertoire. As for the women's Sun Dance singing role, Emily looks for a strong, clear sound. She once complained that the women weren't doing a good job; "they don't sing too good, get soft or quit."

Sun Dance songs should not be too long. After singing one for me, Emily said: "You sing that four times and quit. Same thing over, but four times." The number four, often with reference to the four cardinal directions, has sacred meaning for many Indian tribes, including the Shoshones. The Fourth Morning Prayer Song, already referred to, along with its three companion pieces must be sung exactly four times. Other Sun Dance songs may be and often are repeated more than four times. Listening to her own tapes of herself and Dorothy singing, Emily said that she would tell Dorothy to make it short, but Dorothy preferred to make it long. At home Emily and Dorothy took turns being the lead singer, determining the length of the performance. When Emily led, Dorothy sang an octave above, coming in as soon as she could. When Dorothy was lead singer, Emily sang at the unison, since she was unable to sing any higher. They did not follow the Sun Dance conventions for musical entrance on parts outlined earlier. Vocal range was their only limitation.

The pervasive tension between old and young informs Emily's assessment of Sun Dance songs and performance. Old songs are precious. "There's a lot of Shoshone Sun Dance songs, old-time Sun Dance songs," Emily relates. "They're pretty songs. Looks like somebody ought to sing it, the ones that know it. Now these young people don't hardly hear them sing it. A lot of songs they don't know, the old-time songs."

The Sun Dance Flag Song, which was introduced close to forty years ago, had not yet achieved the status of "old" for Emily. "I don't really sing

17. I have attended the Arapahoe and Shoshone Sun Dances from 1977 through 1982. Shoshone and Arapahoe singers still help one another during the Sun Dance, and in the process songs pass between the tribes. In this respect one notes the use of the Shoshone Sunrise Ceremony Song as a quitting song on the last day of the Arapahoe Sun Dance. Shoshones definitely identify this song as their own; I do not know the Arapahoe judgment about it.

it," she notes. "I know it, but I don't sing it when they're going to stand up too. I don't sing it. I just stand there. It just happened a few years ago, that Flag Song. Never been like that all them other years. It just happened a few years ago after World War II." (Emily did, in fact, sing this song for me in 1977.) How time defies objective measurement! To Emily the Sun Dance Flag Song is as young as World War II. To Lenore Shoyo, youngest singer in this book, World War II, like World War I, happened well before she was born.

On June 22, 1978, I noted the following story passed on to me by the tribal chairman, offering still another perspective on the age of the Sun Dance Flag Song: "Lynn St. Clair slept out in the mountains one night and had a vision in which he 'learned'—was given—the Flag Song. When he returned home he sang it, and some elderly people recognized it as an old Sun Dance song which had been forgotten and not sung for a long time." Shoshones respect and honor their elders; old songs are treated similarly. Thus, at its birth, or rebirth, the Flag Song was respected as an "elder." It was born old.[18]

The tempo of the Flag Song is also affected by generational differences. According to Emily: "It's supposed to be sang that way, slow, all the Sun Dance songs. But now these young people they just go fast. Long time ago, when they're singing, some of them make it fast. Old Indians tell them, 'Slow down. Sing slow.' " Consistent in her complaint, Emily also criticizes old recorded performances if they violate this rule. In her judgment Dick Washakie's 1909 performance of the Fourth Morning Prayer song was too fast: "But now they go like this, like the Wolf Dance songs."[19] Song tempo has changed, and so, too, has the length of some of the older songs. Listening to one Emily remarked, "They sing it now, but forgot part of it." Yet, despite the slow attrition that Emily carefully notes, the Shoshone Sun Dance repertoire—a stock of old songs—remains intact and leaves a distinguishing Wind River Shoshone mark on all five songprints.

Women's Dance (Round Dance) and Wolf Dance (War Dance) Songs

Emily's Women's Dance and Wolf Dance songs come from Shoshone dances of the past. In her mind the songs, dances, dress, and participants

18. The Sun Dance Flag Song is also on the 1951 recording made by Willard Rhodes for the Library of Congress, AFS 14,618B, Archive of Folk Culture. Lynn St. Clair is one of the singers for this performance.

19. The 1909 Edward Curtis recording of Dick Washakie is now in the Archives of Traditional Music at Indiana University, tape 1466; 504, no. 18.

of these older dances expressed Shoshone identity; they were part of the old "Shoshone" way. Although the intertribal powwow is, in some sense, a contemporary counterpart to the older dances, Emily does not see continuity from one to the other, but rather discontinuity. Powwow songs, dances, dress, and participants come from many tribes and supplant the Shoshone precursors in her memory. There is more than a touch of irony here, for although Emily clings tenaciously to a Shoshone past, Shoshones, as we shall see, have a long tradition of cultural exchange. While the particular tribes, their number, and rate of contact and exchange have varied, the actual practice and process remain unchanged.[20] Both the Women's Dance and Wolf Dance of the older Shoshone dances exemplify this practice and process.

At the older Shoshone dances, women were given frequent opportunity to dance. Throughout the evening, after one or two Wolf Dance songs (ancestor of today's Men's Traditional War Dance at the powwow), there would be a Women's Dance, *Waipë? Nïkëp* (ancestor of today's Round Dance). Women chose a male partner, or sometimes two women would choose the same man and dance on either side of him. Emily describes their positions as follows: "The woman holds the man like this [*arm around the waist*], and the man holds her, too [*around the shoulder*]. They stand like this—side by side." Emily's repertoire of Women's Dance songs is testament to the great popularity of this dance in the past.

Scholars have tracked down some of the sources of the Shoshone Women's Dance. In 1912, one year after Emily's birth, Lowie learned about the recent importation of the Women's Dance and noted that "this is a modern dance . . . that came from the Crow . . . not more than eight or ten years ago. . . . There are four or five different singers [men only] with handdrums. The women choose partners, and the men must pay for the privilege of dancing with them" (Lowie 1915:821, 822). Other research reveals Gros Ventre and especially Cree input and influence on the dance (Shimkin 1942:475; Wissler 1913:455). Richard Engavo, an elderly Shoshone man who is Emily's senior by at least a decade, documents this. He remembers the three male societies that were revived early in this century, one of which, in fact, was called *A·no,* "Horn-Packer" (referring to game antlers or horns), the Shoshone name for Cree. All three societies hosted dances, inviting everyone to attend.[21] Engavo recalls one such occasion: "Well, the *A·nos,*

20. Herzog's comments on Plains music written in 1935 still ring true today: "Through warfare, trade and social intercourse between different tribes, foreign songs are introduced, novel dances and rituals spread like our fashions. The result is often kaleidoscopic" (Herzog 1935b:24).

21. Shimkin has described the competitive and social nature of these societies, which

they're going to have a dance. We better get ready and get in there; we'll all be there. Them *A:nos,* they're the ones that Squaw Dance. *A:no* Dance they call that, the women's Squaw Dance." ("Squaw" was an older English translation for *waipë?,* "woman." Many Shoshones today consider it offensive, but old-timers still use it.)

By the time Emily was attending dances, the Women's Dance was established and Shoshone singers had a repertoire of Women's Dance songs. As described by Emily: "This [Women's Dance song no. 1] is what they sang here, Shoshone Round Dance song—not a different tribe. Some of them, they're from different states, but we got some of our own. But they don't sing it; these young people don't know it. The ones that know it all passed away."

Women's Dance Song no. 1

Emily learned all of her Women's Dance songs at the dances just by listening. According to her remembrances, women did not sing these songs with the men, nor did they drum. As reported by Lowie in 1915, hand drums traditionally accompanied Women's Dance songs (Lowie 1915:822; see plate 30 following p. 266 for a picture of a modern hand drum). Only Lenore, the youngest woman of this study, has not seen this tradition. The

---

differed from the military and police functions performed by male societies in nomadic prereservation times (Lowie 1915:813, 814; Shimkin 1942:458).

other four lament its passage. In 1981, prodded by my questions about the drum part, Emily was happy to dub in a drum part over her 1977 performance of Women's Dance song no. 1. She used a pencil on an upturned metal bucket.

Like Sun Dance songs, Women's Dance song no. 1 is in two parts, the second being an incomplete repetition of the first (AA'BC/A'BC). The melodic range is a ninth (g–a'), and the melody starts high and descends by stages. Women's (or Round) Dance songs are set apart by their distinctive rhythmic organization: the drum accompaniment provides the basic un-derlying three-beat pattern (see ex. 1a). If there is any stress or accent on the drum, it falls on beat one.[22] The vocal part often plays against this, either avoiding the first beat through rests (ex. 1b), ties with the preceding beat (ex. 1c), or agogic accents on the second beat (ex. 1d). We defer discussion of subtle asynchronous relationships between voice and drum in Shoshone music until later. Emily's valiant effort on the metal bucket aside, only the two youngest women of the study are experienced drummers.

Example 1. Aspects of rhythmic organization between drum and voice in Women's Dance songs

As in the *Naraya* songs and in virtually all Shoshone music, there are small melodic variants for phrases or parts of phrases in Women's Dance songs. The first half of the B section of Women's Dance song no. 1 appears in three additional forms, as shown in example 2.

Example 2. Variant forms to B section of Women's Dance song no. 1

22. William Powers has published a detailed analysis of Round Dance songs, using Sioux songs as his model. In general Emily's Women's Dance songs conform with Powers's analytical model, varying somewhat in their vocable patterns and the absence of an octave

Women's Dance Song no. 2

(1st verse)
♩. = *ca.* 69

ye____ he ye he ye he ye he____ he ye he ye

he ye____ he ai ____ ya hai____ ye____ he yai e____ hai____

ye oi hai____ hai e____ hai____ e ya hai____ ya hai oi

ya he____ he ai ____ ya hai____ ya he ____ ya he ai e____

hai____ ya oi hai ____ ha ai yi hai____ ya hai____ ya hai oi

EMILY: "Old-time Round Dance song, from the singers, from the old folks singing. These young people, they don't sing that old-time song. It's a Shoshone song."

As we shall see later, Angelina Wagon sings this song, too. She calls it the Goodnight Sweetheart song because she remembers that it was the quitting song for the dances. Another older singer refers to it as the Home, Sweet Home song. For Helene Furlong, next to the youngest woman of the study, it is part of her recognized-but-not-singable category. She remembers it as a cue for mothers to bundle up their children and pack their belongings in preparation for going home.

Women's Dance song no. 3 is transcribed from a tape Emily and Dorothy made in the early 1960s. On their own tapes Emily and Dorothy group songs according to genre, so that one tape or one side of a tape will be all Sun Dance songs or Round Dance songs. It is as though one song brings to mind another, perhaps one with a similar turn of melody or other association. Sometimes in the process songs become entwined, producing a song knot that stops the flow.

Emily acknowledges that song recall can be hard: "Old-time Round

---

leap at the beginning (Powers 1961a:97–104). Library of Congress tapes of Logan Brown singing Women's Dance songs in 1951 all begin with an octave leap. See AFS 14,619A, Archive of Folk Culture.

Dance songs—I know a lot of them. I can't think about them." Often recall, practice, and performance slide from one to the other. After one or several repetitions, the singer comes to a corrected or preferred version of the song, which remains fairly constant throughout the rest of the performance. The following transcription is of the fourth repetition or verse, as Shoshones call it.

Women's Dance Song no. 3

Singers: Emily Hill and Dorothy Tappay

Let us now turn to the Wolf Dance, the predominant dance at older communal occasions. Emily has sung two Wolf Dance songs for me. She once told me she doesn't sing Wolf Dance songs because Wolf (or War Dance) songs were for men. But at another time she confessed, "I know a lot of them."

Wolf Dance Song no. 1

Singer: Emily Hill

EMILY: "The old man, my stepdad, says he sings that song before I was born. That's an old-time Wolf Dance song. These people, they're singing them outside people's songs all the time. These old-time songs, they don't sing them. They don't know them. A long time ago they had dance. Some people, they're not songbirds. They can't get songs. But a person knows, they catch on to songs quicker. Some don't."

In their underlying rhythmic organization, Wolf Dance songs are unlike Women's Dance songs, which move in threes and multiples of threes; Wolf

Dance songs, like most Sun Dance songs, move in twos and multiples of twos. Another connection between Wolf Dance song no. 1 and Sun Dance songs is the use of half steps:

One finds this characteristic primarily in older songs, extinct song genres, ceremonial songs, and, as already mentioned, Sun Dance songs (Vander 1978:101–5). The melody descends by levels within the large range of a thirteenth (a–f'). The song form, once again, is incomplete repetition (ABC/BC). In her solo performance Emily omits the repeat of the opening solo call. Most singers do not do this, even in solo performances. They will usually sing both parts, the lead call and group response. Early in the second section, according to customary practice, accented drumbeats occur every other beat and then resume a straight unaccented beat. Accents, when present, always appear in the second section of the song, often serving as cues to the dancers that the song is about to end. In other ceremonial music the accents cue special dance movements (Vander 1978:41). There are melody markers as well. Distinctive vocal entrances announce the beginning of phrases. The singer attacks the opening note of the melody a fraction of a second "early" or on the beat from a higher pitch, followed immediately by a portamento down into the note. The vocable is sung on the higher pitch before the portamento. The volume remains constant throughout the attack and portamento or, if anything, is stronger on the attack, with the following effect: ♪↓. . This is yet another strategy that separates drum and melody parts.

Wolf Dance Song no. 2

ya hai hai ai___ ha da___ ya he ya ho we yo he___ oi

ya he de he ya he_____ he ai___ ha he yo he_____ ya___ ho

ya he ai___ i ha da ha he ya ha we yo he___ yo

Singer: Emily Hill

Emily also learned Wolf Dance song no. 2 from her stepfather. She described the tempo for the Wolf Dance: "Well, slow dance. That's the way they dance a long time ago. They don't dance like those dancers now, jumping around like a wild Indian. They don't dance like that a long time ago." Although Emily sings two slow Wolf Dance songs, Dorothy remembers two types of Wolf Dance songs in the past: "Some Wolf Dance songs they sing fast; some Wolf Dance songs are kind of slow." A comparison of the tempo of Emily's performance of Wolf Dance song no. 2 with an older rendition also suggests some variety of tempo for Wolf Dance song performances. Emily's tempo is ♩ = ca. 108. In 1951 Logan Brown, a well-known singer of his time (and Angelina Wagon's father), sang the same song at ♩ = ca. 168.[23]

Wolf Dance and Women's Dance, the one focusing on the male dancer, the other on the female, were interspersed at the old Shoshone dances. Several other connections link the two dances. Like the Women's Dance, the Wolf Dance was introduced on the reservation about 1890 by the Crow (Shimkin 1942:456). It was but one version of a dance that spread among many tribes on the Plains, both north and south. Emily relates the Wolf Dance to this movement. "The Grass Dance," she says, "that's what these different tribes call it; it's the Wolf Dance." It is possible to trace and date some of the diffusion routes for the Grass or Omaha Dance. Chart 2 summarizes its dissemination and eventual confluence with older Shoshone dances (Lowie 1915:813–22; Shimkin 1942:456–58). Note the documentation for female singers in the various tribal forms of the Omaha Dance and in the older Shoshone dances. Borrowing, adapting, reviving, renewing—the Wolf Dance is born.

Although Emily and other Shoshones use the terms *Dasayugwe huvië*

23. This song appears on Library of Congress tape AFS 14,619A, Archive of Folk Culture. A musical transcription of this performance is in Vander 1978:127.

CHART 2A
Historical Background of the Shoshone Wolf Dance:
Contribution of the Wind River Shoshone

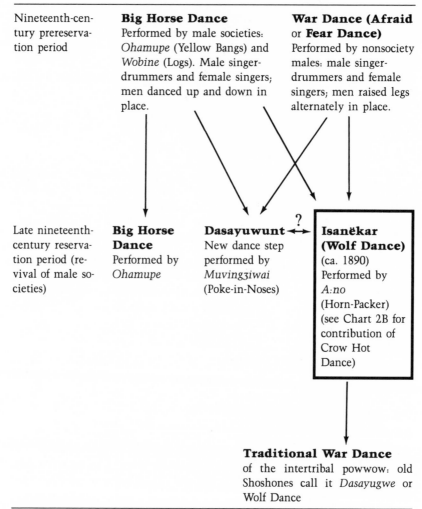

Nineteenth-century prereservation period	**Big Horse Dance** Performed by male societies: *Ohamupe* (Yellow Bangs) and *Wobine* (Logs). Male singer-drummers and female singers; men danced up and down in place.	**War Dance (Afraid** or **Fear Dance)** Performed by nonsociety males: male singer-drummers and female singers; men raised legs alternately in place.

| Late nineteenth-century reservation period (revival of male societies) | **Big Horse Dance** Performed by *Ohamupe* | **Dasayuwunt** New dance step performed by *Muvingʒiwai* (Poke-in-Noses) | **Isanĕkar (Wolf Dance)** (ca. 1890) Performed by *A:no* (Horn-Packer) (see Chart 2B for contribution of Crow Hot Dance) |

Traditional War Dance
of the intertribal powwow: old
Shoshones call it *Dasayugwe* or
Wolf Dance

References: Lowie 1909:222; Lowie 1915:813–22; Shimkin 1942:456–58; and Wissler 1916:865–66, 872.

and *Wolf Dance* interchangeably, the one is not an English translation of the other. The Shoshone word for wolf is *biya iʒapĕ*, literally, "big coyote."

Scholars have tried to learn the derivation for the English term *Wolf Dance.* Lowie reported the use of a coyote tail by a dancer (Lowie 1915:822); Shimkin stated that the name comes from the Crow practice of eating dog

CHART 2B
Historical Background of the Shoshone Wolf Dance:
Contribution of Other Plains Tribes

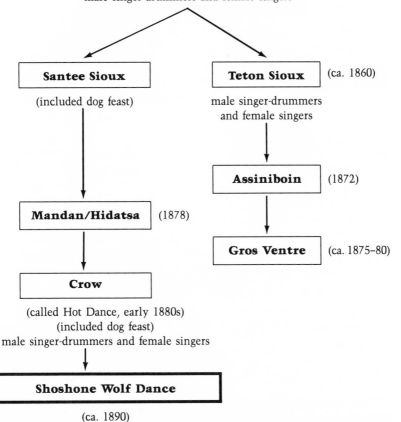

Pawnee

Iruska Society Dance
(later called Hot Dance because of dipping in pot for meat)
male singer-drummers and female singers

Omaha

Hethushka or Omaha Society Dance (Grass Dance)
male singer-drummers and female singers

Santee Sioux

(included dog feast)

Teton Sioux (ca. 1860)

male singer-drummers
and female singers

Assiniboin (1872)

Mandan/Hidatsa (1878)

Gros Ventre (ca. 1875–80)

Crow

(called Hot Dance, early 1880s)
(included dog feast)
male singer-drummers and female singers

Shoshone Wolf Dance

(ca. 1890)

References: Densmore 1918:468–72; Fletcher and LaFlesche [1905–6] 1972:460–61; Lowie 1913:200–203; Murie 1914:629; Vennum 1982:54–55; Wilson 1914 in Vennum 1982:55; Wissler 1912a:266–67; Wissler 1912b:48; and Wissler 1916:865, 868–73.

meat as part of their Hot Dance (Shimkin 1942:458). Shoshones, who do not eat dog under any circumstance, rejected that aspect of the Crow Hot Dance. *Dasayugwe* simply describes the dance step. It means kicking your legs around. Unfortunately, the relationship between the older *Dasayuwunt* Dance and the *Isanĕkar* (Wolf Dance) in chart 2A remains unclear.[24] The *Dasayuwunt* Dance step—"dancing in place, then leaping forward with long steps to the center, hopping back into position"—was a late nineteenth-century innovation (Shimkin 1942:458). Perhaps the two older dances used the same step, or perhaps they were actually the same dance but with different names and meanings for the two different societies, Poke-in-Noses and Horn-Packers. Shimkin stated that the same dance step was also adopted at that same time in the Sun Dance.

Shoshones today associate the Wolf Dance with their own older form of War Dance. They interpret its motions and meaning with Plains warfare: the dancer bends low and swivels his head like a warrior searching for and stalking his enemy. One older Shoshone man likened the warrior to the wolf who searches for his prey. This echoes Densmore's comment about a Sioux Wolf song she recorded in 1911 (L23, Library of Congress): "The Indian warrior wandered like a wolf, and his war songs were often called wolf songs" (Densmore 1951:7). It is interesting to note that among the Crow, from whom Shoshones learned the dance, war scouts were referred to as wolves (Laubin and Laubin 1977:149). In 1916 Wissler wrote: "There is an almost universal association between a ceremonial wolf concept and a war party. It is not only that the wolf is simulated by scouts and wolf songs are sung by warriors, but there is back of it all a definite concept of a supernatural wolf, or wolf power that presides over the affairs of war. . . . The Pawnee are the probable center of its development since it is among them that we find a fundamental mythological basis for the association between the wolf and warfare" (Wissler 1916:873–74). We glimpse some of the Pawnee correspondences between wolves and warriors in Murie's accounts. Scouts on a war party gave their signals "as wolf cries" (Murie 1914:595). After the enemy was spotted, the men sang and danced. "All these songs have a peculiar rhythm and end with wolf calls, from which they take the name wolf songs (see vol. 7, 267)" (Murie 1914:596). This reference leads us to Wissler's Blackfoot research, in which he stated: "All the wolf songs end with a howl, or wolf call, which expresses or symbolizes whatever the

24. From research in 1937 and 1938, Shimkin reported a later function added to the Wolf Dance — the restoration of happiness and well-being for those in mourning (Shimkin 1942:458). It is another example of Shoshone concern for health. Shoshones today do not make any reference to this earlier practice.

Plate 1. Emily Hill, 1981. Picture taken outside Emily's house by the author (Vander 1986:4).

Plate 2. Emily and her sister Millie Guina, inside Millie's tepee encampment for the 1980 powwow at Ft. Washakie, Wyoming. Picture by the author.

Plate 3. Emily Hill, 1981. Emily takes the author to pick currants and gooseberries in a field near her home. Picture by the author.

Plate 4. In 1910 Virginia Grant posed as Sacajawea (Shoshone guide to the Lewis and Clark expedition) for photographer A. P. Porter. The star and crescent moon patterns in the shawl were important motifs in Ghost Dance clothing and ritual objects (Petersen 1976:30, 47–82). Courtesy of the Smithsonian Institution, National Anthropological Archives, no. 56787.

Plate 5. This 1941 Sun Dance picture shows the women who sit behind the male singers around the drum. The women hold willow branches, which they wave while singing Sun Dance songs.

Plate 6. A picture of a Women's Dance on the bank of the Little Wind River above Ft. Washakie in early spring, possibly taken by Lewis E. Webster in 1912. Courtesy of the Archives – American Heritage Center, University of Wyoming, Laramie, Wyoming, no. 0530.

Plate 7. A. P. Porter took this photograph of a Shoshone Women's (Round) Dance in 1910. Courtesy of the Smithsonian Institution, National Anthropological Archives, no. 008687.00.

Plate 8. This 1910 picture of a Wolf Dance by A. P. Porter may be a companion to plate 7. The angles of the roof beams over the dancers' heads suggest that the dance took place in a many-sided dance hall (see plate 9). Courtesy of the Smithsonian Institution, National Anthropological Archives, no. 008686.00.

Plate 9. This many-sided, turreted dance house was photographed on the Wind River reservation in 1926. Its architectural design followed Hidatsa and Crow models (Vennum 1982:120, 121), thus reflecting historical influences in the development of the Shoshone Wolf Dance (see chart 2B, p. 45). Courtesy of the Archives — American Heritage Center, University of Wyoming, Laramie, Wyoming, no. 20605.

singer wishes to obtain, because the wolf howls when he is out on quest.... After the war party has been out a few days... the leader announces, 'Now, it is time to sing the wolf songs. They will give us good luck in getting horses' " (Wissler 1912a:267).

Shoshone mythology carried its own rich associations with the wolf. Wolf is a hero in Shoshone tales, along with his younger brother Coyote, the trickster-hero (Shimkin 1947c:331, 335, 336). Note that in chart 2A the Shoshone name for the Wolf Dance is *Isanёkar*, a compound abbreviation of *iʒapё*, "coyote," and *nёkar*, "dance" (Shimkin 1942:458). However, over time Shoshone distinctions between *Dasayugwe*, Wolf Dance, and Traditional War Dance have faded and blurred. They are now one category, validated with tribal historical overtones.

Emily, in her remembrance of Shoshone Wolf Dance and Women's Dance songs, stands like a rock in the moving stream of Shoshone history and cultural life. Unlike the other women in this book and most Shoshones on the reservation, she has never traveled to other reservations. With the exception of her hospital stay in Denver, she has not ventured much farther than the nearby towns of Lander and Riverton, Wyoming. Emily's distant ancestors were nomads on the Plains. Her descendants — grandchildren and great-grandchildren — have once again taken to the road, no longer by horse but by car and pickup truck. Emily's formative years fell between the two periods of great movement, a time when, for better or for worse, life on the reservation was much more insulated and isolated from the outside Euro-American world and from extensive contact with other Indian tribes. World War II opened the world to many Indian servicemen, and post–World War II tides of change washed onto the reservation. The mass production of cars, building of interstate highways, and per capita allotment of tribal earnings meant that Shoshones had cars, money, and roads to travel. Other Indian tribes were on the move, too. A strong intertribal Indian movement swept the country, generating an important Indian institution, the powwow.

Today, the powwow is a large intertribal gathering for two or three days and nights of singing, contest dancing, games, and a concluding feast, given by a host tribe. During its early development there was great input and influence of Southern Plains tribes from Oklahoma who had rich traditions of dance and costume. Cultural contact led to cultural exchange and borrowing. Two important new elements in the powwow — dance competition and cash awards — even show Euro-American influence (Young 1981:222–23, 243–44). Looking outward and forward, the powwow proudly asserted Indian versus Euro-American cultural traditions and identity. But for Emily, an elder who looks inward and backward, the powwow has obliterated many practices of the older Shoshone dances. It has effaced tribal traditions, meaning, and identity. It is an adversary.

"This powwow business," Emily comments, "is coming from different tribe, not from here. [In the past] they call it, 'we're going to dance,' *nïkarò,* that's all. They don't have different people around, just Shoshones. They don't have different tribes around 'cause they didn't have no money or cars. Nowadays it's powwow. They don't dance like they used to. Now all they want is money. They can't dance without money.[25] They're all spoiled with money. Long time ago the Indians dance in springtime; they dance about two, three, four days—daytime, too. They dance daytime when they're going to quit dancing. [See plate 6 following page 46.] They say, them dancers and drummers, 'Well, we're going to dance, we're going to have a dance. Everybody join, 'cause we come to the spring. We come out good to the spring day—all through the winter. We ought to be glad, dancing for our spring days.' Now, no good no more. They don't dance for that. Now they're just waiting for that powwow. There's so much money for Fancy Dancers. They're all ready there to go. A long time ago women never danced Wolf Dance songs, just men. They got it from some other tribe. They don't even Round Dance anymore! Like last time, last year, they didn't even have no Round Dance. You don't hear no Indian talking. All talking English, telling them through the microphone English. No Indian words. It don't feel good."

The decline of the Round Dance mentioned by Emily is one of several factors that has profoundly affected who participates in the dances. Although there has always been participation of men and women in both old and contemporary dances, the types of dance appropriate for men and women and the age of the dancers differ. In the past women had ample opportunity to dance the very popular Women's Dance. Women of all ages participated, not just young women. After World War II the fast Fancy War Dance moved from the Southern to the Northern Plains. Its flashy style and cash prizes for dance competitions ensured its success and popularity. War Dance competitions pushed aside the Women's Dance and, as we shall see, predominantly middle-aged and older women. Breaking with tradition, Shoshone women began to dance to the slow Traditional War Dance, but although some older women took to this new dancing role, others did not. Eventually, women danced the fast Fancy War Dance as well, called the Fancy Shawl Dance in female competition. The fast tempo and rigorous physical demands

25. Elected members of the Entertainment Committee receive funds from the Shoshone Business Council to support their work in running and managing the powwow. The Entertainment Committee decides the size of the cash prizes awarded in any given year.

make this a young person's dance. Thus, for the bulk of the powwow evening, female participation is mainly younger women who dance both types of War Dance. Very occasional Round Dances draw some of the older women, but many remain in their seats in the outside arbors. There is really no opportunity to get warmed up for just one or two dances an evening, and old bones and muscles get stiff in the progressively colder night air.

Cars and roads and powwows have provided one mode for cultural contact. The popularity and prevalence of tapes and tape recorders have provided another with equally potent impact. Emily has had a tape recorder since at least 1960. She buys commercial tapes of War Dance and Round Dance songs. As in all things, Emily listens with concentration and care. She can document the journey of songs, recognizing older Shoshone songs when performed by singers from other tribes. Emily partakes of cultural exchange, too, for she has learned War Dance songs from tapes of Blackfeet and Sioux music.

Songs Emily Does Not Sing

Naraya songs, Sun Dance songs, and Women's Dance songs — these are what Emily sings. They often accompany her as she works: "I sing, sing, whistle while I'm working everytime." Emily recognizes but does not directly participate in such Shoshone ceremonial songs as the Pointing Stick, Chokecherry, and Giveaway. Women, however, play an important part in the War Bonnet ceremony. Certain women are chosen to sing and others to dance. Although she has never been asked to join in this ceremony, Emily remarks: "I know the songs, but I never — it's just for certain ones. It ain't for young girls; it ain't for anybody. It's for grown-up womens." The increased participation of younger women in the War Bonnet Dance in recent years again reflects a modern trend, a countercurrent to traditional Shoshone values. It may be that Euro-American preoccupation and emphasis on youth feeds this countercurrent.

Emily's Musical Roles

Emily is traditional to the core, and it is fascinating to review her at times eccentric blend of men's and women's musical roles. Within the communal context of the Sun Dance, Emily used to sing the traditional women's part, and she participated in *Naraya* performances. Although in conversation she maintains that only men received *Naraya* songs in dreams,

Songprint 1: Emily Hill

Sample Size: 213	
Naraya	147
Sun Dance	48
Peyote	0
Women's Dance	16
Wolf Dance	2
Handgame	0
Giveaway	✪
Chokecherry	✪
War Bonnet	✪
Euro-American	0

Key: 0 does not know, does not sing
      ✪ knows but does not sing

she, in fact, sings a *Naraya* song received by a Shoshone woman. At home Dorothy and Emily shift to male musical roles, singing Women's Dance songs that, in actual performance at the older dances, were sung only by men. Singing these songs and Sun Dance songs by and for themselves alone, they do not strictly follow conventional singing roles for either men or women. Although Emily is unconventional in these matters, she is not in others. Even in the privacy of her bedroom, Emily does not sing ceremonial music that she knows, because it is traditionally sung only by men. Nor does she sing Euro-American songs, for "Indian songs, that's all Indians used to sing." Emily keeps within her culturally defined musical bounds.

Angelina Wagon

"I'm always singing with my dad — every song like
every War Dance, Round Dance, Sun Dance. Any
kind of song he sings, I'm right there supporting him."

— Angelina Wagon

Angie was born March 29, 1921, in a menstrual hut, the oldest of ten children. "My grandparents raised me," she recounts. "They had a little cabin, that was the old man's, Pevo's [her grandfather]. They had dirt floor — some had dirt floors and dirt roof on top. They had these clay around their logs. They used to put it around their logs between the cracks. Of course, we had a lot of chickens. I had a chicken of my own, a pet white chicken and a dog, black dog. Called it black Pete, *du* Pete. There were some others staying there right beside my grandfather and them. They had children. Nellie was my first cousin, and she was my friend. She's the one I used to lay around with all the time when I was small, I and her. Probably we were about seven, eight years old. We used to go out, walk around, sing Sun Dance songs. We'd sit and we'd sing Sun Dance songs. We used to take blankets, and she had a red blanket that she'd always wear around. She would never get rid of that. My dad called her Red Blanket, *Engawanhagant* [literally, "she who has a red cloak"]. He never called me anything. Angelina. I never had no Indian name. I wish they did call me — [*laughter*] I don't know what they'd call me!

"He [her grandfather] used to tell a lot of stories. That's when my dad always told that you ain't supposed to tell stories until you got a lot of wood. You must always finish the story. Because if you don't, he says it might have been getting, oh, all kinds of things that, you know, some bad luck or whatever. He told us you got to finish the story. And the old man [Pevo] said no, we could keep it. We got words to say, you know, before we finish that. We can just keep it for our next night for another story.[1]

1. Angie's grandfather, Pevo Brown, was among the principal informants for Shimkin's

51

He told stories about coyote and buffalo and beaver, otter, and elk. Mostly of those, like bats, and some kind of evil lady, some kind of *waipë*? [woman]. Water lady, that's another one he told about, a water lady, and *tsoap."*

JUDY: "The ghost?"

ANGIE: "*Hā* [yes], and that *honovich."*

JUDY: "Is that a man-eating cannibal?"

ANGIE: "I think that is. He told a real lot of stories."[2]

After her grandmother passed away, Angie returned to live with her parents. "I don't know when my grandma passed away, maybe I was seven years old, and then I came back to [live with] my mother and my dad. My mother took over after I was going to school." Like Emily, Angie attended the reservation boarding school. Young and adaptable, she quickly adjusted to the rigors of school and the challenge of learning English for the first time. The school was converted into a day school when Angie was in the fifth or sixth grade. "I liked that boarding school better than the day school," she recalls, "because we stay there and learn a lot of things." Cooking, baking, cleaning, sewing—Angie enjoyed learning all the life skills that were part of the boarding school program. Her formal education ended with the completion of primary school in the eighth grade.

Angie's childhood held many happy hours spent with friends and devoted to play and games. Emily's half sister Dorothy was her closest companion: "I and Dorothy, we walk around, we sing. She was my best friend."

At school Angie played jacks and baseball; on the weekends she watched and joined Shoshones who played Handgame and card games. There was no hard dividing line between the ages. "They used to have gambling down here," Angie relates. "I go over and play with them. That was a long time ago. Later, I guess they had a law [imposed by the Bureau of Indian Affairs and prohibiting children from the games]. There was also betting." As a teenager Angie played Shinny (*Nïdoink*), a traditional ball game for women of all ages. At fifteen she was the youngest member of her team of five

classic study "Wind River Shoshone Literary Forms: An Introduction" (Pevo, spelled with an *e* according to Angie, appears as Pivo in Shimkin's article). Water images and water control, so important in the Shoshone *Naraya* and Sun Dance, are also part of Shoshone storytelling. According to Shimkin: "Magical control of weather is intimately connected with the narration of myths. . . . Tales must be told to the formal ending and not beyond, lest it storm. The ending itself is a statement obscurely hinting at melting snow, which results from properly told stories" (Shimkin 1947c:330).

2. According to Shimkin *honovich,* "bat," is not a cannibal but a benign and sexually superpotent creature (1986, personal communication). From her grandfather Angie also heard historical accounts of Indian wars in Montana and how Shoshones came to choose what they called Warm Valley as the location for their reservation.

players. The game is played on a large field, and each team tries to hit a buckskin-covered ball with sticks and knock it through the opposing team's goal lines. Angie describes the game as being "real popular a long time ago. The Shinny ball was round, little bit bigger than a baseball, but not too hard, you know. It's gotta be soft, just so it don't go real far. The sticks were slanted this way and bigger at the bottom, dished out more like that. [A picture of a 1900 Shinny stick collected on the Wind River Shoshone reservation matches perfectly with Angie's description (Shimkin 1986:324).] Nowadays they don't even know. We had to cut our own sticks. They weren't really long, just the same size that you could hold." Shinny is now played only during the Shoshone powwow each summer. Just old pros like Angie note that the sticks used today more closely resemble hockey sticks than Shinny sticks. (For a picture of Lenore Shoyo playing Shinny during the 1982 Shoshone powwow, see plate 31 following p. 266.)

At home Angie received crucial lessons in the value of work, as she helped farm, garden, gather wild foods, and hunt.

ANGIE: "[Pevo is] the first one anyway to have this place here. Of course, he was younger then. And then Dad took over later, when he got a little older. I go out there and help Grandpa, you know, we irrigate water up there. And the old man, he had to get that prairie dog hole. We had a lot of prairie dogs up there. He'll hold that shovel down and get all the water on this side and let it go. And then it'll go in there and flush 'em out. That's what the old man used to do, flush them prairie dogs out. People like those. They used to be really fat. It tastes good. I like prairie dogs."

JUDY: "Did Pevo used to hunt other animals?"

ANGIE: "The deer, elk, mountain sheep, antelopes, them pheasants, quails. Well, they go hunting for those rabbits and jack rabbits."

Angie's grandparents dried the butchered meat on dome-shaped drying racks. The poles resting on top of Angie's kitchen cupboards serve the purpose today.

ANGIE: "A long time ago we used to get those wild onions, wild turnips, the wild potatoes, the wild carrots. And bitterroot and there's one other wild things—just about looks like a potato, too, but it tastes good. And the wild rutabagas, it's got some sharp points on there, and it's got a purple flower. They skin them and eat that, but I don't know what it's called. They eat all kinds of wild food: chokecherries, bullberries, currants, elderberries, gooseberries, and there's another little red berry, and wild plums, wild raspberries. They used to grow along the river here, a lot of raspberries. Wild strawberries, I used to gather, too. There is really a lot of wild food around here. I don't think people ever know nothing about them things now.

"My mother and my dad, they used to have a big vegetable garden here. They put it way up there where the trees are now. Corn, turnips, carrots, peas, beans, rutabagas, radishes — all kinds. They had a big patch of watermelon, Indian watermelon, too, yellow ones and they got black seeds in them. They really taste good.

"When I was about eight years old, I started going out and helping my dad, stacking hay, cut hay. I usually used to be busy working out there. That's what I was raised on, working, too. That's why I never get tired of working."

In addition to their large vegetable garden, Angie's folks farmed and ranched. They grew crops of wheat, oats, barley, and alfalfa. The Bureau of Indian affairs (hereafter BIA) encouraged this, sending around an extension agent known as a "farmer boss," who distributed seeds and farming advice. Children were encouraged to garden and compete in annual fairs for prizes. When only nine years old, Angie won a heifer.[3] The BIA also issued cows to families. The ten years that separate Angie and Emily are crucial here. The extension service of the BIA began in 1929 (DeRiso 1968:15). Whereas Emily's parents could not afford to own a cow during her early years, Angie's family received cattle through the BIA program. In addition her folks raised chickens, pigs, and horses.

As with Emily's family, Angie's received food rations issued by the tribal agency: sugar, flour, coffee, canned meat, slab bacon, and macaroni. (Because macaroni was freely rationed out, it was always added to the soup served at tribal feasts. Long after the agency stopped dispensing rations, soup with macaroni continues to be served at tribal feasts. It has become traditional, a Euro-American sister to chokecherry gravy.) Freshly slaughtered beef was also issued to families. The Shoshone names for days of the week document the importance of these rations in daily life one-half century ago:

Thursday: *Du:tinwaravE*, "penning the beef day"
Friday: *DuwĕsedavE*, "slaughtering day," or *GohoiyïgwïdavE*, "getting the entrails day" (a Shoshone favorite)
Saturday: *Mu?davE*, "ration day"

As Angie grew up, she learned her proper future role as an adult

3. Angie corroborates DeRiso's assessment of the program for children. DeRiso writes: "There is some indication that . . . young girls engaged in farming with greater enthusiasm than boys. . . . This fact is supposed by the distribution of prize heifers, which were most often won by girls" (DeRiso 1968:15).

woman. "My folks used to tell me that inside the house is woman's, that's their business. They'll stay and cook, wash, and clean up. And the man's would be outside, building fence and doing farm work and all that. So they say the man's part is outside. That's what they used to tell me a long time ago." Within the home Angie learned to tan buckskin and to do beadwork. Her mother taught her the latter: "It was my mother. My grandma sews, but I never did watch. I learned that from my mother. See, when it [boarding school] just come to be day school, when I come home in the evening, Mother would be sewing. And on Saturday and Sunday she'd sew. And then I'd do all that with her. I see how she do it, and then from her I learned all these beadwork." Observation and imitation, the typical Shoshone way to learn, counterpointed verbal school lessons. The importance of visual-spatial perception in Shoshone culture is, in fact, a theme I shall return to later.

Courtship presaged the final act in Angie's childhood. At age seventeen she married her childhood sweetheart. "Then we fixed our own frame house, frame tent," Angie recounts. "I had my own place, 'cause my dad, you know, he says when you get married, he says, the man is going to be the head of your family; he's the one that's supposed to take care of you. He just let me go then, 'cause I was under somebody else, not under him. Because he says when you get married you make your own living. And so that's what we done. We built our own house, just a little ways from here. Because this one was my land, you know, and I have to keep my house over here. My grandfather willed this to me, my own allotment [term for inherited land on the reservation]."

Angie has spent most of her adult life raising children, four of her own and, at different times, seven of close relatives. Shoshone reckon kinship differently from non-Indian Americans: besides the biological mother and father, aunts and uncles are also considered and called mothers and fathers.[4] Following this logic, first cousins are brothers and sisters. This is not just a matter of kinship terminology; in practice, children may stay for varying lengths of time in one or several of their "parental" homes. (Angie's own early upbringing by her grandparents is another common pattern.)

An experienced mother, Angie really warms up to her memories of caring for babies and children. I have collected a scant two lullaby-ostinato

4. Although this applies specifically to kinship terms for mother's sisters and father's brothers, there are also distinct special relations and kinship terms for mother's brothers and their nieces and nephews and for father's sisters and their nieces and nephews (Shimkin 1986:316).

fragments from all five women. One is from Angie. She created a gentle motorlike sound for the following lullaby fragment, vibrating her lips as she hummed:

Lullaby Fragment no. 1

(lips vibrating)   a o_____   a o_____

ANGIE: "I used to say that to my little kids. They go to sleep."

Angie had her four children baptized at the Episcopal Mission, just as she herself had been baptized there by its founding minister, the Reverend John Roberts. In raising her children, Angie followed her father's advice. "My dad used to say, 'You girls, don't ever learn your children that English before their Indian words. Whenever they go to school they're still going to learn it from the white man. But your Indian comes first. They could just go ahead and talk Indian any time they want.' So that's what I done to my kids. They all know how to talk Indian."

While raising their family, Angie and her husband worked the land, putting in a vegetable garden in summer. But by the late 1940s summertime also became a time for traveling. "We traveled a lot," Angie relates. "We go up Montana to the Crow Sun Dance. And then we'd go to Pryor, Montana, for that Sun Dance. And we'd go clear down to Lame Deer, Montana, those Cheyenne people's Sun Dance down there." Their frequent attendance at Sun Dances was, in part, due to Angie's father, Logan Brown, a well-known singer who was often called upon to sing at Sun Dances. Then, too, powwows and the powwow circuit were not yet fully developed. Angie continues: "They didn't have powwows too much then, but we used to go up to the Crow Fair [currently among the biggest powwows on the Northern Plains]. They used to have all kinds of games: spear throwing game, rock throwing games, Shinny game, and the Handgame contest. All kinds. And you could hear all them drums going."

At a certain point summertime travel conflicts with working the land. To do one is to neglect the other. In their efforts to turn nomadic hunters such as the Shoshones into settled farmers and ranchers, government agents in the early 1900s viewed Indian dancing as an enemy of settled agricultural life. They sought to control and contain the dancing by placing it within "educational" Indian fairs. (With historic overtones the Crow powwow is still called Crow Fair.) Ironically, Indian exposure to Euro-American values of competition with cash prizes, which first appeared in these fairs (rodeos and Wild West shows), helped set in motion that which it sought to suppress (Young 1981:219, 221–23, 233, 244). The popularity of War Dance competitions and prizes, in conjunction with renewed pride in Indian identity, proliferated powwows and the powwow circuit and season. The circuit spread and flourished, often at the expense of gardening and farming. Of the five women in this book, only Emily, who has not traveled, has most consistently raised a large garden each summer, until her own health made this impossible.

Angie has weathered many losses in her life. Only one of her four children survives, and the rest of the children she has raised at various times have all scattered. In 1979 her husband died. Despite it all, Angie maintains a remarkably sunny outlook on life in general and her life in particular. Something of her spirit and values shines through the following catalogue of the happy times and activities of her life: "Well, maybe my traveling, see other people around, you know, what other people's doing are — Sun Dance, dancing, you know, powwows. And besides that, riding horses, putting up gardens, and working on the farm. I think I enjoyed everything, everything. Even my beadwork, you know, learning my cooking. I think everything is all good. Taking care of my kids; raise them myself. Everything like that was all my happy life. Even when I got married, we'd go here and there with one another. No hard feelings towards each other. Happy, all good. Nice feelings towards my family, towards my relatives, towards everybody."

Angie's Songs

Angie's father shaped her lifelong involvement with music. "I never back off when my dad is singing, 'cause we always got to support him, sing with him — every song, any kind of song he's singing. That's the way it's always got to be. 'Cause he says, 'OK you girls, you're my supporters. You got to sing with me.'" Her expression of support for his singing effort reflects more than just a father-daughter relationship. It is part of a broader sociomusical ethic, an ideal of a cooperative group effort. This, in turn, springs from music's essential function at all communal occasions, social and religious. A powwow is, in part, judged by the number of dancers out on the dance floor. Good singers arouse and inspire the dancers to dance. Sun Dance singers lend critical assistance to Sun Dancers in their quest for health and power. In contrast to many types of music within Western traditions, Shoshone songs do not express individual feelings, and singers

do not seek personal recognition and admiration for their public performances. Singers "help" one another and contribute to the success of each
occasion through their cooperative musical participation and presence.[5] Music is the stuff of tribal survival, a central and defining element of the
culture.

Angie's father personified her model of a good singer. "My dad had a
good voice, loud singer, knows lots of songs — all kinds of songs — War Dance,
Sun Dance, Round Dance, long-time-ago Memorial songs, Flag songs. He
had a good memory, singing those songs right along. Gets it right away, too.
My dad could hear a person sing a song once, and he's going to catch that
song. He's what they call a song catcher, *huvia uru*? [literally, "the song
he knows"]. Catch that song right away, if it's real. That's what he used
to tell us. He said, 'If that song's real, got a meaning to it, I'm going to
catch it. But if it's a fake, a song that's just made up — no, that song ain't
good towards me. Make-up songs don't come to a person, it don't stick with
them. It'll take off.' That's what he used to say. My dad don't wait to sing —
to catch on or which song he wants to sing. He sings them right along,
one right after each other."

"A long time ago," Angie continues, "when he was a young boy, he
was blessed with singing songs — his throat. Somebody gave him a throat,
a songs, a singing, drums, dance. Some old man blessed him — that dirt,
and then up to him, and then the dirt up to the throat. An old man gave
him all that. That's the way he was blessed, and that's the way he sings
good. And this old man told him to use *doza* [see *Naraya* song no. 8, pp.
22–23] when you sing. Each time your throat's not going to give away,
you're going to sing really loud and good. And my dad even used to eat
these little crickets alive that are around here. He says this is mine, it's my
throat. But later, twelve years before he passed on, he just couldn't sing
good. Somebody took that from him, and he said it was these — the tape
recorder.

"He sang all his life. I had no trouble singing with him. So it's just
like I sing good with him, too. I'd sing with him, and then I know them
songs. All of us family sing, even my sisters — they all sing good. We never
make up songs or anything, just learn from my dad. He goes all over. He
knows about songs where he gets them."

---

5. William Powers notes that Oglala Sioux use the same expression and ideals of
"helping out" in relation to music and other aspects of social interaction (Powers 1982:16,
17). Elsewhere he reports: "An informant told me that a good singer was a man 'who doesn't
start a song too high, or too low, and who helps you out all through the song' " (Powers
1961c:161).

Plate 10. Angie and her husband, Jim, posed for this picture in 1952 at Thermopolis, Wyoming. On this occasion they and many other Shoshones dressed in traditional costume to participate in Marie Montabe's "Gift of the Waters," a "Historical Indian Pageant."

Plate 11. Angie at home, 1981. Photograph by the author.

Over her lifetime Angie, like Emily, has learned and sung a large repertoire of songs. Her guess is that it exceeds 100. I have recorded her singing 32 songs: 7 *Naraya*, 8 Sun Dance, 6 Round Dance, 1 Forty-nine, 3 War Dance, and 5 Handgame songs, along with 1 lullaby and 1 hymn — the last a relic of early missionary zeal. The omission of Peyote songs is noteworthy. "I sing those too," Angie states, "but I don't think I want to sing them. Somehow there's a law on those that you don't: their sacred nature. They're religious."

Beyond her particular reasons for not wishing to record Peyote songs, Angie has ambivalent feelings about recording songs in general. On the one hand she wants to tape songs in an effort to preserve them. She uses a tape recorder for preservation as defined by Western scholarly traditions. But on the other hand her Shoshone notions concerning the animate nature of song and its intimate connections with power and meaning argue against taping. This came out during our first taping session, when Angie had difficulty recalling a Sun Dance song that her mother had received in a dream. Frustrated, Angie used a tape to jog her memory, and then she sang it for me. Later I asked if she often used the tape recorder as a memory aid.

ANGIE: "No. That was unusual the other day. But I don't know, it might have just didn't want me to sing it, or something that way. You know, some old people, they kind of don't like to sing songs on the tape recorder. Just like my dad used to say, he said he don't care to use the tape recorder for his song. That's why I never got all of his old songs, like Flag songs and the Chief's songs and like these old Memorial songs. I never got them 'cause he didn't want to be taped. I tried to tape some songs from him, but each time he sees me he quits. He said it's no good to tape his songs, tape songs from people long time ago. Just like me, see, I couldn't remember all those songs. That's the way it happens, too. You can't get out with songs because these songs might be the ones to hide away from people. Like that song that my mother sang, maybe it didn't want me to sing that song. I just [usually] get it right away, but that time I couldn't. So I guess it don't want to be taped. That's why it hid, you know. They always say songs hide. Any songs that do that, they don't want to be taped. Maybe that's what happened."

Another song, a Round Dance that customarily ended the old social dances, also eluded Angie and my tape recorder during our first recording session. Note in the following comments that the dichotomy between sacred and secular in Western culture is not present in Angie's thought; "meaning" may adhere to any song genre: "I know it [the concluding song], but it didn't come to me that time. You know what I said about songs. Some of them's got big meanings to it but they don't come to you. They hide away. They got a lot of meanings to social songs. Well, us young people, we don't know. Old people know the meanings in it. They talk about it. Some don't listen to what the old people tell them. They don't realize what it means and all that. But me, I listen to my old people. So nowadays when things happen—wrong doings—I see it happening, the meanings that the old people used to say. I believe in them old people. I listen to them, and I do what they tell me."

On our final recording session, Angie remembered and sang the Round Dance song that signaled the end of the old dances, as well as many other older songs. Later she commented that the old songs had come to her so that they could be passed on to her son. The songs themselves had resolved Angie's ambivalence. They came out of hiding. They wanted to be taped, much to Angie's, her son's, and my delight.

Naraya *Songs*

In her youth Angie attended *Naraya* dances, which she describes as follows: "They are religious, you know. They tell some people to put it up, just like Sun Dance. It's for healing, or they put it up for somebody, to heal them. They would dance for four nights. It's got a meaning to that. It might be in a building or out in the open, maybe out in the brush someplace, in a circle, just dancing. There was a fire on the outside or in the center. They would hold hands, and they could get partners, too, or maybe just ladies dance. It depends on what they think. Well, they just go dance, oh, probably in the evening, not too long—probably until about 12:00 or 1:00 A.M. Some of them had a feast at the end. Some will furnish food like having a feast with them, you know, it's been said to him or her. It's got meanings to that." Angie demonstrated the *Naraya* dance step—a sideward step as in the Round Dance but smoothly executed with no up-and-down motion. Men clicked the heels of their boots together after dragging the right foot back into position next to the left.

Although Angie knows many *Naraya* songs, it is hard for her to estimate the exact number in her repertoire. Five of the seven she has sung for me are part of Emily's songprint as well.

We had listened to a 1909 recording of Dick Washakie, Chief Washakie's son, the day before our first recording session.[6] Angie had recognized one

6. Edward Curtis's 1909 recordings of Wind River Shoshone music are on file at the Archives of Traditional Music at Indiana University (accession no. 57-014-F).

of the *Naraya* songs on the tape and wanted to sing it for me. "My grandfather sings that song," she noted. "When I was a little girl I used to listen to him sing, and I even help him sing it, too—that same song."

Naraya Song no. 12

(1st verse)

Na-ya-su-yag e-hom-bi na-ya-su-yag e-hom,_ Na-ya-su-yag e-

hom - bi na-ya-su-yag e-hom._ Sĭ-nam_ bo-gom-bi en-ga-na

to-do-wain-da sĭ-nam bo-gom-bi en-ga-na to-do-wain-da.

Na-ya-suyag ehombi,		*na-ya-suyag ehom,*	
Desirable	(?*wongovi,* pine tree)	desirable	(?pine tree),

Na-ya-suyag ehombi,		*na-ya-suyag ehom.*	
Desirable	(?*wongovi,* pine tree)	desirable	(?pine tree).

Sĭnam		*bogombi engana todowainda,*	
(?Tree, shrub, not *sĭnav,* "aspen")	berries	red	ripe and burst open,

Sĭnam		*bogombi engana todowainda.*	
(?Tree, shrub, not *sĭnav,* "aspen")	berries	red	ripe and burst open.

ANGIE: "Something like those little red pine berries. Just like, you know, when you have holly—those same kind of berry. *Na·suyag* means it really looks good. You want it when you see it. *Engana* means something like red, busting, bust, or whatever. Burst open, really ripe, and really nice.

"They got to find those songs. They got to have a real meaning for it, too. They just come from people to people. I don't know where that song started from. My old people, they sing those. I learned those songs from them a long time ago. They're not really hard to learn. I sing them sometimes when I'm just walking around."

It is interesting to compare Angie's performance of this song with Emily's (taped as much as ten years earlier) and with Dick Washakie's 1909 recording. There is remarkable constancy in the three performances over time.

Songprints

Three Performances of *Naraya* Song no. 12

Angie's remembrances of *Naraya* performances document the transition from a religious to a social dance as well as the eventual disappearance of even the social form of *Naraya.* "When I used to go to them dances," she states, "you put your blanket over you. Maybe you got your boyfriend in there with you. That's that kind of dance that one is. Some might be religious in it, too. Or some just go up there — either way, whatever they think, you know." Angie also saw this quasi-social, abbreviated form of the *Naraya* performed after the Sun Dance. Shimkin reported the brief inclusion of the *Naraya* as a social dance after the Sun Dance. He also noted its two forms, religious and social (Shimkin 1953:433, 451, 458). According to Angie: "It was someplace in the '40s that kind of quietened [*sic*] down. Some of the people around here, I don't think they give that dance. I don't know why. Maybe the people that all gave that dance passed on and all that. But these young people, they never did get that dance. Maybe they don't know the songs or something. Not like them old people that used to give them dances. I think some of that still goes on in Idaho, because they give that dance. Last year [1980] my uncle gave that dance back there. They still have that dance, but us people here, we don't do it."

Angie's son Lawrence remembers a *Naraya* performance in 1959, but it remained an isolated event. All links to earlier contexts and meanings had been irrevocably severed.

Naraya song no. 13, conspicuously absent from Emily's repertoire of 147 *Naraya* songs, expresses the social and nonreligious nature of later *Naraya* performances. Angie explained the text: "It says you're not a pretty, good-looking girl. Around on the other side [of the *Naraya* circle], there's a pretty, good-looking girl. It's good to hear about that. *Nünzie dam biya-rïn gaiyo,* I don't know what that means. It says something about our mother."

Naraya Song no. 13

Geya güza geya güza tsa   vuïndïn nevi.
Not   very   not   very   good- looking girl.

Eangwarïnda   zu   tsana vuïndïn nevi.
On the other side (?very) good- looking girl.

Nünzie dam biya-rïn gaiyo.[7]
?   our   mothers ?

Tsan narangë soagïnt.
Good words   thinking.

Using Emily's *Naraya* repertoire as a standard, many things mark *Naraya* song no. 13 as unusual. In place of a spare text and images of water, plants, animals, and the soul, there is a much wordier, proselike text with suggestive sexual allusions. The musical style of this song is also unusual, combining *Naraya* and non-*Naraya* characteristics. Although the use of shifting rhythmic organizations is not the rule for *Naraya* songs, we have already seen this in nos. 5 and 9 (pp. 19–20 and 24). But the very thumbprint of *Naraya* style — repeated phrases — is missing. Links to traditional texts and musical style, like links to earlier contexts and meanings, broke apart.

Sun Dance Songs

ANGIE: "Jim [Angie's husband] used to talk about that big prayer, because he says that the Sun Dance is a big prayer. People always got to sacrifice to it. Have big prayers. When some sick person goes in, they're going to come out feeling good, healed himself. Well, that's what he believed, you know. He believed in that."

And so does Angie, who has sung with the women and performed all the essential supporting tasks for her husband, son, grandfather, and other relatives who have been Sun Dancers over the years. The following Sun Dance visions of her husband and grandfather strengthen Angie's belief in the religion and her strict observance of Sun Dance taboos: "My grandfather looked at the buffalo head [attached to the center pole] and saw water and shiny green grass coming to his place in the lodge. [How closely this vision echoes the imagery in *Naraya* song no. 5: "the water shining and the grass on the earth green."] My husband, he had [seen] that little good luck doll or baby. Everytime he Sun Dance it comes to him, plays around with him. He sees that little doll. [If a menstruating woman were nearby,] well, it

7. Shimkin suggests the following translation of this line: "Maybe (*Nunkie*) Our Mothers are departing (*gai'yu*)." He therefore believes that this may have originally been a religious song and prayer to Our Mothers (Shimkin 1986, personal communication).

would walk away from him, or it could do damage to him, too, you know. He don't want to lose that, 'cause it's a good luck doll."

Angie's involvement in the Sun Dance has been lifelong. She sang Sun Dance songs with her cousin when she was only seven years old; with friends she used to act out the Sun Dance. Angie remembers parts of the preliminary ceremony no longer performed. Before erecting the Sun Dance Lodge, Shoshones used to hold a sham battle that culminated in the symbolic "killing" of the cottonwood center pole. After this battle Angie's father went among the Sun Dance camps with a drum and sang old Victory or Scalp Dance songs. Angie and her sister trailed along making war whoops. She remembers, too, the ululation (piercing tongue trill) of the women, often touched off by the remembrance of dead relatives. One older woman referred to it as "their worship."[8]

As an adult Angie joined her family in their yearly pilgrimages to the Sun Dances of other tribes. They often attended the Ft. Hall Shoshone Sun Dance in Idaho, where since at least 1935 women as well as men have been Sun Dancers (Jorgensen 1972:26). Angie explained why she herself has never been a Sun Dancer: "I don't have no vision for that. I don't have no vision, and I can't say that. You can't promise, you can't say it, if it's not real. That's what I tell them when they tease me: 'Oh yeah, this year Angie's going to go in.' No. It can't be said because I didn't see it, and I didn't get the feeling or anything."

At home Angie sings Sun Dance songs with the women. Like Emily, she joined the women who used to sing with the men the Fourth Morning Prayer song for the raising of the Sun Dance Lodge center pole. She notes that women who sang during the Sun Dance would encircle and face the Sun Dance drum rather than follow the more recent custom of facing the dancers.

Comparing contemporary Sun Dances with those of days past, she sees a greater percentage of young Sun Dancers, including some boys in their early and mid-teens.[9] The Sun Dance is one of many aspects of Wind River Shoshone life witnessing a growing prominence of younger people.

8. War whoops and ululation are further examples of different musical roles for women that complement male song performance. Powers reports this same relationship of song performance and female response (ululation) for Oglala Honor songs: "Women ululate at the moment that they hear their male relatives' names mentioned by singers in the honor songs" (Powers 1984:460). A very different context, in the Mescalero Apache Girls' Puberty Ceremony, provides still another similar example. According to Farrer, "As the [male] Singers chant to each Grandfather, the women 'send forth a voice', a high-pitched ululation of reverent praise and pride" (Farrer 1980:130).

9. Shimkin has reported that in 1937 the mean age for Sun Dancers was thirty-seven

The presence and acquisition of power influences every facet of the Sun Dance. Songs, which themselves have power, help the Sun Dancer in his quest. [May 27, 1982. "Angie's dad sang in Idaho, and two women and one man were knocked down with power. One woman credits this to him — since then she doctors people."] Not only do songs help Sun Dancers acquire the power to heal, they help the Sun Dance Chief as he doctors during the ceremony. A former Shoshone Sun Dance Chief, for example, commented, "There is one [song] if they sing, I can do almost anything" (Voget 1984:178).

Angie's father timed his singing of the more powerful songs to the Sun Dancers' physical-ceremonial progress. "A long time ago my dad used to say, the old songs — they're more powerful than the new ones that come out. So he used to sing old songs on the second day, because he says they got power in them. Give 'em more blessings to the dancers. Maybe some of these old people will find something that's going to be blessed to them that day, 'cause that's the day when they're already dry. And then maybe that buffalo head [on the center pole], he's going to bless some of the old people in there that day. That's the time buffalo head is watching each one, which one he's going to bless. That second day is the time my dad usually sings."

Sun Dance songs thus come from the world of power and vision, and, in turn, they can also be instrumental in tapping into that world. Recorded in my log notes is one incident where the absence of Sun Dance singing actually aborted a vision, including the sacred talisman of a vision song. [July 26, 1978. "Angie's son once danced in the Sun Dance, and he was getting a vision of a white buffalo running, and he could hear a song far off — but the Sun Dance singers stopped singing so the vision slipped away, and she [Angie] feels that because of it he never learned his vision song and wasn't 'blessed.' "] Angie described the origins of a Sun Dance song that came to her mother. This was the song that hid from my tape recorder during our first taping session. "My mother, she found that song. When the sun was coming out and she came into our kitchen and then she heard that song. She was sleeping the first time she heard that song, so she start in singing that song. And when she sang that song, well, she thought that it was a prayer song. Something mentioned to her that it would be a prayer song. That's the way they do, too, for the Ghost Dance songs. It's got meanings to them or something like that, to somebody that found that song. So she got up and was singing that song, and she went in there to

---

(with a range of sixteen to eighty). There were two significant clusters: seventeen to twenty-five years and fifty to fifty-eight (Shimkin 1953:466). In recent years the younger group predominates, with relatively few older Sun Dancers.

the room where my dad was sleeping; and she sang that song for him, and my dad just caught that song all at once [the sign of a true visionary song]. He just sang it once, and he knew that song and that's what they sing. And my dad sang that song 'cause it was my mother's song. The old man said, 'Well, if it's given to you, maybe it's been a blessing for you. We should have it for a starting song, call it a Prayer Song, *Naishuntai Huvia*.' And nowadays you hear this Prayer Song all over, even in Idaho, Utah. They sing that song; they have that Prayer Song when they start that singing, opening. The Sun Dance Chief prays at the pole. They [the Sun Dancers] just stay in one place. [This takes place after the Sunrise ceremony and just before the morning's Sun Dancing.] And sometimes now, they use it for a quitting song, too."

The Prayer Song, like *Naraya* song no. 1, demonstrates that women tapped into the realm of vision and power. Again, the song reached the community through a man, in this case, Angie's father. Although the Prayer Song is one of the few Sun Dance songs that people refer to by name, no one, except for Angie, has ever mentioned its connection with her mother.[10] The Prayer Song and most songs that Shoshones sing are like growing plants. They spring up and spread wherever there is fertile soil; their origins remain unimportant, often unknown. Of the 425 songs collected for this study, only one exceptional example in Lenore Shoyo's songprint reveals song ownership and includes restrictions on performance.

Power, if misused, can affect a person's singing ability. Once when Angie was singing out with a good clear voice during the Sun Dance, someone became jealous of her ability and, using power, took away her voice. Since that time she feels that she sings with a strong voice for one song but then rapidly loses strength. Bad thoughts trigger harmful physical repercussions and lead to undesirable social consequences. Because Shoshones value group solidarity and harmony above all else, boasting or calling undue attention to oneself is discouraged, since such behavior may lead to jealousy and friction. The vicious circle of jealousy brings physical harm back to the one who is, in some sense, too conspicuous. Abused, power breaks down social harmony. This intricate network of beliefs and values is at odds with Western ideals of competition and personal fame. Angie's behavior was beyond reproach; she was supporting ("helping out") the Sun Dance and Sun Dancers. Nevertheless, she inadvertently placed herself in danger and suffered the consequences.

10. This song is not to be confused with the four Morning Prayer songs sung by the Sun Dance Chief at the Sunrise ceremony and for the erection of the center pole of the lodge. As to meaning, Shoshones say that all Sun Dance songs are prayer songs.

Of the thirty-two songs Angie has sung for me, eight are Sun Dance songs, a small sampling from her large Sun Dance repertoire. "I think I know a large amount, a lot of Sun Dance songs," she says. "I just can't get to one of them, they're all tangled up. I learned the songs from my elders and my dad. The older people, like my dad, they sing them slower, not too fast. Now, they got fast rhythm in them. But the old people, they sing slowly 'cause, you know, the dancers a long time ago, they dance slow— forward and back. They danced slower than nowadays."

All agree that the large body of Sun Dance songs one hears today has been passed down from generation to generation. But because Shoshones are very sensitive to relatively small rhythmic and melodic variations and to vocal timbres, the perception of individual songs shifts; identified as old, they are, at the same time, new. The following comments by Angie demonstrate something of the complexity of this issue, especially for a knowledgeable older singer: "Well, some of them singers don't know the old songs nowadays. They catch on to the new ones; they want to sing the new songs. The new songs that they put out now, they're the old songs, and sometimes they're ended in a new meaning, new sounds. Sometimes they put the new song and the old together. I don't know where they get the new songs. Maybe just people coming from here and there bringing them and then they learn the new songs. Maybe Ute, maybe people from other tribes. They sing some of them new ones, but they got 'em all crossed, the old and new together. They just sound like they're new, but they come from the old songs, too." The practice of combining different parts of old songs in the creation of new songs is another complicating factor in the separation and recall of Sun Dance songs. It is no wonder Angie complains that they get "tangled up."

Shoshones talk about songs in visual linear terms. Angie, for example, remarks that the old Sun Dance songs "don't have very much curves. Some, they're kind of straight, you know, singing. But the new ones, you'd say they got curved in those, more zigzagged. The older ones, they're kind of straightlike." During a Sun Dance practice session, one woman laughed at her own singing error, chuckling and complaining: "Oh, I got lost in the curves of that one."

As reflected in their language, Shoshones cultivate a strong visual-spatial perspective. Different pronomial forms, for example, indicate the relative distance of the pronoun from the speaker: *idE*, "very close," *sidE*, "close," *sadE*, "slightly removed," *madE*, "removed but in sight," and *sudE*, "out of sight" (Shimkin 1949a:178; Tidzump 1970:38). I noticed the sharp perception of space and land during my first days of fieldwork when I asked for directions to people's homes on the reservation. City-bred, I depended on road signs and measurements by blocks and miles. But Shoshones gave me other kinds of directions, detailed topographical descriptions that faithfully recalled all the dips, curves, tree clumps, and stream crossings on the way to someone's house. Shoshones carefully observe and talk of songs much as they do of their landscape.[11]

Round Dance and War Dance Songs

Unlike Emily, Angie has accepted and actively participated in the contemporary powwow scene. As the section heading suggests, she has adopted its terminology, Round Dance replacing Women's Dance and War Dance replacing Wolf Dance. What then is the powwow? First and foremost, it is a large gathering of Indians who come to enjoy a weekend of Indian singing and dancing and who seek companionship and good times together. The ninety-year-old Shoshone man who opened the 1979 Eastern Shoshone Indian Days (powwow) expressed it this way: "Well, my friends, those that didn't understand in my language, I was telling my people that this dance has been placed here by our old people which you call as Shoshones. They were the ones that first lived here, right here where we are. They are not with us today. And so this is the dance which they used here. And so I'm glad to see there's many of you here, all gathered together with all your dancing outfits. And I'm glad to mention that my people are so pleased that you visitors, you people are here with us. Let's have a good time, enjoy ourselves. And those visitors from far off may go back home and say, 'We have a good time with our friends, the Shoshones.' Let's all join hands and make ourselves a happy gathering here. That's all." Scholar Vine Deloria, himself a Native American, wrote: "It is important to understand that the more tribes claimed, the better the powwow. . . . This was unity for all of us. What, after all, is unity but the fellowship of people?" (Deloria 1970:220).

The schedule of events structures the powwow. An evening of powwow dancing falls into two main categories: (1) dance contests restricted to enrolled

11. "The primary function of metaphor is to provide a partial understanding of one kind of experience in terms of another kind of experience. . . . Since speaking is correlated with time and time is metaphorically conceptualized in terms of space, it is natural for us to conceptualize language metaphorically in terms of space" (Lakoff and Johnson 1980:126, 154). Music, like speaking, is also correlated with time. Shoshone speech about music reflects the implied natural correlation and conceptualization suggested in the above quote. Beyond this — for whatever specific combination of historical-cultural factors — Shoshones have especially selected and focused on this particular mode of perception.

costumed contestants and (2) so-called intertribal dances (mostly War Dances) open to any and all dancers.

The first War Dance competitions on Friday evening (liberally interspersed with intertribal dances) are for the youngest dancers. Cash prizes are commensurate with the age of the contestants. On successive evenings the contests move on to older age groups with larger cash prizes. The Fancy War Dance contest on Sunday evening carries the largest cash prize. Energy and momentum steadily build. Saturday daytime activities include foot races, rock throwing, tug-of-war, Shinny, tepee-erecting races, and Handgames. On Sunday morning there is a parade: horseback riders in elaborately decorated outfits (both horse and rider), floats, and costumed walkers of all ages slowly move across the east-west axis of the powwow arbor. After lunch Giveaways take place (especially by the families of the powwow queen and attendants), with their lavish distribution of blankets, shawls, towels, fabric, and so on to Shoshones and as many visitors from other tribes as possible. Often a Handgame is simultaneously underway on the sidelines. Activities pile up, tucked into the last available time before the Grand Entry Dance and the final climactic night of singing and dancing. The powwow peaks. Monday is the day after; there is a communal feast for lunch, but the excitement and energy are spent. Everyday life resumes.

The powwow crescendo is set against a background of ongoing activities: camping, visiting, hospitality — feeding and being fed — eating at the stands, buying and trading at craft stands, joking, teasing, waiting, watching, being, being there. These are the essence, the soul, of Indian doings, and the powwow is an Indian doing par excellence. A random and rambling array of activities take place according to "Indian time." Things happen when they happen, and not a minute sooner or later. Scheduled powwow events stand in relief against this ambience.

Now we return to Angie's participation in the powwow and her knowledge of its songs. Although Angie may know and be able to take part in some of the most recent Round Dance songs, the six she chose to sing for me are of an older vintage. Perhaps these songs, which were part of a musically active home when her father was still alive and singing, retain a clarity and come to mind when she wants to sing. Perhaps, too, being older, they hold special value. Angie half-jokingly referred to Round Dance song no. 4 as the Goodnight Sweetheart song: "When people heard that, they get all their kids ready, telling them, 'OK, we're about ready to go home. That's the last song.' And everybody would get up on that song, too, and Squaw Dance. That's the last song, the ending song they call that."

(See Women's Dance song no. 2, p. 39, for Emily's performance of this same song.)

Round Dance Song no. 4 (Goodnight Sweetheart)

(3d verse)

♩. = *ca. 84*

E____ he wi hai____ hai ai we e ya wi ya wi

ya hi ai ye____ ha hi yo ha wi hai ya ya wi ya wi

ai yai ya o__ ha wi ya wi ai ya i yo e yo i yo e

yo we____ ha hi yo ha wi hai ya____ ha wi ya wi hai

yai ya o__ ha wi ya wi hai yai hi yo he yo wi yo he yo

ANGIE: "Long time ago they never let the women War Dance. Just the Round Dance was the woman's dance. My dad, he sang that song [Round Dance no. 4]. He had his own little round drum — Squaw drum [see plate 30 following p. 266]. That's what they just used to use all the time. He says he don't care to use this big drum [bass drum] for that Round Dance 'cause that ain't supposed to be the drum for that Squaw Dance song. He says it's these little ones, Round Dance drums, that's all they used to use a long time ago. He had a drum group of his own. [Each man held and played his own hand drum while singing the Round Dance songs.] They used to stand around these old dance halls, you know, they used to have down here. He sang from there. When my dad and some of them others passed on, I think after that time I never seen them little round drums. That's the time it started to fade out."

Some Round Dance songs from the older Shoshone dances included small portions of English within the vocable texts. Angie relates that "one song that my dad used to sing was 'My Honey Dear.' He used to sing that with the words and make us laugh."

Round Dance Song no. 5

ya we he   ya he ya e   ya e   ya a o e   ya   he yo we yo ho he____

wi yai hai   yai hai   yo   ya we he   de he de__   ya he ya e   ya he yo   he____

we ya he   ya he ya__   ya he ya o e   ya   he ya he ya ho ha   wi ya hai__ ya hai ya

Oh, yes I love you hon-ey dear, I don't care   if you're mar-ried ya e ya o I'll

get you yet e   ya we hai   e ai hai____   ya hai____   ya   ya   we ya we hai

ya   ya e hai   ya he ya e   ya he ya o e   ya e ya e ya we ha   we ya hai__ ya hai ya

Oh yes I love you hon-ey dear, I don't care   if you're mar-ried six-teen times I'll

get you yet   e   ya he hai   we yai hai   ya hai   yo   ya we hai   ya he ya we

ya he ya o we_____   ya we ya e hai   e ya hai   ya hai   yo

ya we he   de he de__   ya we ya e   ya e   ya we hai   ya   ya we he

de he ya we ya he ya we   ya we ya we hai____   ya e ha   ya he ya we

ya he ya we yai   ya   he ya we ya he ha   we ya hai____   ya hai   yo

That Angie recalls and sings this song by starting in the middle is understandable. This is the place in the song where women normally enter, waiting until the men perform the opening solo call and repeated group response. The words in Round Dance song no. 5 are tucked away in the second part, the usual placement in Plains music (Nettl 1954:30). Round Dance song no. 5, which did not originate with the Shoshones and was popular with many tribes, testifies to the intertribal movement of songs and singers, even in the "old Shoshone dances." According to Angie one still occasionally hears this song, but without the English words. Both Angie and I suspect that the English text struck a dissonant non-Indian note within the contemporary powwow. "For Indian doings," Angie states, "they don't want English words in it. I think that's the reason." Vocables replace the English words.

The form of Round Dance song no. 5 as performed by Angie is idiosyncratic, making it difficult to sort out each verse. In older Round Dance songs, an octave leap to the highest note commonly marked the very beginning. Meaningful words replacing vocables in the second section (B′) before the final cadence functioned as ending markers (Powers 1961a:99–101). In light of these conventions, Angie's performance could be analyzed: BCABCB′C BCB′C BCAABC.

Note, too, that the melody moves in twos and not threes. (This will also be the case for Round Dance song no. 7.) When I asked Angie at a later time to add a drum part (spatula struck on kitchen table), she marked time in groups of threes. We shall see later that the combination of a melody moving in twos accompanied by a drum part moving in threes is common in Forty-nine Dance songs, a closely related genre to the Round Dance.

Round Dance Song no. 6

ye de ye___ i he ye___ i he ye ya he ye___ i

he ye wi___ he ye ye ye___ wi he he ye___ wi ha wi

ha wi ha wi ha wi ha o ho wi ya we ya wi yo he yo

ANGIE: "Nobody sings that one now. My dad used to sing it. Those old songs, at the ends they're kind of slowlike. Because steps, different ways nowadays. They got these fast steps."

Angie demonstrated the older way of performing the Round Dance step. Beginning with both feet side by side, the left foot moves to the side (as performed today) but is placed with the foot turned in, pigeon-toed. Then, while bending and straightening the knees, the right foot drags sideways to the left as the left foot pivots on the ball of the foot back to a straight position. Both feet finish as they began — in a straight side-by-side position. The motion of the left foot in the older style requires a little more time for its smooth execution.

Round Dance Song no. 7

(1st verse) ♩ = ca. 80

ye ya hi de hi ya wi___ wi hai_____ ye wi ye de wi de wi ye oi___

wi hai_____ ye he ye hi ya hi ha o wi hai yai ya ya hi ya hi ya o___

wi ha hi ya___ hai ya hai yo ye e do hi do hi ha o___ wi

hai ya ya do hi do hi do o___ wi ha wi ya___ hai ya hai yo

ANGIE: "My dad used to sing that, and then some of the older people, too. I never hear it too much now, just once in a while."

Round Dance Song no. 8

(5th and final verse)

♩. = ca. 84

ye ya wi we____ ya wi ya wi ai ya ya we ya

he____ ya he ya wi ai ya ya he ya wi ai ya ya he ya wi

hai ya hi ya hai ya he yo he yo yai ha wi hai____

ya he ya wi hai ya ya wi ya hi hai ya hi ya ai ya we yo

he yo ha we yo he____ Why don't you be so true,____ run-ning a-

round for more____ in the ho-ky do-ry way hi ya hai ya we yo he yo

It is paradoxical, but the inclusion of English text dates this as an older song. "I didn't want to put the words in at the end," Angie says, "but I could say somebody's name. I should have said,

Oh, Law-ren-cy

[a teasing reference to her son].

"A long time ago them ladies, you know, when they have that Round Dance, they kind of dance slower instead of just kind of going really fast. Nowadays they just really go fast. A person can't keep up with that. The old people, they kind of go out of step or something with the fast songs." Thus, the fast tempo of the occasional one or two Round Dance songs performed on an evening is another inhibiting factor for older women. By default the Round Dance draws a greater number of younger dancers.

Angie recalls that at the old dances every fourth dance was a Round Dance. Men paid their partners for the dance. Older men kept nickels and dimes in one pocket for older women, quarters and half-dollars in the other for young women. Women rushed to ask older men to be their Round Dance partners.

The musical line dividing Round Dance and another genre, known as Forty-nine Dance, is slender. In fact, one older Shoshone man was not sure whether Round Dance song no. 8 was a Round Dance or a Forty-nine song. The two genres bear a family resemblance in their music, dance, and spirit. But the Round Dance is older than the Forty-nine Dance. It is a traditional part of tribal dances and intertribal powwows. In contrast Forty-nine Dances are performed after events, after a powwow or Sun Dance. They are their own event. The Forty-nine Dance originated sometime between 1911 and 1918 with the Kiowas or Comanches in Oklahoma (Feder 1964:294). It spread to many Northern Plains tribes, including the Shoshones by the 1930s and 1940s. Angie enjoyed Forty-nine Dances. "They are fun. I used to dance and have fun. A long time ago for a Forty-nine Dance they'd use a big old canvas. They hit on those canvas a long time ago. Or later, when they were having a Forty-nine, they'd use a bass drum. They danced in a circle; some would be going in back of one another—two, three circles, or four circles. And the singers would go round and round holding that drum. They used to like that, but I don't know, they just don't dance that anymore." Without going into detail Angie alluded to drinking problems often associated with the dance and that eventually led to its suppression among the Shoshone.

Forty-nine Dance Song no. 1

e yo e   Meet me to - night in the moon - light hi yai ha you

know the place where we meet_ ev - ery night e o e___ yo e yo

ANGIE: "I couldn't say if that's an old one. The Forty-niners still sing that one. I would say it's still old and new. Still sung."

The structure of Forty-nine song no. 1 is indistinguishable from Round Dance songs. As in Round Dance song no. 5, the melody moves in twos. The coupling of a melody in twos with a drum accompaniment in threes (𝄾 ♪ 𝄾) is not unusual in Forty-nine songs (Borst 1975:6, 7). The tempo of Forty-nine songs is faster than Round Dance songs (Powers 1968:355). As a result there is not time to step to the side and draw the feet together during one group of three. Instead, the Forty-nine Dance step uses two groups of three to complete this motion:

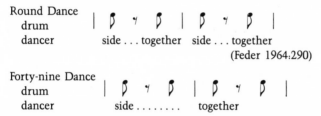

Round Dance
drum
dancer   side . . . together   side . . . together
                                  (Feder 1964:290)

Forty-nine Dance
drum
dancer   side . . . .   together

The romantic text of Forty-nine Dance song no. 1 makes the piece a kindred spirit to Round Dance songs nos. 5 and 8 and *Naraya* song no. 13.

The powwow, for all its innovations and differences, still bears many similarities and lines of continuity with the older Shoshone dances. Although the Round Dance once constituted a significant fraction of the older dances (according to Angie, one-fourth), male War Dancing was the principal activity. War Dancing remains at the heart of the powwow, but the Fancy War Dance imported from the Southern Plains became its central focus. (In recent years Shoshones have raised the cash prizes for Traditional War Dances to encourage a greater balance between the two types of War Dance.)

The musical roles for women at the older Shoshone dances and the modern powwow present a mixed picture. Angie remembers that women used to sing in back of the drum for War Dance and Round Dance songs. Emily's contention to the contrary may reflect the ten years difference in their ages, both women holding a slightly different frame of reference for the "older" dances. That Shoshone women today do not sing behind the drum for War Dance and Round Dance songs is a curious reversal to the general trend of an enlarging musical role for women. Angie explained: "Over here, the Shoshone drummers never have no lady singers. Other people come from other tribes, even the Shoshone-Bannocks, and ladies sing with them. I see there was one drum group from Montana—those ladies singing with them, too. Boy, that sounded good. But us people, I don't know. I can't understand why Shoshone drums have no lady singers to sing with them. But there is some problem there, people's ways, I guess. Probably people would be talking about that person, saying, 'Why is she singing with him' or something. It's just criticizing one another. Makes people afraid to sing with them." The fear of gossip and criticism inhibits Angie and other Shoshone women from singing with the men, but singing with family members is another matter. Angie feels free to sing with her nephews (sons by Shoshone reckoning) from Idaho. "I and my sister, we sing with our sons there, too—A and W Singers. We sing with them." Although knowledgeable of contemporary songs, Angie chose to sing for me three older Traditional War Dance songs.

Traditional War Dance Song no. 3

ANGIE: "That's an old-timer. I just heard a few of them singing that song [now], not too much. My dad sings that one. He sings most of those songs, too. There's just not too many curves in those. They [the older Traditional War Dance songs] were straight because they just have a straight War Dance. That's what they call a Omaha Dance a long time ago, but they call it Traditional War Dance now. The Omaha Dance, that's just a straight War Dance."

There are interesting parallels between the contrasting metaphoric terms used for the Traditional War Dance and song and the more recent Fancy War Dance and song: straight/not many curves versus fancy/many curves. The straight War Dancer may jerk and swivel his head and upper torso from side to side, but his methodical light pat followed by a full step on each foot leads him in a big circle around the dancing area. He may veer momentarily to the side, but his forward motion continues. The Fancy War Dancer also moves around the circle, but he interrupts his forward motion with all kinds of spins, twirls, and up-and-down and sideward motions. A comparison of musical transcriptions graphically illustrates the analogy of straight versus curves in Traditional and Fancy War Dance melodies (see ex. 3). It is a study in contrasts between two types of War Dance songs and, by implication, between old and contemporary musical preferences and styles. The melody in Traditional War Dance song no. 3 (ex. 3a) descends by long notes (like the steps of the dancer). After arriving at a long note, the melody always begins anew by going to a higher pitch and then moves consistently downward to the next long pitch. By comparison, the melody of a 1979 Fancy War Dance song (ex. 3b) also moves down by long notes, but between these pitches the melody descends with an undulating curving motion.

While these two particular songs illustrate Angie's point, other examples do not fit the pattern as neatly. A complexity arises from the practice of making new songs from old ones.

Example 3. A melodic comparison of Traditional and Fancy War Dances

a. Excerpt from Traditional War Dance song no. 3

b. Excerpt from a 1979 Fancy War Dance song

ANGIE: "I think the old [songs] and the new are together now."

JUDY: "You mean they take the old songs and add some dips or curves in it?"

ANGIE: "Yes."

Older singers, like Angie, have to differentiate and separate the two. This complicates the process of recalling songs. "When you know a lot of songs," Angie acknowledges, "you don't know which one to sing or maybe one of them will get tangled in one. That way you can't even barely well sing one song out of a whole bunch. You got to try and get the same music all in one, but in a way, when you know a lot of songs, you can't just get only one string, like one song only. Most of all these songs, they come, or something, when you know a lot of songs."

Traditional War Dance Song no. 4

ANGIE: "My dad sings it. That's an old song. But lately they have a different sound to them. They've got a faster music and different music. They start higher, and it's got more curves. See, this song that I sang, not too many curves in it. Just straight. In the past some War Dances were slow, but some of them were kind of fast. And at the end, the tail part — in Shoshone that's what we call *nduah* [son] — there was only one and then they quit. That's a War Dance song."

The "son" of the song, or "tail" as other tribes refer to it, is an additional repeat of the second section tacked on to the final verse of a song. Instead of AA'BC/BC, the last verse is AA'BC/BC/BC. Angie is contrasting the older Shoshone name and practice with today's "tail," in which the extra repeated section may lead to many repeats of the entire song. Again, her imagery is visual and linear. Songs, like necklaces in an overflowing jewelry box, are "strings" that get intertwined and "tangled." It is hard to pull out a single strand. The use of linear figures of speech to describe music is consistent with Shoshone visual art, in general, where a linear style of representation, common to many tribes on the Plains, is characteristic. Plate 20 (following p. 178), depicting War Dancers and singers at the center of a buffalo herd, exemplifies this style.

Angie, like many other Shoshone women, enjoys dancing. Since Round Dances are now infrequent, the intertribal War Dances interspersed among contest dances provide the only opportunity for noncontestants to dance. Angie comments on the consequent change: "Long time ago people say ladies ain't supposed to have that dance. They never let the women War Dance. Just the Round Dance was the woman's dance. Now it's different." The War Dance is one of two older taboos for women that has been discontinued in recent time; Shoshone women began War Dancing in the 1950s and beating the drum for powwow dances in the 1970s. Angie is old enough to remember the tongue-in-cheek warning for women against drumming. [September 23, 1981. "They used to say that if a woman played the drum, she would get big tits."]

That women can now dance to War Dance songs, combined with several other factors, has influenced the relative percentage of men and women dancing and their age. Because there are comparable contest categories for men and women, the number of male and female contestants may be roughly equivalent. However, the dress code for intertribal dances (those open to noncontestants) works as a limiting factor on male participation. Women need only toss a shawl or blanket over street clothes to take part in an intertribal dance. But men can wear street clothes only for the occasional Round Dance performances. They must be in costume to participate in War Dances, and because this entails an elaborate outfit, most men who are not contestants never dance at all during the course of an evening. Moreover, the fast tempo of contemporary Round Dance songs (see Angie's comments on p. 75) inhibits older people from dancing. All told, the type of dance, dance tempo, and dress code favor female participation, especially of young women, in intertribal dances and discourage male participation. Angie has moved with the times and dances to War Dance songs.

Traditional War Dance Song no. 5

(1st verse) ♩ = ca. 104

ye   ye   he   ya hi yo   ye   ye   he   ya hi yai   yai   yai hi ya o

hi ai ya hi ya   he   ya   he   ya hi ya o hi ya ya hi yo

[10th and final ending]

ye   ha   he   de   ye   de hi ya   o   hi ai ya hi yo   gŭ-ra we-ki-nin.

ANGIE: "That's an old song. A long time ago they look for wood and make a fire before they have their dance in the old dance hall down here. [For a picture of the old dance hall, see plate 9 following p. 46.][12] They had pot-bellied stoves. And then, you know, they sing that song because it says, looking for wood [*gura wekinin*]."

The picture is now complete: War Dance song no. 5 and Round Dance song no. 5 (Goodnight Sweetheart) were musical frames, markers and cues for the beginning and end of the older dances.

Handgame Songs

Dances and other occasions that draw the community together often spill over into a variety of games. Angie's initiation into Handgame, an ever-popular recreation among the Shoshones, began when she was home from boarding school on weekends. As a grown woman she and her family played Handgame on the reservation and during their travels to other Indian doings.

For a Handgame two teams of equal size face each other, sitting behind parallel logs placed about three feet apart on the ground. One side chooses two players who each hide a pair of bones in their hands, one bone marked and the other unmarked. A member of the opposing team tries to guess which hands hold the unmarked bones. When the guess is incorrect, the guessing team hands over one stick from its initial supply of five. When the guess is correct, the hider hands over the bones to the guessing team. As soon as the guessing team wins both sets of bones, that team, in turn, chooses two members to hide them. The teams alternate hiding the bones until one side wins all of its opponents' sticks, thus winning the game.

12. Wissler noted that one can trace Omaha or Grass Dance history and diffusion through a comparison of dance halls (Lowie 1913:200). About 1890–1900, Mooney photographed a Sioux dance hall, an octagonal domed building resembling the earth lodge of the Omaha from whom they received the dance (reprinted in Vennum 1982:119). About 1913 Lowie photographed the similarly shaped Crow Hot Dance building, but with additions of a turret and windows on the top (Lowie 1913:201). The old Wind River Shoshone dance hall seen in plate 21 is almost identical to its Crow model.

Before play begins, players and onlookers place their bets. The amount wagered on each side must match exactly before the game can begin. As soon as the hiders arrange the bones in their hands, the whole hiding team sings a Handgame song. As they sing they tap with a stick a steady pulse of fast, light beats on the log in front. (Lacking a log, people tap on anything at hand—soft drink cans, the leg of their chair, and so on.) These are the basic rules; in actual performance Handgames are as various, elaborate, and filled with humor and whimsical motions as the moods and personalities of its players.

Handgame Song no. 1

ANGIE: "That's an old one from here. The old people used to sing that song. It's a ladies' song. The old ladies, they Handgame with that. Just the ladies used to Handgame by themselves. They had their own old songs. They used to call it *waipë? naiyawhi huvia* [women's Handgame songs]. They're ladies' songs. They don't belong to the men, but the old ladies, they sing that.[13] Now, ladies and men, they're together. Some of these fast kind [of songs], the men they have that. But the old ladies' songs, you know, they're kind of slow. The old ladies, they go: [*Angie pretended to hide bones in her hands and slowly jiggled her closed fists up and down*]."

Although there are no longer special women's Handgame songs, sometimes one or both teams will have only female players. When this occurs, Angie will sometimes lead off a song for her team.

Shaped by the game they serve, Handgame songs have their own distinct musical style. The vocal range in Handgame song no. 1 is a sixth (d'–b')

13. The separate Handgame repertoires that Shoshone women and men sang, however, were stylistically indistinguishable. Vennum documents this same practice in the western Basin and California (Vennum 1986:689).

compared with the ambitus of an eleventh, found in many other types of songs. Confined within a relatively narrow range, the melody moves step-wise, mostly by intervals of a major second. Handgame songs are generally short songs made up of small musical sections, which, in turn, are based on tiny musical ideas. At the base of Handgame song no. 1, one finds a musical motif (ex. 4a) repeated, expanded (ex. 4b), and sung at different levels (ex. 4c). There is a breathy, almost breathless quality in Handgame song no. 1, achieved through the use of rests (ex. 4d) and sometimes combined with a softer arrival on the note preceding the rest (ex. 4e). Many Handgame songs share this breathy quality, which is absent in most other songs in Angie's repertoire.[14]

Example 4. Musical elements forming basis of Handgame song no. 1

Handgame Song no. 2

The form of Handgame songs and the mood they create bear strong relationships to the game itself. In play the Handgame song is to be ever present, a kind of musical curtain or screen, enfolding play as the hands enfold the bones. Handgame singing begins just after the bones are hidden and stops immediately upon the correct identification of the hand holding the unmarked bone. Handgame song no. 2, like Handgame songs in general, goes round and round in a circle with no strong ending markers such as the vocable *enĕ* in *Naraya* songs or final notes that trail down, as in War Dance songs. The opening pattern of the first section (ex. 5a) and the closing

14. In his study "Special Song Types in North American Indian Music," Herzog also pointed out the breathy quality of Handgame songs (Herzog 1935b:29).

pattern of the last (ex. 5b) parallel each other, one high, one low. The use of the same pattern for the beginning and ending ties the two together, obscuring the musical seam and easing the singers into another round of the song. Only the game itself determines when and where the song ends: the hand opens, the musical curtain vanishes.

Example 5. Excerpts from Handgame song no. 2
  a. Opening pattern of the first section
  b. Closing pattern of the last section

Handgame Song no. 3

ANGIE: "A long time ago they sing those Handgame songs. I don't hear them anymore. They used to have tents sitting down there by the old dance hall, and they'd Handgame all night."

In addition to no strong ending markers, Handgame songs have no strong beginning markers. From start to finish Handgame song no. 3 has no accents on or portamenti into notes that begin sections (see p. 42). The log tapping also provides a seamless pattern: a constant beat at a constant speed and volume. In some indefinable way the music resembles the deadpan face of the hider. The constant tapping and short, repeated melody seem, at times, trancelike, somnolent — slowing, dulling, lulling. It is as though the music itself conspires to confound the guesser.[15] And yet Handgames and Handgame songs can have many moods. I especially remember a Handgame after the 1979 Shoshone Sun Dance when a group of Ute women beat a Shoshone team. The principal Ute singer accompanied herself with a small hand drum. Each time the Shoshones guessed the wrong hand she

15. "One might see some relation between the make-up of the songs and the 'psychology of gambling'" (Herzog 1935b:30).

hit some hard drum accents and sang more loudly, humorously taunting and teasing her frustrated opponents.

Handgame Song no. 4

(1st verse)

♩ = ca. 108

ye   he   ye__ ye__ he____   ye__ ye   ye__ yi ye ye__ yai

yai   yo__ hai   ai   yai__ yai yai   yai__ hai   ai   yai__ yo   ha

ANGIE: "They still sing that. It's from around here, an older one from a long time ago."

When asked whether these older Handgame songs sound different from the newer ones, Angie answered, "No, I don't think so, because the old ones, the new ones, they seem just about the same."

Shoshone Ceremonial Songs

Wind River Shoshone ceremonial music is also part of Angie's repertoire, in the sense that she recognizes all these songs and, wherever appropriate, has sung with the men on ceremonial occasions. Angie and her mother have both participated in the War Bonnet ceremony (*Dezŏwe Nïkěp*, literally, "Hat Dance"), which includes female singers and dancers. For the first two songs, male dancers pantomime warfare: searching for the enemy and striking at war bonnets, which symbolize their foe. The third and final dance is a kind of victory dance performed by women, who put on their war bonnets and dance the Round Dance step to a concluding War Bonnet song (Vander 1978:34–39).[16] In the past Angie's mother danced in the ceremony, and Angie sang with the female chorus, an essential part of the musical ensemble for this occasion. (Women sing the "lady's" part for War Bonnet songs, entering after the opening call and response.)

ANGIE: "When my dad sings that War Bonnet song, then I have to go up there and sing with him."

JUDY: "Could you sing that song now by yourself, or do you have to hear a man start it?"

16. In structure and rhythmic organization, the War Bonnet songs are indistinguishable from Round Dance songs. However, as with other older songs and ceremonial songs, there are half steps. For musical transcriptions, see Vander 1978:114–18, 122, 128, 129.

ANGIE: "My dad singing it."

[August 19, 1981. "One of the last times that Angie's father sang for the War Bonnet ceremony, J. cut him off after he sang one of the songs only three times (thus, breaking the ceremonial rule of four repeats). Logan Brown felt that made him go against his sacred trust. Soon afterward he became sick and felt it was related to the incident."] Music, ceremony, power, and health are an interrelated chain; mistakes court danger. Mistakes are intolerable, but change may be acceptable. Angie notes that, formerly, only women danced to the final War Bonnet song. In more recent times Shoshones have asked visiting men from other reservations to dance between each woman on the final song.

Women are an essential part of the musical ensemble in the Sun Dance and War Bonnet ceremony. Their singing participation in other ceremonies such as the Chokecherry and Giveaway, while possible, is rarely practiced. The songs are stored away and catalogued in Angie's musical memory.

Miss Ross's Hymn

Only Angie's songprint contains Miss Ross's Glory Hallelujah Hymn, a hymn that has undergone many changes on its historic pilgrim's progress. It is of no great importance to Angie now; she sings it as she works around the house. (That is, in fact, how I first heard the piece.) The song itself is not important here, but rather the different perceptions and meanings that surround it. Songs take on different meanings within different contexts. Cultural contexts yield one set of meanings; at an individual level, within a personal context, another set emerges. Angie's comments on how and why she learned Miss Ross's hymn suggest some of the psychological and historical factors and associations that give the song meaning to her. Angie is one of four generations of her family to have brushed elbows with Miss Ross or her song or both. In each case the perception of, interpretation of, and response to the song differed.

Angie recounts how she first came to learn Miss Ross's hymn: "Miss Ross, she's an Episcopalian missionary. [Adeline Ross lived and worked on the reservation in the 1930s and 1940s.] She goes around to the homes where old people stay. Miss Ross was singing that Glory Hallelujah, and these old people, well, they started singing that. Like they said, 'Well, that Miss Ross is coming, we better start in singing. She's going to be coming around, telling us to sing that song.' So the old man, my grandpa, and some of these older people used to go to church. My grandpa used to tell me about that. So he start in, you know, singing that song. That's when I caught that song, and then I keep it in remembrance of my grandpa, Pevo Brown. He used to sing that song for me. That's where I learned it." Because only Angie lived with her grandparents during early childhood, she was the only one among her siblings to become acquainted with the song. Interestingly, her father never learned it. He sang only Indian songs. Thus, the song traveled from Miss Ross to Pevo Brown, skipped a generation, and went to only one of the grandchildren, Angie. "And I started in singing it for my children. They think it's real cute. They tell me to sing it. And sometimes I still want to sing it 'cause they want it. They laugh at me and all that."

For Miss Ross, no doubt, this song was to win and teach Christian converts. For Pevo Brown the song was associated with Miss Ross, her religious zeal, and whatever Christian identification he felt. For Angie the song is a family heirloom, a loving memento of her grandfather, detached from its religious origins and use.[17] For Angie's children, who could only focus on the song itself, bereft of its early connections, it seemed something of a humorous curiosity. Eventually, this colored Angie's response to the song as well. When I asked her to sing it for me, her unexpected reply was, "That's going to make me laugh."

Miss Ross's Glory Hallelujah Hymn

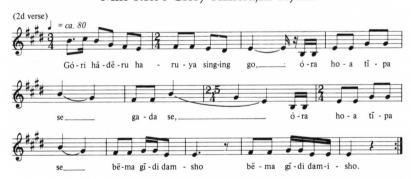

Why is Miss Ross's song funny? Humor always involves a particular combination of unexpected or inappropriate elements. Miss Ross's hymn is a cultural hybrid, a peculiar combination of Euro-American and Indian musical-textual elements. And like some of the bestiaries that artists have imagined—with head of lion, reptile body, and eagle wings—Miss Ross's

17. The Reverend John Roberts baptized Angie. Most Shoshones are Episcopalian, but in practice Episcopalian ceremony only enters their lives at the beginning and end: baptism and funeral services.

song provokes laughter. Both from the Euro-American and Indian standpoint, the song is neither precisely fish nor fowl.

First the text. The Shoshone language does not have an *el* sound. There is a certain grim humor, albeit unintentional, in attempting to incorporate "glory hallelujah" into a text for Shoshone speakers. Either Miss Ross or the Shoshone singers changed the phrase to *gòri hädĕruya* — not quite English and definitely not Shoshone. The next word of the text, "singing," stands out as the only unaltered English word. The phrase ends, inexplicably, on the word "go." The *o* sound in Shoshone songs is used almost exclusively as an ending marker, for example, *heyo.* Shoshone songs with lexical texts, for example *Naraya* songs, often contain ending rhymes. (In *Naraya* song no. 9 on p. 24, *doihïn* rhymes with *wogïn.*) Thus, while strange to Euro-Americans, the final syllable, "go," satisfies Shoshone singers on various counts.

The rest of the text remains an enigma. Under the strong leadership of the Reverend John Roberts, the Episcopal Mission taught Christianity to Shoshones in their own language. Devising his own way of spelling Shoshone words, the Reverend John Roberts translated religious prayers and catechisms into Shoshone. The text for the second part of Miss Ross's hymn resembles the sound of the Shoshone language, but to Angie it makes no sense. She thinks she hears the word for shoelaces, *damisho,* but this seems an absurd possibility to both of us. My hunch is that it is a religious text in Rev. John Roberts's Shoshone, which may or may not have been intelligible to Angie's grandfather. Through time, alterations in the perception and singing of the text blurred all connections to recognizable Shoshone words. Angie learned this song by rote; her children giggled as their mother sang what must have sounded like Shoshone gibberish to them.

The musical setting for this quasi-English, quasi-Shoshone text deepens the strangeness and humor of the song. Drawing on my own Western musical background, I can easily guess the hymnal musical style and sound of the song as Miss Ross sang it. It would have had a strong underlying isometric organization, perhaps 2/4 time with two beats in every measure. Such unvarying rhythmic regularity is not characteristic of Shoshone songs, and it is interesting to see in Angie's performance additional beats here and there that conform with Shoshone musical style, just as the text is adapted to Shoshone language through substitutions for *l.* For example, the rendering of hallelujah as *hädĕru haruya* adds an extra beat in the first measure. In Western musical terms the result is a mixed meter, one measure of three beats followed by a measure of two (see ex. 6).

Example 6. Mixed meter in Miss Ross's Glory Hallelujah Hymn

Gŏ - ri hä - dĕ - ru   ha   -   ru - ya   sing - ing   go,_____   ó - ra

If the text and metrical organization fall at varying points on an Indian–Euro-American continuum, the melody retains the unmodified imprint of its Euro-American origins. Is it the melody that tickled Angie's children? As in many Indian songs, the first phrase begins high and descends to the tonic, but the cadence follows strictly Euro-American musical conventions, moving from a leading tone, D-sharp, up to the tonic, E. Half steps such as D-sharp to E are rarely found in Shoshone songs today, with the exception of a few old ceremonial and Sun Dance songs. But to my knowledge (with one notable exception in the Sunrise Song of the Sun Dance), the placement of the half step never occurs between the tonic and the note just below it, as is the case here—D-sharp leading up to E. Finally, the up-and-down melodic movement of the second phrase, outlining the implied tonic and dominant chords in the key of E major, is also completely foreign to Plains musical style (see ex. 7). Are these inappropriate elements funny?

Example 7. Implied tonic and dominant chords in Miss Ross's
Glory Hallelujah Hymn

I   I   IV   I

By the time Angie sang this piece for her children, it was a relic. Over time some of its Euro-American musical edges were worn down, with no Miss Ross or hard-pumping organist to herd the tune back within the isometric hymnal fold. Abandoned, any further unconscious process of adapting it more closely to Shoshone musical style was likewise arrested. The text, too, fell into a state of rigor mortis. It speaks "in tongues" and funny accents. A curiosity.

Angie's Musical Roles

While both Emily and Angie looked to a parent as a musical role model—Emily to her mother and Angie to her father—the gender differ-

Songprint 2: Angelina Wagon

Sample Size: 32	
Naraya	7
Sun Dance	8
Peyote	◑
Round Dance	6
Forty-nine	1
War Dance	3
Handgame	5
Giveaway	◑
Chokecherry	◑
War Bonnet	◑
Lullaby	1
Euro-American	1

Key: ◑ knows but does not sing

◑ sings, but not represented in sample

ence had a direct effect on their public singing roles. Angie's father not only encouraged but really depended on his family for musical support. In public Angie sang Sun Dance, Round Dance, War Dance, Handgame, and ceremonial War Bonnet songs. Because of her singing role with her father and later with her nephews at powwows, Angie sings more War Dance songs than Emily, including those of recent origins. (Unfortunately, the three War Dance songs in my sampling do not justly represent the full extent of this genre in her songprint.) Angie sings contemporary War Dance songs, and she dances to them as well. She has even participated in the Traditional Shawl or War Dance context for senior women at the local Crowheart powwow, taking third place. This also sets her apart from Emily. The detailed information on the Sun Dance Prayer Song received by Angie's mother demonstrates again the potential role for women in sacred music.

Angie's song sample reveals the breadth of her songprint but only touches the surface of its depth.

Alberta Roberts

"When we really need a prayer, that's when we go to
that Native American Church. 'Cause that's one thing we
have here that we survive on. And the Sun Dance, that's
the two main things that's here — our spiritual way."

— Alberta Roberts

In my mind's eye I can still see Alberta Roberts as she introduced herself
to me in August 1977: short, stocky, with shiny black hair parted in the
middle and neatly pulled up in a bun in the back, and wearing pants (setting
her apart from Emily and Angie and the generation of "older ladies"). Like
Angie, she wished to make copies of my tapes.

Born on November 27, 1929, Alberta is eighteen years younger than
Emily and eight years younger than Angie. She has lived her entire life on
the reservation. Her earliest memories are of moving about and living in
a tent with her parents and younger brother and sister. She attributes the
infant death of three older siblings to the cold shelter of their first home.
Eventually her family moved into her grandmother's log cabin. Alberta
recalls that when her grandmother was over 100 years old, "she was still
a working woman. She used to go out and, you know, pack wood on her
back. I seen her do all those stuff. I grew up seeing it that way."

Despite her family's financial difficulties, Alberta led a contented childhood. "Well, in those days we had hard times, but we were happy all the
time. See, we never got the per caps [per capita payments] until lately. We
never got this big oil money what we're getting now. My dad used to go
out and plow ditches. That's how he earned his money. And my mother
would do some loomwork, beadwork, and sell it." Daily food for the family
still came from hunting, gathering, and gardening. Alberta's grandfather
hunted deer and rabbits. Cow intestines (gwichĕmüngoih), unwanted and
discarded by neighboring non-Indian ranchers, were highly sought by Alberta's family and other Shoshones who enjoy cooking and eating them.
Vegetables from the garden and wild fruits and vegetables complemented

93

their diet. "My mother and grandmother used to dig those *gan*? [bitterroot]
up with little iron pins. They grow way out on the deserts. They put it in
water, and they peel the little pink toppings off. Then they'll dry it out in
the sun. They have a little heart in there, little red ones, and they call that
the heart. When my mother was living, she's the one that really picks
them bitterroot. She used to cook it with soup, meat." Even cooked in soup,
bitterroot remained too bitter for Alberta's taste. She remembers that an
average evening meal might have consisted of potatoes, dried meat that was
boiled, bacon, and greasebread (or frybread). She comments: "Of course they
used to like to eat Indian way, you know. Not like nowadays, us young
generation. We're kind of modern-type now." Rations, so important to Emily
and Angie's family, ended when Alberta was a toddler.

Alberta began her schooling at the Episcopal Mission Boarding School,
an all-girls' school established on the reservation by the Reverend John
Roberts in 1890. (See plate 12 following p. 114.) Alberta's brief attendance
of two or three years in the late 1930s came in the final decade of that
institution. "At first I liked it," she states, " 'cause see other girls were there.
But when I started growing up, well I thought it was funny, so I quit going
to school there. 'Cause see, they make us go to church and Bible studies
and stuff like that. We'd go home on Friday after school. We'd go home
and be with our parents. But we had to come back Sundays, Sunday morning
to go to church. When we'd go to church in the mornings, we'd have black
stockings and blue dresses. And we used to have little red tams. [See plate
13 following p. 114.][1] But as I was getting to grow up, well, I was kind of
sad and would cry when I was supposed to go back to school. I didn't want
to go back 'cause see, I had to stay there a whole week. I'd cry when they
wanted to take me back."[2] Unhappy at the mission school, Alberta left and
enrolled in the government day school on the reservation.

Alberta describes how she and her cousins would play adult games
while living at home: "And we'd be all together playing cards, like that

1. The uniform that the Reverend John Roberts chose for his pupils reflected his own
Welsh, British Isles background. In the earlier picture of Rev. John Roberts with his pupils
(plate 12), note that he has dressed his young son Dewi in a Scottish outfit, with a plaid
kilt and tam. The red tam and uniform Alberta and classmates wore (plate 13) likewise
bear European influence.

2. According to the following comments in a history of the Episcopal Mission school
prepared by the mission, the Reverend John Roberts was not insensitive to the stress of
boarding school life on his young pupils. "To combat homesickness, a circular cabin of logs,
in the fashion of a tepee, was built in the Mission yard. . . . In this imitation tepee, the girls
were allowed to practice their native songs and dances during that wonderful hour between
supper and evening prayer" (Guild and Ward 1973:21). Apparently, for Alberta, this was
not enough.

Squaw game [an ever-popular card game]. We play that. We'd have little round things, little washers, we'd have those for money and have a little purse. We'd put it in there, just like how we seen them do it. Once in a while we'd play Handgame, you know. And then we'd have little dolls, you know, on our back, and we'd even have little cradle boards and have our little dolls stuck in there, just like we seen these elder people, you know, the way they do. So we'd get carried away and start playing those things ourselves. And once in a while when we would get together, we'd be Sun Dancing. We just had old tubs — we'd be beating on that."

Aside from playing games herself, Alberta also remembers accompanying and watching as her mother and grandmother played their games. "There were some ladies that used to have Handgames every day and night," Alberta recalls. "And that's when me and my mom and my grandmother used to walk from Wind River to there. Everyday, and sometimes when they got carried away, well, we'd stay overnight. And that's what they had, just lady Handgames."

Shinny, a popular game played by Angie, was all but gone by the time Alberta grew up in the early 1930s. She can only remember hearing stories about the games and the skillful players. They took place before her time or when she was too young to remember.

At night Alberta's father told stories; some were oral history of Shoshone settlement on the Wind River reservation, others were to settle and coax children to sleep. Alberta listened to stories of the *Nüwĕrĭka*, "Indian eater," a giant who comes and eats naughty children. Also during childhood Alberta received an Indian name, an old custom that survives today among the Shoshones and other tribes. When she was twelve, one of her uncles from Idaho named her *Basĕgip*, "Waterlily." A water plant seems a particularly apt Shoshone namesake, carrying with it cultural associations of water, fruitfulness, health, and life.

Alberta has lived in a variety of locations on the reservation, each marking a piece of her life. After residing at Wind River for many years, her parents moved to Mill Creek, into a home built by the tribe. (By the early 1940s the Shoshone Tribal Council began building houses for tribal members.) At their new home Alberta's folks farmed and ranched. "When we moved down Mill Creek," Alberta reminisces, "well, that's when I started riding horses. We didn't have no car at that time. My dad used to own quite a bit of horses, and he breaks them himself, to be on a team. He had cattle by then, at that time, about ninety head. I had to ride horse just like a boy. I had to help my dad, and, you know, we used to have hay, too, at that time. I had to help hay, just like a boy. That's how I was raised, with horses and stuff like that, doing heavy work. Even in wintertime I had to take them cows about two-and-a-half miles towards the south. 'Cause see, that's where the water hole was. My dad had to work hard cutting water holes for them; and then after he had did that, he'd come home and get me, and we'd be ready and get on our horses and then, you know, lead them to that water. And then we'd have to be bringing them back. At first I was just kind of cold and didn't want to ride, but I had to. I got used to it. That's kind of hard work. That's how I was raised.

"When we moved from the reservation clear on down to Mill Creek, they had a school there by the highway. That's where I went with my brother and sister. That was the public school. [Unlike both the mission school and government school on the reservation, this was a non-Indian school.] I kind of like it, 'cause see, we played with white girls and had friends. When I came to ninth grade, I was supposed to go to high school, Lander High School, but I didn't want to go. I just quit."

Ending her formal education in eighth grade, Alberta continued learning at home important life skills and cultural arts. She learned to gather and cook many different kinds of berries, make frybread and an oven-baked Indian bread (*nüwě ndoshstikěp*), make dried pounded meat, process hides into buckskin, and sew beadwork. Alberta pointedly comments that, in every instance, she learned through her own observation and by trial and error. In her mind these were her teachers, rather than the person she observed doing the task. This is how Alberta describes learning beadwork: "I seen my mother beadworking, and I thought I'd start beadworking. I didn't learn from her, but just when I got out of school, I just started doing beadwork myself. Just taught myself. When I started, the first part, I wasn't really too good. The beads would just go crooked. Later on and later on I kept getting good."

Near childhood's end, in her mid-teens, Alberta joined other girlfriends of the same age for weekend dances on the reservation. She recalls these weekend outings as follows: "I was in my young days, about like fourteen, fifteen, sixteen. Every weekend we used to come in buggy and team from Mill Creek up towards Ft. Washakie, where my grandmother was living there at the time. We'd spend weekends with her. They used to have a dance hall down here. They'd be having dances there, so there's a bunch of us girls would get together, put our moccasins on, and we'd just start walking over there, and then pretty soon we'd be dancing. Our moms would make us moccasins, but at the bottom they'd rip out—our soles. We'd have to run back home and sew it up, and then we'd come back and dance again. It was fun in those days, but they're all gone." Dipping back further into the stream of time, Alberta's father adds that gone, too, are the velvet dresses with flowers beaded on the back that adult women used to wear for dances and special occasions.

Marrying at age eighteen, Alberta closed the door to her childhood. She met her first husband at the Shoshone Sun Dance. While its main function and meaning are intensely religious, the Sun Dance draws people together and creates its own social environment, often serving as a meeting ground for courtship. During the next seventeen years of marriage, Alberta raised her family of five children. But the marriage foundered. "When I was with my first husband, I never did nothing. I didn't go to no dances; I didn't sing [at the Sun Dance]. So I used to enjoy nothing. I lived with my first husband, maybe for about seventeen years, and then we divorced."

About that same time Alberta's mother began to ail, and her sister died, leaving behind young children whom Alberta helped to raise. "I used to cook dinner in the morning. Every night I'd soak beans and when morning comes I just put it on the stove and cook it. And we'd have that corn bread. So that's how they were all raised." Surprisingly, the stories Alberta told to her family were traditional Euro-American stories such as *Goldilocks and the Three Bears,* rather than the exploits of Coyote and other characters in traditional Shoshone tales. She explained: "They say don't ever tell [Coyote] stories like that, or it's going to snow or rain hard. That's what our people tells us. 'Cause that's why we never told stories like that. I never did tell them stories, just, you know, once in a while, 'cause that's what my grandmother used to say."

Three years after her divorce Alberta remarried, and her life-style changed dramatically: "So when I got with Richard, well, go dancing, go to some of the powwows, Sun Dance time, well, I sing." In part Alberta also felt greater freedom to enjoy some of these activities because her children were growing older. Her interest in Handgame, which had lain dormant since she was a child, was also revived later in life, and, swept along with the powwow tide, Alberta competed for and won prizes in the senior citizens' division (forty-five years and older) of the Women's Traditional Dance contest. Although her own children are now grown, Alberta assumed new responsibilities in the early 1980s for the youngest generation of her family. She is currently raising two of her seven grandchildren. This has inhibited her ability and inclination to compete in recent years. With good humor and teasing, Alberta states: "Too many grandkids. Can't be taking 'em in the middle of the floor. They'll cry for me. Grandchildren! So you'll probably be having some [*a hearty laugh*]."

Alberta's Songs

Alberta has two public musical roles: she is an important Sun Dance singer, and, in a more passive way, she sings along with her teammates when she plays Handgame. She supports each occasion through song, always as part of a chorus or team. She blends into the musical scene and follows musical conventions, both publicly and privately. It is, therefore, perfectly understandable that she would feel reticent about singing alone on tape for me, since she does not sing alone for herself. In this regard and in other aspects of their musical experience, Emily and Angie are idiosyncratic and individualistic. Alberta's reticence is perhaps more typical of Shoshone women in general, closer to a hypothetical norm. In 1981 she sang fourteen Sun Dance songs for me in a special recording session, but not alone. We had arranged a small Sun Dance ensemble: two male singer-drummers, Alberta, and two other women with whom she frequently sits and sings during the Sun Dance. In this more normal group setting, Alberta was happy to sing.

Alberta's repertoire of Indian songs falls into several categories: songs that she listens to and performs at certain prescribed times (Peyote, Sun Dance, and Handgame songs), songs that she primarily listens to (War Dance and Round Dance songs), and songs that she recognizes in performance but does not listen to on tapes (Shoshone ceremonial music and lullabies from her childhood). As for *Naraya* songs, Alberta recognizes the genre but does not know, sing, or listen to any of these songs — Emily, a torrent of *Naraya* songs, Angie, a gentle stream, Alberta, dry memories of the last *Naraya* performances.[3]

Because Alberta is, at times, captive to the taste and tapes of her children and other young people, she also has some familiarity with non-Indian, popular American music. Reflecting on the musical interests of contemporary youth, she comments: "Sometimes I listen to these young teenagers now. You can't hardly play your Indian songs and here they'll be coming along putting their jazz music on. That's how I listen to them. Like my Aunt Emily [Hill] said one time, she said, 'Our young people, nowadays, all they know how to sing is just white songs. They don't even know how to sing an Indian song. They just like to hear and put it on tapes.' " Music widens the gap between the generations.

Alberta's comments also imply a different use of tapes by young and

3. Alberta's father suggests another reason why Shoshones abandoned the *Naraya*. He became disenchanted when he saw that winter *Naraya* performances did not prevent illness but actually brought on colds and sickness. This invalidated the *Naraya* in his judgment, just as related illness and death invalidated the Native American Church in Emily's.

old. For many of the younger generation, tapes are a substitute for personal experience and knowledge of Indian music. They build on no prior partic- ipation and lead to no future involvement. In this sense they are a musical dead end. For Alberta and others who know and sing Indian music, tapes extend experience and knowledge. Listening to her own homemade tapes, Alberta learns new Sun Dance and powwow songs. Listening to tapes of friends and relatives, she hears songs and singers who perform at powwows, Sun Dances, and Native American Church meetings that she was unable to attend. Tapes are a surrogate for travel to these performances and occasions.

Alberta grew up hearing songs at home. Her mother used to sing Sioux lullabies she had learned from Sioux girlfriends. In 1982 at a local school conference, a visiting Sioux woman sang one of these songs, and Alberta immediately recognized it as a lullaby her mother had sung to her years ago. A trace of the song lingers, half-remembered, still recognized.

Describing the pervasiveness of music in her home as a child, Alberta notes: "A long time ago in his early days, my dad used to Sun Dance, and he sings in the Sun Dance. Well, you know, when he lays around [at home], maybe doing something, he'd be really singing. But I don't pay no attention 'cause I was a kid then. And he used to sing these War Dance songs. His aunt's husband, he was a warrior, I guess, at one time. He used to sing all these warrior songs. I said I wished he was still living. I could have taped it from him.

"When I was about fifteen, sixteen years old, there was a bunch of us girls got together and go over there [to the Sun Dance] and just sing. We just enjoyed it. It was something like our hobby."

Although Alberta's father was a singer for the Sun Dance, she does not connect her own musical Sun Dance role to him in the way that Emily cites her mother and Angie her father. Girlfriends, rather than a family member, played an instrumental role in Alberta's musical debut in Sun Dance singing as well as in powwow dancing.

Sun Dance Songs

JUDY: "The Sun Dancer that goes in — it could be for himself, for his family?"

ALBERTA: "Just for all everybody, for the whole United States, different tribes. They pray for one another. Like the army boys, soldiers, for everybody. Not just for one person. For everybody. Well, you know, I really believe in these ways. Sometimes I'd sit there and pray for that center pole. And that's something powerful, that center pole that they have in there. I have beliefs in them. And when I go there sometimes I pray too, pray for all the boys, that they'd be alright in there. Get something that they want. See, what they went in there for. Maybe some of them don't really — you know these younger generation — some of them just go in there just to think they're fancy, or something like that. But a lot of older men, they respect it, and they go in there for some reason, like for getting healing power and all that. 'Cause see, that's a blessing, what they're asking for. Whatever they're seeking, maybe sick or something, well, they get what they want from there. Even you, too, when you go over there, like when you're feeling sick, well, when you go over there and pray with them — you fan yourself off with your hand and you'll be alright. That's how it goes. The way I understand it."

Alberta explained Sun Dance rules that directly affect women. "They say when you got your menstruation you're not supposed to walk in there. You're supposed to stay outside, not go in there. But like a few times, I guess, there was young girls that was like that; and they walked in there, and it just knocked them all down. 'Cause that blood, they can see the blood come dripping down from that center pole. So R. was Sun Dancing one time, and he said there was a girl walked in there and he seen the whole thing. And I guess, just knocked everybody down and they were just asleep. And we wondered how come they were doing that, just asleep all the afternoon until evening time they woke up. He said they just felt heavy. So finally, I guess, somebody announced that, you know, talk to your daughters and tell them the ways — they can't do that. And if you're pregnant you can't be in there either. And then when you just had your baby, you can't be in there 'cause you're bleeding. But like nowadays, our young generation, they don't know about these things. I've heard about that when my grandmother was living. She'd tell me those things like that. And I also tried to tell my girls about it."

Log entries and conversations during the 1980 Sun Dance reveal how Alberta and her father think and talk about water, blessing, vision, and power, in the context of the Sun Dance and in everyday life. [July 25, 1980. "Alberta says to drink water first thing in the morning — get a blessing. She might also drop some water on Mother Earth. She says the old people used to pat water on their heads in the morning." July 22, 1980. "Saw R. E. (Alberta's father). He recounted being in the Sun Dance next to an old man who had a vision of water and was blessed — R. E. felt two drops of it on him."] According to R. E.: "The Shoshones used to have their Sun Dance in June, when the sweet sage leaves were damp and green. [Now it is generally held near the end of July.] Everything was green and everything was damp. But now, along in July, everything's burned up. Everything has no leaves on it; it's all dried up. Just has no power, nothing in it." Water-associated vegetation helps the Sun Dancer endure dryness in his quest for visionary water and power: cottonwood center pole,[4] the sweet sage, and bunches of cattails, which families bring to Sun Dance members. Sun Dancers sometimes chew the sweet sage to moisten their mouths, and Alberta and other singers who chew it maintain that it helps prevent a sore throat during the long demanding hours of Sun Dance singing.

Willows, like cottonwoods, grow along stream and creek beds and carry associations with water. Thus, the bunches of willows that women singers hold and wave during each song represent another surface manifestation of the underlying water-power nexus. (For a picture of women singers holding willow branches, see plate 5 following p. 46.) Alberta believes that the willows have power, and her Sun Dance singing companion adds that songs come to you while holding the willows. Jorgensen reports similar interpretations by the women who sing and wave willow branches for Ute Sun Dance performances:

> Women use willows to fan themselves, but, most important from the Ute point of view, they use willows to attract power to themselves and to the dancers. Just as the willows in the crotch of the centerpole give water to the pole and to the Buffalo or whatever else may be attached in its stead, so the women think that their willows will bring them power to sing well, power so that their throats will stay moist, cool-wet power so that they can endure the hot-dry power and encourage the dancers, and power for their own good health and happiness. (Jorgensen 1972:267)

According to scholarly accounts of the older Shoshone Sun Dance of the nineteenth century, women brushed away the tracks of the Sun Dancers with willow branches (Johnson 1968:42; Shimkin 1953:423). Although women no longer perform this action, a Tribal Council member and Alberta's father connect the shaking of the willows with this older custom. In both cases—the one real, the other symbolic—the women cover the Sun Dancers' tracks so that no power could harm the dancers and no one could steal their power. There is still another possible meaning for the use of willows by the women. Following Shoshone thought, willows are associated with water and, by implication, with abundance. For example, Shoshones explain the use of willow branches attached to the center pole as

4. An anthropologist who Sun Danced on two occasions reported that the prayer following the erection of the center pole for the 1966 Shoshone Sun Dance sought blessings from Mother Earth, Our Father, *living water,* and Elder Brother, Jesus (Johnson 1968:6; italics added).

follows: "A bundle of willows . . . are placed and tied in the large cottonwood fork, as a sign of abundance or lots of luck, etc." (St. Clair and St. Clair 1977 1/2:5). From data collected in 1948, one scholar concluded, "Thus, according to aboriginal conception the willows moved in unison by the women's chorus promote abundance; but to achieve the abundance of fruits of the earth prayer today is directed to God through the willows" (Voget 1953:497).

As a final balance to the philosophic and symbolic, Alberta's father suggests a musical role for the willows and, typical of Shoshone humor, an amorous one as well. "When they're shaking the willows," R. E. states, "they're helping the singers sing and keep time with the drum. Instead of having a drumstick at the drum, they have this brush, see, and they're singing. They sing when they have that. And a lot of them old people used to kind of joke and say, 'Get a lot of brush so you can see your boyfriend through that brush.' But that was kind of like a joke. Years ago the women never sat towards the dancers [as is customary today]. They all sat with their backs towards the dancers."

Water-vision-power is one Sun Dance axis, a legacy of the Great Basin environment and its central concern and image. Buffalo-vision-power is a second axis, a legacy of Plains life. According to Alberta's father: "Well, you know, the buffalo, he's the chief of everything on earth. And they put [buffalo head on the center pole] up there. If you're going to get power you look at that. They put the sweet sage on [and sticking out of] his nose. That's blowing his nose when he's on the fight, see. Phew!! Like that. They say he's got his head down. You just keep dancing around there, maybe he hook you and knock you down. That's when you're blessed."

Alberta adds: "When my great-great-grandfather was living, he used to give Sun Dances, the old man, my mother's grandfather. They used to call him *Boho [O] gwe tsugupĕ* [literally, "Sage Creek old man"] because he lived in Sage Creek. He used to give Sun Dances, and he was a doctor, a medicine man. I just barely seen him; he died. I just remember him like a dream. So I guess he used to give Sun Dance. And at one time, I guess, the [BIA] superintendent that was put here didn't want the Indians to have the Sun Dance and fasting things like that.[5] So they went without nobody knowing it. They had a Sun Dance clear up Togotee Pass someplace, towards

5. Still in the waning days of the Indian wars and perceiving the Ghost Dance movement and other native religions as a threat, the Interior Department enacted a criminal code in 1884 prohibiting the performance of the Sun Dance and other religious ceremonies. This code remained in force until 1933 (Collier 1947:137).

Mt. Moran, down below there. They said they were Sun Dancing up there, 'cause I remember I heard stories about it.

"I think Richard's dad [her husband's father, Toorey Roberts] was often a leader from what I understand—Sun Dance and the Ghost Dance. When Richard's father sponsored a Sun Dance, he used to have four days and four nights. [Now it is three days and nights.] That's when my brother, he used to Sun Dance with them. In those days they used to have two Sun Dances in one year. I remember when we used to move to the Sun Dance we used to be moving to the Sun Dance on a wagon and camped there."

Alberta's family and many Shoshones still camp on the Sun Dance grounds, setting up a tepee or tent, or parking a trailer. Camp often includes a separate shade house made of brush sides and poles that support a canvas or brush roofing. Shade houses contain tables, chairs, cupboards, dishes and silverware, Coleman stoves and lanterns, coolers, wash basins, large water containers, cots, and sometimes even rug floors—rustic but suitably appointed.

Alberta finds it difficult to estimate the number of songs in the Sun Dance repertoire she sings. "I couldn't even tell you," she says. "There's so many of 'em." From the five women, I have recorded eighty Sun Dance songs: forty-eight sung by Emily, eight by Angie, fourteen by Alberta and friends, five by Helene, and five by Lenore and her uncle. I believe this is only a fraction of the entire repertoire. The source of Sun Dance songs remains, for the most part, anonymous.

ALBERTA: "I guess no one knows. From the old ancestors, I guess. The way I understand, well, I think it comes to them. Like when they're dreaming or something. But then sometimes they just make up a song."

JUDY: "Would the Sun Dance Chief make up some of the songs?"

ALBERTA: "In the past they used to, like when Richard's dad, he was the one that used to run Sun Dances over here. I guess he used to make songs, like these regular Sun Dance songs that they sing.[6] In the longer days, that's when they used to dream about it, I guess. But like lately, well they just make up songs, some of them."

In recent years Shoshone Sun Dance Chiefs have not been a source of new songs. Since 1977 the one or two new Sun Dance songs that have been introduced have come from singers from visiting tribes such as the Utes.

6. Quoted in Shimkin's Sun Dance monograph is a 1902 manuscript by H. H. St. Clair referring to this older practice: "Some medicine man has a dream that he has led a Sun Dance, and tells the people when it shall take place. He then composes songs which he teaches to the people during the four days preceding the dance" (Shimkin 1953:475).

New Sun Dance songs come from the very tribes who had themselves
learned the Sun Dance and Sun Dance songs from the Shoshones in the
late nineteenth and early twentieth centuries.[7] As Alberta notes: "They're
all over the reservations. Even clear down to Colorado, I guess, they sing
the same songs I understand. And those [four Morning] Prayer songs, that
always comes along with the Sun Dance. No matter where, in different
states [it's the] same."[8]

As a final footnote on new Sun Dance songs in recent times, I have
been told of one that was sung during the 1977 Sun Dance. A Shoshone
woman in her thirties recounted to me that while sleeping she heard a
Sun Dance song. She awoke her older brother, a well-known singer, and
asked him if he had heard the song, too. He said no, got a tape recorder,
and had his sister sing the song that she alone could hear. Learning from
the tape, the brother taught other singers the song, and it was performed
during the 1977 Sun Dance. After that one year the tape was lost, and the
song was forgotten; it has not been sung since that time. The story behind
this song presents an interesting anomaly, combining two traditions and
sources of knowledge — dream and technology. Like the tale about Virginia
Grant and Angie's mother, it is another example of a Shoshone woman
receiving a sacred song and bringing it out to the community via a male
singer.

JUDY: "Do you like to hear the older songs?"

ALBERTA: "Uh-huh. They're pretty. They say that them songs got
powers in them. When somebody sings it, well, them old-timers, they're
going to be doctoring with it and heal somebody with it. My mom told
me that when her great-grandfathers do that doctoring when they're Sun
Dancing, well, that's the time they have a special song for it, I guess. But
the older men, like the age of my dad and all them older men, they're all
gone. So I guess they were the ones that used to do them things. Like now,
they just sing any song, and anybody sings, I guess. Out-of-staters, too, and
Arapahoes."

JUDY (*listening to a tape of Sun Dance songs*): "Is that an old Sun
Dance song?"

ALBERTA: "I don't know if it's old or not. It might be. Well, the songs

7. The Wind River Shoshones taught the Sun Dance to the Northern Utes about
1890, and the latter, in turn, passed it on to the Ute Mountain Utes, who passed it on to
the Southern Utes. About 1901 the Wind River Shoshones passed the religion to the Ft.
Hall Shoshone bands (Jorgensen 1972:196). Voget documents the further diffusion of the
Wind River Shoshone Sun Dance to the Crow Indians in 1941 (Voget 1984:134).

8. We see documentation for this in Fryett's study of Crow music, which includes a
transcription of the Fourth Morning Prayer song (Fryett 1977:224).

all come from the old songs. But they make it sound good. That's why it sounds like a new song."

JUDY: "They sometimes change it a tiny bit here and there?"

ALBERTA: "Yeah, and that's what makes it sound good."

Thus, according to Alberta there is a large stock of old Sun Dance songs, with very few actual additions of brand new songs over the years. But note in the above and following comments how Alberta's great sensitivity to small changes in Sun Dance song performances influences her perception of them.

JUDY: "Are there many new Sun Dance songs?"

ALBERTA: "No, I haven't heard of no new songs yet. But when they sing the [old] songs pretty, well it's just like it's a new song with some peppy guy singing."

JUDY: "Do they sing them pretty much the way they used to, or has there been a change in the way people sing those same songs?"

ALBERTA: "Oh, they make a lot of changes in the songs, the endings and probably in the parts somewheres."

For Alberta variations in Sun Dance song performance over the years have gone beyond revitalizing the old songs; relatively small changes create quasi-new songs. Fresh performances and variations of old songs occur commonly in Euro-American music as well as in Sun Dance songs, but I do not think Euro-Americans perceive variant performances of old songs as actually constituting new songs. Schooled Western musicians and even those who have no formal training are aware of notated scores for musical pieces. Someplace out there is *the* song, an authoritative or standard model (Lord 1974:101). Variations are mentally checked against it, but the integrity of the song remains intact. Even unnotated Euro-American folksongs with multiple models retain their identity. Song texts composed of words rather than vocables and song titles aid this process and perception.

Tempo is a key indicator of new versus old Sun Dance performance and songs. Alberta, after listening to a tape of Emily singing a Sun Dance song, commented: "That's an old song. It's slower, and I never heard it before, so probably that's a real old song." On another occasion we listened to a 1951 Library of Congress recording performed by older singers of that time. Alberta compared and explained the difference between older and contemporary performances of the song. "They're just about the same," she noted, "but he's kind of slowlike. But see, like now, maybe just because they're used to the powwows, they just really sing like them powwow songs. Now they really beat that drum and sing so fast. But like in those days, probably they sing like his ways."

Data gleaned from scholarly studies of the Wind River Shoshone Sun Dance corroborate Alberta's assessment. Shimkin states that in the 1937–38 Wind River Shoshone Sun Dance, song tempo moved at approximately 160 beats per minute (Shimkin 1953:444). Thirty years later Jorgensen documented Ute and Shoshone Sun Dance song tempos from 180 to 220 beats per minute (Jorgensen 1972:189–92). (Jorgensen also describes a "rest song" at 120–60 beats per minute used to terminate dance sets. I have not observed this practice during the 1977–82 Wind River Shoshone Sun Dances.)

Besides faster tempo, Alberta distinguishes contemporary Sun Dance performances by their shortened phrase ending. Interrupting her own taped performance with the Sun Dance ensemble, Alberta remarks, "See, cut short there. [*Alberta sings the longer cadence and at the next cadence notes:*] He got it right there." Alberta illustrates this point again after we listened to a 1951 performance of the Sun Dance Flag Song. "When he's singing it, well, he sings them *aho* at parts. You know how he does,

They don't do that now. They don't have those little drop-downs. Now they just sing it straight on through." Despite small changes in its more recent performances, the Flag Song maintains its identity. For other songs the modern version crosses the hazy boundary into a new or quasi-new song.

JUDY: "Do you still sing that song [a song Emily sang on tape]?"

ALBERTA: "No. C. [lead singer] sings one that's similar to that, but he kind of makes it short and fast. So probably that's the song."

Although Alberta suggests a possible direct relationship between the two songs, her immediate response to my question was, "No," they don't sing that song.

Alberta enjoys both the older song performances, characterized by slower tempos and longer cadences, and the more recent, faster and shorter versions. Her ultimate judgment of a performance depends on its function. "They're all so pretty," she notes, "when somebody like C. sings it. That just really makes it prettier. Nice voice. When somebody like that sings a song like that, it just makes it sound really good. But like some other person, well, they just drag along and make you feel sleepy. But that one's peppy. Like when he sings, all the dancers will get up and dance." For Alberta the last criterion defines a good performance.

JUDY: "And always the women have ended the song?"

ALBERTA: "Uh-huh. The men stop and then you know, the women make it sound pretty."[9]

JUDY: "Is there supposed to be a meaning to that, the way the women end the song?"

ALBERTA: "Well, they're singing for the Sun Dance songs. There's probably prayers all in there and then you sing the songs and that's what makes them get up and dance, and that's what goes with that—songs. So you have to pray a little and sing for them, too. So then they won't get thirst and all that.

"It's from the [male] singers, that's how we learned Sun Dance songs. When they sing it, well we set in the background and listen to them. We got to maybe sing it a few times, and then we catch on. See, they've been sung so many times every year, you just really know what they're singing."

In performance the lead male singer renders his version of a song, and the other men follow his lead. The women enter and likewise follow this version of the song. Alberta, who has sung Sun Dance songs for close to forty years, has learned to sing old and new renditions. At times this can cause confusion during a performance. "I'm used to singing it this way now," she states. (*We listened to her performance on tape.*) "See, like C. always sing it like that so he learned us that now. But sometimes, like some guy from out of state, maybe he'll sing it the old way. Then we'll be singing with him. That's why we all get mixed up like that in songs like that. Sometimes we'll get carried away and we'll be going straight like the old way, and we'll start laughing, you know."

Male singers may have difficulties, too, but etiquette inhibits helpful intervention by Alberta and the other women. "Sometimes they [the men] get mixed up, too," Alberta points out. "But then we can't just go and, you know, sing it for them. 'Cause they might get after us. One time [the lead singer] couldn't get that Prayer Song, he couldn't quite get it. So somebody [a man] had to come over there and start him off. Of course, we know it, but we didn't want to, you know, go way ahead of him and sing it. He would kind of get mad at us. So we just stayed put until he sang it again; then we sang with him again."

Other rules govern the songs and accompanying action of the Sun Dancers. Alberta notes some recent infractions in Sun Dance observance:

9. From his 1937–38 fieldwork, Shimkin described the women's musical part in the Sun Dance ensemble. At that time, in addition to ending every song, the women had a distinctly separate part at the beginning of the song. "The women now have joined in, but their song goes its own way, being merely the continuation of a single high-pitched note, broken by occasional trills, grace notes, and accidental quavers" (Shimkin 1953:444).

"One time when we were singing they started singing the Prayer Song [the song Angie's mother had received]. So the dancers all got up 'cause they know what it's for when you start singing that song. They'll all get up and blow their whistles. See, nobody's supposed to dance 'cause the Sun Dance Chief has to come up to that center pole and prays, prays for everybody. When we all stood up to sing and were already singing, and I seen this boy just run up to the center pole and he was just dancing. He danced about three, four times. And there was another one standing beside him, and then he took off with him and danced. We couldn't just say, 'Hey, stop,' you know. So that's what these two boys did. Well, see, they didn't realize. Nobody told them, I guess, 'cause they were just beginners. That's what happened one year, and I seen it."

The Shoshone reaction to this breach in conduct is as significant as the act itself. There is great reluctance to directly and publicly correct someone. Another scene that I witnessed underscores the same point. A non-Indian who has worked with people on the reservation on various occasions and who was very familiar with the Sun Dance decided, on the spur of the moment, to join the men at the drum and sing Sun Dance songs for the first time. He drummed and sang for at least an hour, until the next group of singers came in. Later, one of the men in charge of the nonsacred aspects of the Sun Dance took him aside and politely suggested that the next time he wanted to sing Sun Dance songs he should come and see him first for a lesson in singing and drumming. That was the only comment made to him. From other sources I heard the unvarnished reaction to his performance. The other singers at the drum were very upset and angry. The non-Indian was totally inexperienced; his first attempts at drumming were very distracting, and his effort to sing songs he did not know and could only roughly follow was equally disruptive. Typically, everyone quietly tolerated him, even in the midst of a religious ceremony.

Tapes, especially of Sun Dance and Peyote songs, play an important musical role in Alberta's daily life. They serve as companions when she is alone doing beadwork and as background when she is working around the house and caring for her grandchildren. On Sun Dance tapes recorded each year, Alberta preserves a fragment of ceremonial, communal time and place. She is free to enjoy Sun Dance tapes in private throughout the year. "I just listen. Maybe sometimes, like going on the car, well, I'd hum it." For Alberta and others who sing and appreciate Indian music, the tape recorder is a standard household item. She bought her first tape recorder about 1940.

Alberta notes some of the consequences from the popular practice of taping Sun Dance songs.

JUDY: "Did that Sun Dance song come from Idaho?"

ALBERTA: "I don't know. Well, they sing it here, and maybe some person from another state comes here and maybe tapes it. They learn it, and they go to some other state and go sing it. So you don't even know where that song came from."

In 1944 Alberta's father recorded himself singing the four Morning Prayer songs for Alberta and her family because he was concerned that these songs were not being performed correctly. Shoshones use technology where it is appropriate and suits their needs. This particular tape is part of Alberta's personal Sun Dance archive.

In 1982 I went with Alberta to several of the Sun Dance singing practices held during the week before the Sun Dance. I sat next to her and taped as she and her usual Sun Dance companions sang with the men. I did not have an opportunity to listen to this tape for quite some time. But when I did, I noticed a woman's voice that I had never heard before. Intrigued and puzzled, I tried to reconstruct the scene in my mind, remembering the women and where they had sat in relationship to my mike. Slowly I began to recall the evening, how at a certain point I could no longer restrain my impulse to sing. I pointed the mike toward Alberta, turned my head the other way, and sang softly, at least at first. In the end I was swept along by the songs, and I no longer sang softly. I was the mysterious voice! On the tape I had assumed a new identity: I was a Shoshone woman singing the Shoshone way — tight throat, pulsation, nasal quality. It was, and remains, a strange moment of recognition of another me.

Peyote Songs

Alberta's oldest daughter explained the origin of the Native American Church to me: "The way this Peyote culture started was one time, this Indian lady, she was just really depressed, really down and out and helpless. She just didn't have anything, you know. Her life was so bad she was just going to lay down and die. So I guess she was way out there in the desert someplace. The Creator blessed this spirit to come to her, I guess the spirit told her, 'Don't be afraid. Don't give up.' Just told her a lot of good things about life. And showed her the way to use this medicine, that this is a good herb [peyote]. And that you take care of it. There are ceremony ways that go along with it. And that's how this church started. So she went back to her people and she told them, told her people about this thing that came to her. And that's how this religion started. So basically this Native American Church belongs to a woman. A woman has every right in there. That's how come in the morning time [at the conclusion of the all-night ceremony] the woman is the one, she brings in the water of life, and she's the one that puts everybody's prayers together and talks to the Creator for them. That morning water — the sun's going to come out — so she has the final prayer. And then sometimes, too, like if it's just an all-men meeting and there's no woman in there, the spirit of that woman comes in. You could hear her singing with the men, even if there isn't a woman in there.

"The Sun Dance is a self-sacrificing ceremony. It's between you and the Creator. 'Cause you're the one that's fasting, you're the one that's sacrificing yourself for whatever kind of vow that you've made — sickness of person or in family or wanting to break bad luck. Just one person and the Creator. Whereas, in the Peyote meeting, in this Native American Church, you go in there — if you're not the sponsor of that meeting — well, you go in there to be of some service, to be of some help to those people that are sponsoring the meeting. Your prayers, you're adding your prayers to their prayers, so that in return, whatever good blessings that they get, that good blessing could be shared with you."

Alberta adds: "I've been to a lot of Peyote meetings, and I even had one for the family, you know, for sickness." For all their differences in history, form, and meaning, twentieth-century practice of the Native American Church, Sun Dance, and *Naraya* reveals certain common elements in Shoshone religious experience. Health — both physical and psychological — is inextricably connected with religious ceremony. There is a great concerted effort not only to cure illness but also to prevent it. Health comes through prayers, songs, and ceremony performed in a group context.

As a consequence of attending many Peyote meetings, Alberta has extended her family. She and a man who often serves as a Peyote Chief have adopted each other as brother and sister. "At the meeting," Alberta notes, "they prayed for us. Told the Creator about it. So after that we were taken as brother and sister."

The notion of lending support, coupled with Alberta's feeling for family ties and her emotional response to Peyote gatherings, all influence her singing role during a meeting.

ALBERTA: "Sometimes I, you know, feel real good in there. And like when my [adopted Arapahoe] brother, when he runs a meeting I always help him sing 'cause he's got pretty songs. He has a starting song, and then in the morning he has quitting songs. So, you know, I really like his songs 'cause I'm supporting him to be there with him. So I sing with him. And they even got these Arapahoe words in their songs, and somehow it just gets to me and I'll just be really singing [Arapahoe words] with him.

Miracle!" (Peyote songs may have all vocable texts or combinations of vocable and lexical texts [McAllester 1949:79].)

JUDY: "Are those songs that come to him?"

ALBERTA: "Yeah, I guess he got gifted with that—songs."

JUDY: "Do you sometimes sing those songs by yourself?"

ALBERTA: "No, just when somebody's singing it, well, you know, I could sing it. But to myself, I can't memorize it or, you know, it won't come to my mind."

Although Alberta does not initiate and sing Peyote songs by herself, she immediately recognizes them when she hears them. As we listened to a 1951 Library of Congress tape of Shoshones singing a Peyote song, Alberta commented: "They still sing that, some people, you know.[10] Whenever they think about it, I guess they sing it." Alberta singles out Peyote tapes as those that she listens to the most. "They're all pretty songs," she remarks. "Some of them songs came from the Comanche [Southern Plains Shoshones], Oklahoma, so that's why they got them Shoshone words in 'em. They tape themselves and pass it on, or tape from one another. The songs, they're just carried here and there, you know, like the powwow songs are—from one place to another."

Handgame Songs

JUDY: "What makes a good Handgame song? Is there anything you like or look for when you're listening to a Handgame song?"

ALBERTA: "Well, I don't really know because they don't even hardly have no Handgames around here. Maybe if we had it every now and then, then we'd go for it. I'd be setting over there really singing and Handgaming. But now, it seems like, just feels like we're not even interested in nothing. It just seems like we're losing our culture, Indian culture."

JUDY: "In the past was that very popular?"

ALBERTA: "Oh, just like to some old people. Then when they all left and died, nothing more. Seems like it just vanished with them. I don't think the young ones Handgamed at that time, just older people. Just recently the young ones started in. So in my [young] days, well, we never did Handgame. Just lately I started. Well, I had my little kids to raise. I couldn't be going to all those things. And I even stayed home when, like powwows came along and things like that. I stayed home until they all grew up."

10. In 1951 Willard Rhodes recorded Logan Brown singing four Peyote songs (Library of Congress tape AFS 14,610A, Archive of Folk Culture).

Handgame Song no. 5

Source: Library of Congress tape AFS 14,618B, Archive of Folk Culture.
Singers: Nesbit Weeks and Logan Brown

Songs bridge the hiatus between the Handgames Alberta watched as a child and those she plays as an adult. After listening together to Handgame song no. 5, a 1951 Library of Congress recording,[11] Alberta commented: "I remember they used to sing that song. And then lately, well you know, I can still sing that song. About two, three years ago we got some group there, and we were playing with them Idaho Shoshones. We were against each other, and we didn't have no song! So that was the only song we had [*laughter*]. We just had one song, and every time, you know, it'd be our side to sing, well, we always sing that [*chuckle*]. But we won 'em! Me and my cousin, that G., well, me and her sing. And when I start off, well, she'd start singing. And C. [male singer] was just laughing at us. He said, 'Them ladies got one song, but they sure could win on it [*cackle*].' "

JUDY: "Could you sing that song without G.?"

ALBERTA: "I don't know. I can't remember any songs; I don't know why I can't remember songs unless somebody sings it. Well, then I know. But I can't memorize it myself, like right out and sing it. I can't."

On another occasion Alberta described her customary Handgame singing role: "Well, I sing along with the singers, but I never lead them off. I just stay behind."

JUDY: "When you hear a Handgame song, can you tell if it's from Washington or another state?"

11. Willard Rhodes recorded Logan Brown and Nesbit Weeks singing several Handgame songs, including Handgame song no. 5. These songs are on file at the Archive of Folk Culture in the Library of Congress, AFS 14,618B.

ALBERTA: "Yeah, I think I can. 'Cause you know, these Washington people, they got different songs. Some's got some words in it, you know [not just vocables]. So then I can tell they're from other states, like Washington, Oregon. But the Utes, Idaho people [Shoshone-Bannocks], and people here, they're most similar, close. They got the same Handgame songs. They're all over the states — Utah and Idaho and here."

The Powwow: Round Dance and War Dance Songs

ALBERTA: "What makes a good powwow is the dancing, and everybody joining in, and like contests and all that. Well, mostly everybody from other states coming and enjoying everything and enjoying themselves. That's what's really good about it. The Giveaway, parade, drum groups, big crowd. Everybody enjoying themselves and having quite a time. They never used to have powwows here on the reservation. But in other states they did, and maybe that's how they caught on. I guess all summer long they used to have dances up this valley, right around here at North Fork. You know, they'd make big fire in the night, they'd dance. They'd just have dances anytime they feel like it.

"When old Dewey Washakie, Logan Brown, and all them men were still living, that's when they used to have them little [hand] drums. In their times, that's when they used to have Round Dances mostly a lot. They used to come and stand in the middle [of the dancing area] and hit them small round drums. They used to hit them kind of slowly like. I was in my younger days, about like fourteen, fifteen, sixteen. They called that song *A:no huvia* [Cree song]. They say that's where these Round Dance songs come from, the Crees. *A:no huvia, A:no* songs, all of them."

JUDY: "Now in those days when you danced the Round Dance, women took their shawls off."

ALBERTA: "Yes. When the old ladies used to dance, they used to wear just a dress and moccasins, belts, handkerchiefs, you know, put them around their necks."

Today women always wear a shawl or blanket to dance. It is a symbol of Indian identity and, as such, is unaffected by the temperature or indoor-outdoor location of the dance. There is an exception to this rule. If a woman wears a buckskin dress, itself a symbol of Indian identity, she need not wear her shawl. Nevertheless, she is expected to carry one neatly folded over her arm.

Alberta's comments on the older dances and the 1912 picture of an outdoor Round Dance performance (see plate 6 following p. 46) suggest a less symbolic and more pragmatic dress code in prepowwow days when women habitually wore shawls and blankets and Indian identity was perhaps not an issue. The early dances that Alberta remembers were held in the old dance halls. It is easy to imagine the women, warmed by the potbellied stove, the crowd and activity, and their velvet dresses, preferring to leave their shawls off as they danced. Going back even further in time, the 1912 picture shows us one of the dances held outside in the early spring, with patches of snow still on the ground. All the dancers are wearing blankets. It would seem that in the past the physical environment shaped the woman's outfit as much if not more than the cultural environment.

Enough time elapsed between the old dances from Emily's youth and those of Alberta's for there to be some significant changes. Alberta has heard of the older custom of payment for the dance, but it was before her time.

ALBERTA: "They say the men used to pay. Like if a woman goes and gets a man over there, you know, and dance with him, well, he'll maybe give her fifty cents or quarter. So I guess they used to fight over men [*laughter*]. That's the way I heard about it when my dad tells stories."

JUDY: "When they used to Round Dance a long time ago, was it always in couples or two women and a man dancing?"

ALBERTA: "I guess it was. But when I seen it, well just women danced together."

Even in the 1912 Round Dance photograph (plate 6), we see a partial Round Dance circle of just women. This suggests that two ensembles — one all-female, the other with male-female partners — have always been possible. Only their relative proportions have shifted over time.

Alberta expresses a sense of loss over the waning fate of the Round Dance and suggests some reasons why this has happened: "Oh, you know, there's too much jealousy. See, like a long time ago them older women, they go and dance with this guy. They don't think anything. But now, seems to me like there's nothing but jealousy going on now. Like if I go and get somebody's husband and dance with him, maybe they'll get mad at me. That's the way. I like to listen to Round Dance tapes. They're pretty. I tape some of 'em. But I haven't taped very many of them 'cause, see, they don't really come out with the songs. Not too much, maybe one or two [during the course of the powwow evening] and that's it. I'd really like to hear them singing the Round Dance songs more, but I guess they can't 'cause they'd be [disrupting] the dance contests. They're more interested in the contests and stuff like that. Maybe that's why they don't hardly sing those Round Dance songs. Maybe just rarely, once in a while when you make a request."

While the number of powwows each summer has increased, the num-

Plate 12. This picture of the Shoshone Episcopal Mission Boarding School for girls was taken sometime between 1893 and 1897. The Reverend John Roberts on the right, the Reverend Sherman Coolidge in the center, Mrs. Mackenzie, a teacher, on the extreme left, and Rev. John Roberts's wife, Laura Alice Roberts, on the extreme right, bracket the pinafored students. (Rev. John Roberts's son Dewi stands in front in a Scottish outfit.) Courtesy of the Shoshone Episcopal Mission.

Plate 13. This photograph of students who attended the Shoshone Episcopal Mission Boarding School dates approximately from the winter of 1939. Courtesy of the Shoshone Episcopal Mission.

Plate 14. Alberta, playing Handgame during the 1979 powwow at Ft. Washakie, Wyoming, holds her hands under her shawl while she hides the bones. Photograph by Arthur Vander.

Plate 15. This photograph of Alberta was taken during the 1978 Shoshone Sun Dance. She stands near some of the tepee encampments on the Sun Dance grounds. Photograph by Arthur Vander.

Plate 16. Alberta, in 1982, on her way to join other Shoshones playing Squaw Game, a popular card game. Photograph by the author.

Plate 17. Alberta at home in 1981, beading a traditional Shoshone design—a rose—on a small coin purse. Photograph by the author.

ber of Shoshone tribal dances during the rest of the year has dwindled. It was at the local tribal dances that the Round Dance enjoyed great popularity. According to Alberta: "They just sing these Round Dance songs Christmas time [at holiday tribal dances]. But like now [at other times of the year] we don't even have no [Shoshone] dances. Like I say, they're just doing away with our Indian culture. They don't do a lot of things now. Like if they'd have weekend dancing, maybe then things would be bringing up, brought up. But to me, seems like it's just doing away. Barely seldom they sing these songs. Once in a while."

JUDY: "And these older Round Dance songs, how would you say they're different from the ones you hear now — the few that you do hear at the powwow?"

ALBERTA: "Well, like when they come here at the powwow from other states, you know, they just really make the drum go fast, and they'll sing it real fastlike. But like C. [Shoshone male lead singer] and them, they do it right. The out-of-state people, they're the ones carrying on just fast, you know. Then the ladies can't barely make their step."

Like modern Sun Dance song performances, recent Round Dance song performances move at a faster tempo, and the endings are shorter. After listening to a tape of Shoshone-Bannock singers from Idaho who sang during the 1979 Wind River Shoshone powwow, Alberta commented: "Well, it sounded pretty. But it seemed like they cut short on them songs, too, you know, like the ending."

JUDY: "Do you like to listen to powwow tapes [i.e., War Dance songs from the powwow]?"

ALBERTA: "Just sometimes once in a while I'll put a powwow tape on, maybe like now, when powwow's coming up. That's when I put 'em on."

JUDY: "Get in the mood."

ALBERTA: "Uh-huh."

For Alberta powwows and powwow tapes of War Dance songs are like seasonal summer fruits. They ripen and are consumed each summer. This contrasts with her use of Sun Dance tapes, which she plays year-round, extending the Sun Dance music and presence beyond its yearly performance.

JUDY: "Do you ever sing powwow songs with tapes?"

ALBERTA: "When I'm around here at home, I'll sing it to myself. Sew or something, and I have the tape turned on, well, I'll just sing right along with it. But I don't sing it when I'm out in the public."

JUDY: "Are there a lot of new powwow songs each year?"

ALBERTA: "No, they're the same songs, over and over. But, you know, some have fancy voices. They make it sound pretty and sound good. You like the way they're singing it. Some old men, you know, they sing it, and it makes you feel like going to sleep. [Too slow for Alberta's taste.] But like when they do [War Dance] competing, well, sometimes it's really too fast for them. 'Cause sometimes I see them [dance contestants] disqualify themselves [for faults such as overstepping when the drumbeat stops], and they'll step out of there. Too tired. It's too fast. I seen that happen."

Paralleling her comments on Sun Dance songs, Alberta touches on other small changes besides tempo that renew old powwow songs; again it involves a complex relationship between the recognition and perception of old and new elements. After we listened to a 1951 Library of Congress tape of an old Wolf Dance song, I asked Alberta, "If you heard that and didn't know what it was, what would you think it was?"

ALBERTA: "I don't know. See, like now, the new generation carry it on, but they'll kind of change some places. So you can't really understand where it comes from. Nowadays these young people go to all of the powwows, and they sing these new songs, maybe add a little more to it. And that's the way it goes now. But like him singing it now, I knew that it was Logan Brown singing it. Just singing it so nice, like the way it should be. Nowadays you can't hardly understand what they're singing. They change maybe little parts somewhere. They put a few little 'ins' [additions] in it. That's the way it goes now. Then you don't know what kind of song they're singing. It's just powwow now."

JUDY: "And his beat, too, was kind of different."

ALBERTA: "Slowly. But like now, it's really like powwow. Everything's changed, to new and old, old and new."

As we have already seen, Alberta's dancing role at the powwows waxed and waned according to the different periods of her life. Free during her mid-teens, she danced with friends. Then, burdened with an unsuccessful first marriage and with long years of childrearing responsibilities, she neither danced nor sang. But after her children were grown and she had settled into an enduring second marriage, Alberta danced and sang. There is a progression in dancing roles from Emily to Angie to Alberta. Emily has never danced to War Dance songs; Angie has and has even competed on one occasion; Alberta dances and has competed in several contests. In recent years, however, childrearing responsibilities, this time for her growing brood of grandchildren, again limit Alberta's dancing opportunities.

Shoshone Ceremonial Songs

There is a natural progression from powwows and social dances to Wind River Shoshone ceremonial songs and dances. Communal occasions provide the appropriate context for ceremonial performance; summer powwows and winter holiday dances are prime examples. Within the context of the powwow, Alberta and her family held a Giveaway Dance and ceremony (*Nahīnwe Nīkĕp*, literally, "Collecting or Donating Dance") in honor of her daughter, who was an attendant to the powwow queen. A Giveaway is just that; a family gathers together a large stack of items—blankets, shawls, dress fabric, towels, cigarettes, and so on—and gives them away to other Shoshones and any visiting Indians who happen to be on the reservation at the time. It honors the person and his or her accomplishment or tribal participation. It also honors those who receive the gift. "The Giveaway in the powwows," Alberta states, "that's just like for the queens, or maybe some little kid just learned how to dance. That's what they do. But it's a lot of work. Of course, people, you know, helped us, some of 'em. It just came to a whole stack [of things to be given away]."

JUDY: "What do you think is the meaning of it?"

ALBERTA: "I think it's just to share their happiness with other people so it would make 'em happy and, you know, feel good when they receive those gifts."

Alberta and all of the women in this book have taken part in the Giveaway Dance on various occasions, joining the cortege of family and friends who dance behind the honored person.

Until recently the War Bonnet ceremony used to be performed at the winter holiday dances. Alberta and her mother participated in it, Alberta singing and her mother dancing.

ALBERTA: "Just one time I sang. After that I never did."

JUDY: "Did you just have to learn the songs as you were singing them?"

ALBERTA: "I don't know. It just came to my mind and I was singing it. There was about eight women, whoever wants to join in. They [male singers] would use them little round drums. They have to stand in the center there and beat them. I remember my mother used to dance in there. They used to pick out some ladies, you know, so my mother was one of them. There was about eight ladies."

While Alberta recognizes all Shoshone ceremonial songs, she has only sung the War Bonnet songs once, and that during an actual ceremony.

Alberta's Musical Roles

Like Emily and Angie, Alberta grew up in a musical household. But unlike Emily and Angie, she attributes her singing and dancing roles more to peers than to parents. She supports religious and social occasions the

Songprint 3: Alberta Roberts

Sample Size: 14	
Naraya	0
Sun Dance	14
Peyote	♩
Round Dance	♩ Only with tape
Forty-nine	0
War Dance	♩ Only with tape
Handgame	♩
Giveaway	♫
Chokecherry	♫
War Bonnet	♩
Lullaby	♫ 1
Euro-American	0

Key: 0 does not know, does not sing

♫ knows but does not sing

♩ sings, but not represented in sample

traditional way, through attendance and participation. And her participation is traditional, as a Sun Dance singer, Handgame singer, Native American Churchgoer, and powwow dancer. Assuming a strong supportive role, Alberta does not sing alone or apart. At home she creates her own musical environment with Sun Dance and Peyote tapes. Even in private Alberta is not alone.

Helene Furlong

"One of my dad's main goals was for his children to
learn Indian ways: to take part in Indian activities like
dancing and singing and Handgaming, all that. Keep
our tradition and our beadwork and beliefs in our religion. He said keep it up, no matter what. Continue
and enjoy life that way, he said. Nobody else is going
to give it to you. You have to do it yourself."

— Helene Furlong

The birthdates of Emily, Angie, Alberta, and now Helene — 1911, 1921,
1929, and 1938 — tick off the decades of twentieth-century Wind River
Shoshone history. In many ways Helene is the fulcrum of this book and
within her culture. Delicately poised, she balances her fluency and ease
within Indian and Euro-American cultures. On the reservation she balances
the past and future, the traditional and the innovative.

Helene was born August 6, 1938, the next to the oldest among her
siblings of two brothers and two sisters. She has lived most of her life at
or near Crowheart, a smaller community than Ft. Washakie and forty miles
north of it on the reservation. "I wouldn't trade my childhood for anybody's,"
Helene proclaims. "Thinking about way back, I could go on and on about
my school days and how much fun we used to have." Helene enjoyed her
early schooling at a one-room schoolhouse, with schoolmates of all ages
(first to eighth graders) both Indian and non-Indian. At home her father
told stories to frighten, enlighten, and amuse. "After we would go to bed,"
she relates, "my dad would tell us some night stories, stories about real life,
about things that happened, and mostly about the *wĕkĕmumbich* [Monster
Owl]. It's just something that you don't know whether he's a man or an
owl or a cannibal. It's just something scaly, ole owl man, you know. There's
more than one story he would tell. I myself had a few favorite, and then
I'd ask him, 'And then what happened, and what about the *wĕkĕmumbich*?' — just to encourage him on to tell the story. And then he'd be still

119

telling it, and we'd fall asleep. I never did hear the end of it. I really valued those stories at that time."

Religion was an important part of Helene's upbringing. Like Emily, Angie, and Alberta, she was baptized by Episcopalian minister Rev. John Roberts. But her religious training at home centered on Indian religions. A turning point in her life actually took place during a Native American Church meeting. According to Helene: "I've been saved, and I wouldn't be here today if it wasn't my beliefs in Peyote. And so I have a strong feeling about my religion. Once when I was about twelve or thirteen, I was given an Indian name right in the ceremony, in the early morning. My cousin G. W., when he was Peyote Chief at that time, gave me an Indian name, *Neewapah* [*Nüwĕ Waipĕ*?, "Indian Woman"], right there inside [the Peyote meeting tepee]. I wasn't prepared for it really. My dad came in about midnight, after midnight water, and told me, 'You must get ready this morning 'cause G. wants to give you an Indian name and bless you.' Then they called me in just before morning water, early in the morning. I went and stood in front of G., he was Chief. He told me from here on out I would have no kind of illness or sickness, because as a kid and up to my teenage life, I was a very sickly person. So he gave me that Indian name and prayed for me and fanned me and all that. He blessed me and told me I'd have a good life here on out. And that's the way it's been. That's the way Indian people are, way back. They say when you're a sick child, well they give you an Indian name for your health. Then you're OK."

Helene's parents taught their children a variety of skills. Helene learned to do beadwork, garden, run a tractor and other machinery, ride and handle horses, and cook. She even learned the same skills as her brothers, for, as her father "always said, 'You never know, you might always be bachelor ladies or you might marry a man that don't know how to do these things. He might be a necktie person,' he'd call 'em."

After grammar school Helene went to Dubois, a neighboring non-Indian town off the reservation, for the first three years of high school. "And when I went to Dubois," Helene recounts, "instead of taking up sports and physical ed. (I wasn't a sports person), I took music and health. I joined the glee club choir and drum corps and all that stuff. That's what I got involved in mostly, rather than team sports. The only thing that I enjoyed was being a cheerleader; that's the only sporty thing I did.

"When I was a kid I didn't care too much to even learn any Indian songs or know Indian songs. Mostly my thing was learning the white man's songs at school, and radio, and so forth. I didn't care too much for Indian songs. I grew up with it. I'd hear it; it was something I took for granted.

I listened to it—my dad singing in the morning. He'd sing when he'd have a break from working, coming in—like lunchtime. He'd sing just before going to bed. And all kinds of songs, anything he can think about. He'd talk about certain people. Like you was asking—if songs rekindle your thoughts—and that's the way he was. He'd talk about it and give a little history on it, and then he'd go into singing it. So it was just a natural thing for me. I just took it for granted. I really can't say when, but as the years got older I started changing my ideas about Indian songs and Indian doings. Most of my interest came from my dad, you know, encouragement. And he'd tell us, 'This is this type of song and this is that type of song.' Go through some of the real important and interesting songs—even toward Handgame, even toward Peyote songs, Sun Dance songs.

"Singing just runs through the family. My grandfather, *Enga Bagadïd,* 'Red Lake,' he was one of the songmakers for War Dance and Sun Dance. He was real active in that. He was one of the songmakers, and he had a singing group. My dad got his interest from him, just as we did from my dad. So we just kept it up. When I was young I never really figured I'd lose my dad. And then when he got ill, he kind of slacked off singing. And then when he got better it continued. So it was really enjoyed. When he died it's kind of a lonely feeling that you get. You don't hear that singing anymore.

"They used to have dances real frequently then [when Helene was a child], like every weekend. Indian dancing was really a thing for the Shoshone people here on this reservation at one time. Everybody would just get out there and dance, and they had scads of dancers then. They were really enthused with their dancing. And they had big circles Round Dancing. I remember I used to like to Round Dance. I'd ask my mom, 'Is that a Round Dance song or is that a War Dance song?' I really couldn't tell at first. And she'd say, 'You just sit back and wait.' Then I learned when they grabbed the Round Dance drums, that meant everybody gets out and dance. Boy, I just couldn't wait then. But the only problem is that I wanted so badly to be just like the big ladies. I wanted to dance with the big ladies. I couldn't. We weren't allowed to. The children had to dance in the center in a circle. And if you got out, that whip man was going to come along and tell you. 'You get over there.' One warning. [Helene is referring to an old tradition in which a dance chief with a quirt used to make sure that male dancers were dancing, whipping them if necessary (Lowie 1915:816; Shimkin 1942:458).] In my time they still had that. He had a stick that had kind of little horse hair on the end. He'd just tap you like that with it. Not real gentle either, no kind of smile or anything, just solemn face.

Boy, you obeyed that guy. You looked at his switch, and you'd better be over there second time around."

As a young girl in the early 1950s, Helene was among the first females to War Dance. She documents how this came about and the mixed reactions she encountered: "I used to dance in buckskin dress. My niece was almost my age level; I think she was something like eight years old, and I must have been something like twelve. Maybe younger than that, because she was quite little. So she got me involved. I remember her wearing a little buckskin dress out there, just dancing around all them old guys. They were just colorful dancers and she'd watch them and say, 'I can do that, too.' And she'd be out there doing that. 'Come on Auntie,' she said. So I had this buckskin dress on. My intentions were good, where I just take part in the ladies' social dance. But she got me. 'Come on Auntie, I don't want to be out there by myself.' So I got involved. So that's how we started. I don't think the men cared too much. If they did, they didn't have the heart to say. But we had some old ladies, my own aunts, say to us, 'Girls are not supposed to dance like that. You guys are dancing like men. You girls supposed to only dance Round Dance, because that's the way ladies here do it, and you girls shouldn't dance like men, 'specially with your buckskin dresses like that, you know.' That's the comments we got then. They were so narrow-minded then, too. It got to be a bigger thing. Then we'd go dancing; my folks would take us to Ethete or Lower Arapahoe [powwow]. And then the fun part was when they paid us to do this special [dance]. They gave us some money, and we weren't even expecting it. But when my niece's grandmother got sick, my niece kind of slacked off [on her dancing] and she started doing other things."

Following the chronology of Helene's life, we'll momentarily shift to the final important period of her formal education, when she attended an Indian boarding school. After elementary school, Shoshone children had two options for their secondary education. They could either attend non-Indian high schools off the reservation or go to out-of-state Indian boarding schools.[1] (The establishment of Wyoming Indian High School on the reservation in 1972 added a third alternative.) Helene left home for the first time at the beginning of the twelfth grade and attended Haskell Institute in Kansas. She stayed on for post–high school vocational training in a sewing program. Although it was a hard adjustment living away from home for the first time in her life, Helene enjoyed the experience and the new friends she made.

1. Carlisle Indian School, established in Pennsylvania in 1879, set the pattern for boarding school education, which some Shoshones continue to elect today.

Upon returning home from Haskell, Helene resumed her dancing activities, for which she received much familial support, especially from her father. "When I came back from Haskell," she states, "my dad made me a feather outfit. He encouraged me into dancing like that. He'd be right there on the positive side giving me feedback. He said, 'Well, if you're going to dance like a man, I think you should wear a [man's] feather outfit.' So he rigged up a costume for me. I used to wear feathers—black, fuchsia, pink, and white. And just kind of a turkey headdress up here. It really stands up, you know. I had shorts with little fringes on there, and I put fuchsia sequins around it and I wore a black T-shirt. And then I wore high-top moccasins with bells on. And I learned to dance that way, too [like the male Fancy War Dancer]. I was, and still am, the only girl to wear a feather outfit to dance around here in Wyoming ('cause girls do in Oklahoma)."

JUDY: "Then when you got this outfit that your dad made for you, you danced more in the manner of the male dancer?"

HELENE: "Yes. They didn't know what to classify me next time. And then my older brother got to saying, 'I don't think you should wear that outfit anymore. You're getting a little bit too old and too big for that.' He kind of discouraged me from that. And so I went back to my buckskin. And then in 1968 or '69 we went up to Poplar, Montana, and I seen these Canadian girls, they was two sisters from the backlands above Hobbima, Canada. They wore what I call my monkey suit of today, long pants with a lot of fringes on and a roach [headdress]. They have a thing for ribbons up there. They don't wear a tailpiece and feathers. It's more ribbons. I think I like it that way because you can watch their movements and their rhythm of the way they hold their body. Because with feathers you can't. All you can see is a bunch of feathers moving. And they were fast dancers, fancy dancers. They move from head to toe. And I was so intrigued with their movements and dress and the way they dance. That's what inspired me. So right there I made up my mind when I got home I'm going to make myself a suit like that. And I'm going to go into ribbons, and I'm going to hang up my feathers for awhile. And I'm just going to do this sort of thing because it just inspired me so much. I could see the beauty in their dancing. So actually my idea of the way I dance today in my monkey suit came from Hobbima, Canada [see plate 19 following p. 178]. So I kind of stole their idea about the way I dress, you know. And today when I get out there and dance, the foreign Indians don't know I'm a girl until they get pretty darn close to me. And then when the young boys dance by men, when they find out I'm a girl, they're going to stay away from me. They won't dance by me. They're scared to death by me. Not that I'm out for competition. I just get out there because I like it; I like to dance. And a lot of people, they kind of look at me cross-eyed, too. Like, 'Huh?' you know. I like to dance in either costume. I haven't used my buckskin dress for quite a while.

"All the inspiration I get for dancing and singing seems to be coming from Canada. I get to analyzing it myself, and I think about it in that way. In 1972, two years before my dad died, we went up to the powwow at Lame Deer, Montana. It was really interesting 'cause we heard new songs come out. They came from Canada. And what inspired me, as a woman, to get at the drum and beat the drum and sing right along with my brothers, is Canadian girls that came from Canada. They had lively voices and they were around the drum and they were singing. One girl in particular was singing with her dad and her three brothers. They were all the immediate family. And she was beating the drum and singing right along with that. I had heard about it, you know, them Canadian girls singing, but that's the first time I seen it for myself. Then I told myself, 'Self, why not?' So instead of discouraging me, my dad would say, 'Yeah, go ahead. Why not? They did it; you can too.' I've heard a lot of people criticize a woman on this reservation among my own people: 'Women can't do that and that.' Well, I thought it's about time, you know, women did this. Women never did vote in the first place until one of our own Wyoming ladies.[2] So I thought why not set a trend? So then I thought, well I'll just try it.[3]

"Instead of waiting two years or longer we came home and picked up our drum sticks. So we got up enough courage and went to Idaho. They were having the festival [an annual powwow], so we went into Ft. Hall. On the trip from Lame Deer coming home, we learned all the songs we'd heard in Lame Deer. And to this day we don't know how we did it, but we sang every one of them new songs in Idaho that they'd sung in Lame Deer. Between that time, too, I had to practice my beating on the drum. I

2. Helene is referring to Esther Morris, who successfully pioneered women's suffrage in Wyoming when it was still a territory in 1869. In addition to the Canadian women who sang and drummed, Esther Morris's example reinforced Helene's courage and served as another female role model.

3. Helene set a precedent for Shoshones when she joined her brothers and father at the drum to perform War Dance songs. However, as a singer, she followed conventions established by precursors of the old Shoshone War Dance, or Wolf Dance (see charts 2A and B, pp. 44–45). While Helene's singing is not unique per se, we shall see later that her particular singing role sets her apart from contemporary female singers who perform behind the drum. Helene's experience as a powwow singer and drummer is part of Hatton's historical overview of mixed (male-female) drum groups on the Northern Plains (Hatton 1986:208–15). See p. 222 of Hatton's article for a discography of some of the groups mentioned in the text.

did with my dad and brothers sometimes, not too much. But that time I had to do some fast practicing. It was exciting for me.

"There was only myself, my brothers, my dad, and G. M., a neighbor. We set up our drum section, and, of course, they didn't seem to have mikes then, no outlets to plug into. Then Lottie Shoyo [Lenore's mother] came over and was kind enough to let me borrow their speakers from off their car which ran off their car battery. We killed off their car battery! Oh that was terrible. The boys had to push Lottie's car around and then jump her car later on. That was before her daughters were singing. Those girls were really interested then. I could tell.

"And then we sang, and I think everybody noticed a new group's come. They all came over, and I tell you, tape recorders were coming out between our legs and under our arms. We couldn't even turn around without getting jabbed on both sides. We had to sit there like stones, only thing that was moving was our mouth and vocal cords and our eyes. And when you've never been recorded singing, it was kind of, you know, spooky in a way. That was the first time we were singing."

JUDY: "Did you receive some criticism for playing the drum?"

HELENE: "If I did, I didn't hear. I don't think the old people who would have had real hard criticisms were alive. But if they were, we probably would have. I think it was a more modern generation gap where we started that."

JUDY: "In your own family have some of the other women joined you at the drum?"

HELENE: "Well, D., she tried it a couple of times. She didn't feel at ease, so she just sit in the back like they used to and help sing, like the ladies do. My mom never said much, but I know she was right there supporting us all the time. That helped, you know. I don't think I would have done it if my mother or dad said, 'No, I don't think you should.' I don't think I would have done it, 'cause I respect their thoughts and their ways."

JUDY: "And then you became, as you realize yourself, kind of a role model for the Shoyo girls and maybe some other girls around here. Had they ever seen a woman around the drum at that time in Idaho?"

HELENE: "I don't think so. And then a couple of years later one girl sang with her dad. That's the first girl I seen in Idaho. Ever since then, when I go and see or hear of some girls having their drum groups or singing with the drum sections, it's a nice feeling as long as I know it, you know, but nobody else knows it."

Helene's family drum group, which came to be known as the Big Wind Singers, suffered a severe blow when Helene's father died. As Helene recounts it, music itself was a powerful healing agent for the family at that time: "So two days before Father's Day my dad passed away. He told us, 'Just go ahead and enjoy yourself, sing and dance and do what you always did. And don't think of me. I'm going to a better place, you know.' And shortly after losing a loved one like that and going to the dance, seeing people, it made me feel lonely first time. When we set up our drum, we had curious glances and people thinking, 'So soon after. . . .' You know, this kind of thing. And then my mother, she's very sensitive I know, and all this she knew. So she went up to the loudspeaker when we set up our drum, and she more or less told people what he had said, and for all his relatives to go ahead and take part and don't think of him being gone. So she went and said that, and I think a lot of people kind of relaxed and had a good feeling about it. And so when we sang, well, there was tremendous action out on the ground and then same way with our drum group. And it gave us a good feeling. I know it did." [Interestingly, an added and later function of the old Wolf Dance used to be relief and release from mourning (Shimkin 1942:458).]

Helene recounts the last days of the family drum group as follows: "Nineteen-seventy-nine, I think that's the last time our drum group really got together and sang. Since then we've really gotten away from it. Wayland [Helene's brother and leader of the drum group since her father's death] doesn't have much time to come and bring his drum over and sing. And I don't have that much time to go over there and sing. And I. [Helene's other brother] is so busy doing his own thing. It's pretty difficult for the three of us to get together."

Helene still loves to sing even though her family drum group rarely performs today. She returns to the traditional musical role for women, singing the lady's part behind the drum. "I do that quite often nowadays," she says. "And it's nice if you like to sing, don't put it away. Just try, keep going."

During the years when Helene was experimenting as a dancer and drummer, she was also looking for employment on the reservation. After working for two years at a friend's grocery store and café on the reservation, an unexpected set of circumstances led her to apprentice and finally assume full teaching responsibilities in the reservation Head Start program. Helene has thoroughly enjoyed this work for many years as well as the Head Start workshops she has attended at a variety of colleges in the West. Of the five women in this book, Helene has had the widest experience off the reservation in Euro-American situations and settings. As we shall see, this has influenced her musical taste and songprint.

Dancing, singing, drumming, and teaching, Helene has also taken an active part in Shoshone affairs on the reservation. In 1977 she served a term on the Shoshone Entertainment Committee, the all-important group responsible for running all tribal dances and powwows and for making all the nonreligious arrangements for the Sun Dance. Finally, we end Helene's biographical section in 1981, when Helene married. Putting aside her maiden name of forty-three years, Helene Bonatsie, she became Helene Furlong.

Helene's Songs

"I'm what you call a real music fiend," Helene states. "I love music, any kind of music, from instrumental type of music or even operas. I like them. Just everything appeals to me, everything that has to do with music. I really enjoy it." Because Helene loves all kinds of music, she and I struck a musical bargain early on in our relationship. I gave her guitar lessons in exchange for her teaching me about Shoshone music and culture.

Singing is a fundamental part of Helene's life: "A lot of times when I was home before I got married and when I was washing dishes and stuff like that, well, I wouldn't even know that I'm singing out loud. I just enjoy it so much. I don't even mind washing dishes. You can accomplish things when you're singing. And that's what my dad used to say. Even when you dislike doing something, if you're singing you can really go faster. I find it true for myself. It helps. I sing whatever grabs me. Maybe all of a sudden, maybe outside and then I'll think, well, my dad used to sing this certain Sun Dance song, and then I'd start singing it. And then all of a sudden that song is gone. And before I know it I'm on to a different kind of song. Maybe I'll be out there singing a War Dance song. And then it goes on and on, you know. Then maybe there's some other Western song playing on the radio when I come in, and then I'll sing along with that, too."

The eighty songs that Helene has sung for me, some solo and many with her brother Wayland, include thirty-seven War Dance, twenty-four Handgame, six Round Dance, and five Sun Dance songs; one Flag, one War Bonnet, and one *Naraya* (Ghost Dance) song; and one lullaby, two country-and-western, and two Euro-American children's songs. While the relative numbers in each category roughly reflect the relative proportion of that song genre within Helene's complete repertoire, recording circumstances also shaped and, in some minor ways, skewed the sampling. Because Helene normally sings in public with her family drum group, she felt more comfortable singing for me with her brother Wayland, lead singer of the group. Influenced then by Wayland's powwow (i.e., War Dance) repertoire, the percentage of War Dance songs is perhaps disproportionately high in relationship to Handgame songs. Also, Helene knows many more Euro-American songs than her sample indicates, but both of us concentrated predominantly on her Indian repertoire.

Helene herself acknowledges the relative proportions of songs in her repertoire: "I think the Handgame songs overdo my other songs, but a lot of times War Dance songs will come into my mind, too. I don't think I could put my finger on it, maybe it's just a mood I'm in. But usually it's between Handgame songs and the War Dance songs. And then after that I think would come white man's songs. And then I would probably say Sun Dance songs and Round Dance songs. I'm very poor in Round Dance songs. I think I could probably say just a very few I know and that stick in my mind. And that's because I think to myself they're a little bit more difficult to learn, 'cause there's so many pretty ones and they're almost identical."

JUDY: "And then the Peyote songs, do you know a lot of those?"

HELENE: "Secretly, I think I know a lot."

JUDY: "How do you think about your songs? What kind of groupings do you have?"

HELENE: "I would probably classify them today's songs, more modernized, you know, something like new hits. And I would say more or less modernized version of that, I would say top 10. The more new songs that people put together I would classify that way. The other ones I would say are kind of way back, old hits. Like myself, I like to hear old songs. I'm very much familiar with a lot of old songs. I think they're much more pleasant and they're much more easier to dance to and they're much more nicer. I can't explain it. That's my feelings about the old songs.

"The curves and all the little dips is the beauty of the song.[4] As time goes on it loses all that because people got too anxious to get in on either the curve and make it curvy before they get to that certain section. And before you know it, you just have a song that barely has a wave to it. And that's the same mistake I make a lot of times. There's one song that we used to sing that really has a lot of curve in there, and all of a sudden there's a curve and then everybody comes to a pause for a minute. And

---

4. Of the five women in this book, only Helene talks of the beauty of a song. *Beauty*, an abstract Western term and concept, has no exact Shoshone equivalent. *Tsand*, "good," as in *tsanĕvuïnd*, "good-looking," is the closest Shoshone translation.

then we start again. It's not ending it, it's just part of the song, and that's what beautifies the song. And a lot of time when that pause comes, what does Helene do? Keep going. I lose the beauty in their song when I do that. That little tiny gap in it where you have to come to a halt and then curve in — isn't it amazing how one little dip or one little curve will throw the whole thing off? And I think the old people really knew about things like that. We're so civilized now that we want to hurry, hurry, hurry. So we just cut things short.

"Like a picture, that's how I look at my songs up in my brain is like a picture, like a painting or a vision rather than words. I don't see little bars or any of those notes. I just think of them as a picture or painting or a dream sort of thing. Like a beauty in it, I find the beauty in it — a song. Going back to art, I would say I think of it as a straight line drawing, like a lot of Indians do. That kind of art I think about. [For an example of this type of art, see plate 20 following p. 178.] And I think about songs as really colorful. You notice when I describe a song I'm always saying real colorful songs, because there's no other explanation that I can give you on the beauty of a song to even tell you how — even pretty don't even sound the place of colorful. It's like real pretty colors, some colors that I can't even describe to you. Just like if there was a rainbow out there and I'd tell you, 'Judy, go describe the colors in that rainbow.' I don't think you could. You could just see what you wanted to see, and I'd go over there and I'd say, 'No, Judy, it looks like it's all purple and then it goes into reds.' And you'd tell me, 'It's all greens and all yellows and it goes into oranges.' We all can't see just exactly the beauty, the same thing we're looking at, but each person has its own beauty in looking at that rainbow. The reason why I said rainbow is because you cannot describe the beauty of nature, something that nature does. You can on, like your dress, something that's man-made. But this other is nature. That's the reason why I say I can't describe the beauty of a song. I feel that Indian songs are nature, because I know a lot of the songs are relating to battles, to religions, and things that nature has a lot to do with, and the Indians have captured that."

For Helene one kind of visual imagery expresses the beauty in songs; another kind, one tied to specific memories, helps her to identify and recall them. This is a particularly keen problem, since, as pointed out earlier, some of the factors that help in the recall of Euro-American songs are absent in many of the pieces Helene sings. In general she performs songs without titles (only song genres), without texts (only patterns of vocables), and without notation.

JUDY: "How do you recall songs?"

HELENE: "Well, I just kind of think about certain people that dance to that particular song. It's like a color tape recorder, just little memories of your own to label songs. A certain song reminds me of a certain person — either a dancer or the person that sang it, or just a certain person, a spectator that's sitting in a particular style, or something that happened that kind of brings back a little memory about a certain song. And when we're at the drum when Wayland can't think of a song, he'll ask me, 'Can you remember that song that certain bunch sang, remember that?' And then he'll go back and explain what powwow it was or where it was. Then I try to visualize that powwow at that time. And then I'll get to humming it and kind of whispering it or singing — first in my mind and then I'll kind of sing it to him into his ear. To me it's easier to think about a song at a drum when there's people, rather than just like this [alone with me]. And sometimes we tease one another. We'd say, 'Well, turn to page so-and-so in your music book.' And I said before long we'll be doing that because Judy is doing that."

On one occasion Helene, Wayland, and I reviewed a tape of some War Dance songs they had sung for me.

JUDY: "What was that one?"

WAYLAND: "I don't know." [*Everybody laughs.*]

HELENE: "He might of got a song on the spot! Some songs don't have memories [*laughs*]. Isn't that awful?"

WAYLAND: "It's like a worn-out shoe."

HELENE: "Or a brand new shoe, you can't get used to it, you know, it rubs you."

Besides people and events, sights and sounds in the natural and man-made world may also draw forth songs. "Maybe the blowing of the wind," Helene comments, "might be kind of singing a particular kind of song that I'm familiar with, or just the way the grass is, you know, kind of blowing. You see a certain kind of rhythm in it. And you say, 'Oh yes.' And then you think, well, that's just like a song, and you get right into it. Sometimes, you know, even the hum of a car wheel will give you a song. That's the way it is with me."

Helene also reflects on the song-making process. "A long time ago back around in 1929, they had their own singing groups of five or six men. I would call 'em professional singers because they would have their own singing parties at their own homes and practicing, what they call making songs. In Indian it's called *huvianai?*, and it means making up songs, new songs. And then the men that belonged to a certain group would say, 'Well, come over every night, or every other night, or every Saturday night.' They used to have chokecherry parties where they'd have *gotsap* [gravy] and fry bread. People would come and sing, you know. Well-known old men that have passed on now would get together and kind of make songs. And they have some opponent singers, too. See, there's quite a few old guys, like my grandpa, Red Lake, he had a group. One of the other groups had the name *Ohapongap*, 'Yellow Pumpkin.' So they're just in little societies, I guess you'd call it, like the old *Ohamupe* [Yellow Bangs], *Muvingȝiwai* [Nose Poke or Digger], and *A:nos* [Horn Packer; see chart 2A, p. 44]. And then they'd try to outdo one another in their singing and all that. That's why I call it opponent singers now. In those days they'd probably have a different trans-lation for it."

JUDY: "Was it in a good-natured way?"

HELENE: "Yes, it was. It's not where they had jealous feeling towards one another. It wasn't like that years ago, from what I understand. They really kind of put themselves into it, and they'd kind of joke around about it and they laugh at themselves as well as with others."

Helene could not describe the song-making process of these singing groups because this all took place before her time. But within her own home she looked on as Wayland and her father made up songs together. "Wayland used to do that a lot with my dad," she notes. "They used to sit around and beat the drum and just, you know, kind of sit there and dream about their song and then kind of try to sing it. A lot of times they'd get carried away, and they'd jump on some old one. It's kind of difficult. A lot of times they'd come up with a good song that I've never heard of, and they'd laugh and they'd joke around about it and that's it. It's gone. They can't think of it again."

In 1981 I asked Wayland about his recent song-making efforts.

WAYLAND: "It's some songs put together on the end and some songs that was this year's and altogether mixed."

JUDY: "You said that C. helped too?"

WAYLAND: "Yes, he added little bits here and there. So it was really the two of us."

JUDY: "Do you usually do that when you make up a song?"

WAYLAND: "Most generally. That was the first time that C. and I ever made up a song together. Most of the time it's with Helene."

Helene, too, has tried by herself to make new songs by piecing together fragments of different songs.

HELENE: "Once in a great while I try to take [part of] one song and put it onto another. Try to jumble it up."

JUDY: "If you can successfully do that, does that make a new song?"

HELENE: "I think it does. And then I kind of pass it on to Wayland."

JUDY: "Is it a common practice to take parts from two or three songs and make it into a song?"

HELENE: "I think the younger generation is doing that a lot. The older people like to have a totally new song rather than just changing here and there."

There can be a certain ambiguity about a song made up of pieces of existing songs. Helene notes that "at powwows, a drum group could be singing a beautiful song, and all of a sudden the head singer jumps onto another song and they just keep a-going. And nobody knows it; nobody knows they changed their song completely. It might be two or three songs or just two completely different songs put together, and maybe they sound almost identical, the two songs. But they jumped onto a different song. And like me, I'm aware of it because I'm familiar with that song. Then somebody would say, 'Hey, they got a new song.' And who knows, maybe they did make a new song at that time? The only thing I can say is that they just fall off from the song. That happens all the time, you know, among our people.

"One time we made up a song right on the dance floor at the Shoshone powwow. We started to sing a song that the Bear Singers had sang way back. (They're from Nebraska.) So we started singing their song. We got on to the first verse, and then all of a sudden we all chimed in on a different song, but it was the same. I don't know what you'd call it, but we all go on the same track that Wayland had started out on. He's the lead singer, so we all just came behind him and we just sang it like we'd been singing it year after year. And when we got through C. says, 'Gee, that's a pretty song. Where'd you guys get that? Where'd you guys learn it? I never heard that one before.' And I said, 'We haven't either!' We never sang it again, and for the life of us we can't remember it. So that was it. We really had fun, though, because we didn't know what we were singing and yet we come up with a song."

[July 10, 1977. "Helene says music given by nature—wind gives you song. Sleeping, a song comes to you."] Over our years of friendship and work, Helene has suggested a wide spectrum of compositional processes: group to solo, conscious to accidental to passive receipt, joined pieces to whole entities.

Sometimes it is hard to classify a song. Is it a new song? Or is it a revised, renewed older song? Helene expresses her own uncertainty about new versus old: "The new songs, the ones we call new, I don't know how new they are. They might be really old songs from other reservations that's recaptured. And then the younger generation or somebody like us guys haven't heard it, you know, so we'd probably think it's a new song. Like these younger singing groups, they're singing songs from way back in the early 1950s. They think they're new songs. They'll be singing it, and yet there's a little difference to their melody, to the way they're singing it [compared with the older version]. So it just sounds like a new song.

"If you're going to learn a new song, it should be right there on the spot. 'Cause if you just stand there and record and you try to learn it later on, it's easier for you to forget. The only time you'll remember is when you play that tape. What's the use of remembering it then? You got it on tape. But this other way, you know, you're there on the spot; you sing it softly, or you sing it with them. Then you learn it, and it's up here in your mind and then it's there to stay regardless whether you record it or not. And I think that's the best way."

JUDY: "Do you use the tape recorder to help you recall songs before you're going to sing?"

HELENE: "No, I don't. Like I was telling you, you might as well not have a brain. And it makes me mad when I can't think of songs at a time like this [when you want to record me]. I don't really think it's the tape recorder or anything like that. Things like that don't really scare me that bad. I like an audience, too, when I do things, but sometimes I like to hide. I just can't recall right now. My mind's so mumbled up with songs that it's pitiful."

Naraya *Songs*

HELENE: "My grandpa used to take part in them Ghost Dances; that's why I'm kind of familiar with that. Although I didn't know my grandpa (he died before I reached the age of two), but my father used to tell me. And on those Ghost Dance songs that we heard [1909 recording of Dick Washakie; see Angelina's chapter, n. 4], that first one, it seems like I've heard it, but I don't know where. I don't know whether my dad used to sing it or what. It's just kind of dreamlike. And then I remember one song, but I don't know where I learned it from or where I caught it from."

Naraya *Song no. 14*

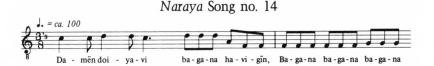

ha - vi - gĭn. Da - mĕn doi - ya - vi ba - ga - na ha - vi - gĭn,

Da - mĕn doi - ya - vi ba - ga - na ha - vi - gĭn en - do. Da - mĕn doi - ya -

vi ba - ga - na ha - vi - gĭn, Ba - ga - na ba - ga - na ba - ga - na ha - vi - gĭn en - do.

> *Damĕn doiyavi bagana havigĭn,*
> Our mountains fog lying lightly,
>
> *Bagana bagana bagana havigĭn.*
> Fog fog fog lying lightly.
>
> *Damĕn doiyavi bagana havigĭn,*
> Our mountains fog lying lightly,
>
> *Damĕn doiyavi bagana havigĭn endo.*
> Our mountains fog lying lightly (ending vocable).
>
> *Damĕn doiyavi bagana havigĭn,*
> Our mountains fog lying lightly,
>
> *Bagana bagana bagana havigĭn endo.*
> Fog fog fog lying lightly (ending vocable).

HELENE: "*Damĕn doiyavi bagana havegĭn,* it's mountains under fog, you know. Maybe I learned it from my uncle from Idaho. I think it was about in 1975 after a Sun Dance, and he was still alive then. And he created Ghost Dancing that one time. There was just a few of us there, and the cops told us we could stay and do it under the light. So that's what we did, and there's where I learned a lot. He showed us how they clicked their heels together. It was so unique that I kept a-wanting to do it. Maybe that's where I learned that song, or maybe it was from my dad. I just can't recall."

Such is Helene's knowledge of and experience with the *Naraya*. The text and music of *Naraya* song no. 14 bear a family resemblance to *Naraya* song no. 2 (pp. 17–18). Of course, we'll never know their relationship — parent-child, siblings, distant cousins, or even variants of the same song. They are short, easy songs to compare and illustrate the degree of similarity among many songs. Helene and all the women in this book often refer to this characteristic in their music, and, without question, it contributes to the difficulty of separating and recalling songs.

There is one final point about *Naraya* song no. 14 that makes it unique within the corpus of 150 Shoshone *Naraya* songs I have collected. The use of a final "o" in *endo,* which conforms with other common cadential patterns in Shoshone songs, replaces the customary *Naraya* ending vocable, *enë.* (See *Naraya* songs nos. 3 and 6.) Like the children's game Telephone, in which a word changes as it is whispered from one child to the next, so the ending vocable in *Naraya* song no. 14 may have changed over time, heard and sung in a way that makes sense to the last ones in line.

Sun Dance Songs

HELENE: "The old Sun Dance songs, they're the prettiest. I don't think they'll ever die out unless the people lose the Sun Dance itself. But I think if the younger people keep it up, watch it carefully, and see how it's done, it'll really come out good. 'Cause I think it's something really special and it's a religion that should be carried on.

"I remember when my dad was going to go in the Sun Dance years ago when I was a kid. When he said he was going to go in the Sun Dance, I'd really get scared. Because I knew they never got any food or water for three days and three nights, and to me that's a long time. Was my dad going to make it through, you know? As a little kid all this kind of stuff worried me. And I knew my dad wasn't young at that time either. He'd say, 'Well, I'm going to ask the Sun Dance Chief if I can go in.' You know, tell him the purpose he was going in for and get OK'd before he went in. Now, it's not that way anymore. They don't ask. Whoever wants to go in just gets ready and goes in. But as I recall, during that time the Sun Dance Chiefs were tougher. You didn't go Sun Dance to prove your manhood, you know, that you can do it or on a challenge basis. I guess that's the reason why when I was young I never seen no young teenagers in the Sun Dance at all, just mostly young men and older men. I would say over twenty-five, or something like that, nothing below eighteen and down. You went in for your health or your family health or a death in the family, that kind of thing. You had to have a purpose, not an excuse, to go in. And the Chief would really think about it, and if the reason for you going in was a good reason, he OK'd it. And then there you start getting ready, get your aprons and your blankets ready. And it was just a thing you done for two or three days, you know, getting ready for that time, and getting your family all situated and camp set up a week before.

"When I was a kid, when they had old guys Sun Dancing in there, they used to go on and on and on. There was no break. They were made to stay inside. The only time they go out is when they went to the bathroom and back again. They weren't even allowed to socialize with their families. The only time they did was right in front by the entrance, where their families wait for them with a change of outfit or cattails and sweet sage [which the men find cooling and refreshing during their dry ordeal]. And then there used to be old ladies when we camped; they used to walk early in the morning just before sunrise come, and then they make their war whoop. They do that. And my dad said when you're so dry and in that lodge laying down early in the morning, he said, 'That just goes right through you from head to toe. It gives you a good feeling, but that really stabs you in the heart when an old woman comes towards the lodge making that noise.' He said, 'Nŭ rukushinwĭtatsua,' which means everything just lifted away from me. 'Tinglelike feeling, and then I felt real down in the dumps, real depressed. And then a good feeling came over me.' That's how he would express it. Then, he said, you hear old men singing way out. Maybe, he said, that's just in your mind, I don't know. And I've heard other men say that, too, other than my dad.

"They used to go through the night, the dancers. By the last day they're pretty dry. The old people knew it; they just keep singing. They just keep a-going, keep 'em going. And then the Camp Crier says, 'OK guys, get up. Keep getting up. Keep getting up. This is what you're in here for, for your health.' In Indian he'd say,

> YorIyorI duivichane   nĭkĕpfuint   nĭkĕpfuint
> Get up, young men, keep on dancing, keep on dancing,
>
> nzananĭ nŭsŭnga.
> good   feel.

They say that [dancing] makes you feel good. And then he'd turn around [to the singers] and say,

> Duivichane duridwad   wituwache   wituwache.
> young men start singing, drum louder, drum louder.

That means pound it, get louder. Put your whole self into it. He'd say, 'Come on, sing. What's the matter? Sing for your boys.' Even old ladies, they'd stay up all night Sun Dance singing. It just goes on and on and on. And on the last day they'd go around the camp telling everybody, 'It's almost time to go out. Get whatever you're going to give away ready, or prepare what you're going to give away ready, or prepare your food and everything.' That kind of thing. They don't have that anymore. That was beauty in those days. I realize that now. And people came just to observe, watch the Sun Dance. Everyone used to take part in it. Like my uncles, they'd wear their fancy reservation black hats, beautiful scarves. They'd have pretty shirt on, beaded gauntlet gloves, beaded moccasins, and maybe Indian pants. Them Indian pants were made of the navy blue trade cloth, and they're beaded around here [by the cuff]. Just all decked out. You would think that they were going to a powwow, but this is all Sun Dance. And then my auntie, she'd put on her best velvet or silk dress, her beaded belt, and her high-top moccasins. And her hair was braided real nice, a scarf around her neck. Just beauty in itself. For me, sitting in the car or standing in the background watching these old couples come over to look on at the Sun Dance, that's the time I really loved. 'Cause I loved to watch these people's outfits. Each person had a different kind, but they were all beautiful. It gives you a good feeling, you know. You ought to look good. That's what the white man, when he goes to church, he looks the best. Everything is clean and everything is nice when he goes before the altar. Well, that's the same thing with the Sun Dance."

JUDY: "Do they sing pretty much the same older Sun Dance songs year after year?"

HELENE: "I think so. And then they kind of modernize it a little bit, you know. I understand that way back, years and years ago, whoever's going to run the Sun Dance comes up with a new song. He makes a new song and sings it to the drum group, and then they pick it up from there."

JUDY: "Is that still done?"

HELENE: "I don't know. I haven't been taking too much part in the singing and all that since my dad passed on. I've kind of slacked off."

In the past both Helene's father and grandfather made Sun Dance songs, but Helene points out that women, too, have always played an important part in the Sun Dance musical ensemble. "For the Sun Dance, the women, they're going to go in there [sit behind the drummers] and sing for their boys or their grandsons or whatever—support that person. Explaining it to you, I would say there's about three categories when you tear it down to basics. The guy that sings the first verse—he's not exactly the lead singer. In War Dance songs, yes, he's the lead singer, but in a Sun Dance song he's maybe the head singer; but I wouldn't specify it like that. He's the one that's singing the song for the group of men to catch that song or think about that song. Because someplace they know that song, or if it's a new song, it gives these people a chance to pick it up. That's the reason why a Sun Dance song, like I've always heard it, starts low and slow. It's not coming out full force. Now that's the way I've heard Sun Dance songs sung by the old men. They're not practicing, but they give each a chance to pick up that particular song. So it's the whole verse so these men could know it. And then it picks up speed when they think they've got it. Then it gets a little bit forceful and it gets a little bit faster, and all these men chime in. Then when they pick it up and it's going on good, that's when the ladies come in. They chime in where it comes high and where they're needed. And then they end it. That's where it's beautiful that way. And then the men do that [nonsynchronous drumbeats, a brief and irregular tremolo] and end it. And then the ladies pull out the cigarettes,[5] and they start talking amongst themselves, laughing at their own selves." Helene later added a comment on the vocal quality used when the ensemble is at full tilt: "Certain songs you have to sing with your heavy voice, and Sun Dance songs, that's one of 'em."

JUDY: "When you're going to sing Sun Dance songs, when you're beadworking or doing something, do you have trouble remembering that first part of the song that usually women don't sing?"

HELENE: "I usually start in with them when they first start. Then I just hum along or I just sing along with them. I just sing it clear through because I feel if I'm going to learn a song I might as well learn it properly from the beginning. But I still respect the way the ladies sing it, so I don't outdo 'em. I just sing along quietly until it comes to the ladies' turn. But I do want to learn the full song, not just the little chorus in it."

Interviews with Helene often turned into dialogues, as we traded roles. Articulate and analytical, Helene sometimes turned questions back on me, before giving her answer.

JUDY: "When the women wave the willow wands, is that just for the rhythm, or is there a meaning to that?"

HELENE: "Yeah, I think there's more to it than keeping up with the song. It shades you, for one thing, from the sun. As a little girl, you know, I've seen them do that. I think it must have had a real meaning before, a certain kind of reason they do that. But I'm not that up on that. There again, we'll never know the real reason behind it. It's probably what each individual feels about it. Maybe they're too shy, they want to hide behind it. But before [in the past], they never looked at the Sun Dancers that much. How do you feel about it when you hold it? Ridiculous?"

JUDY: "No, it makes me think of growing things. Waving wheat — growing things. It's willow, maybe it's associated with water the way the cottonwood tree is."

HELENE: "Well, when I get over there when I get a chance to, I only sit there when I feel like I need to, when I want to, not because I have to

5. Helene wrote the following note on the manuscript for her chapter: "Judy, long time ago the ladies (old) didn't smoke. Now days they do — modern times."

and not because somebody says come on. Then I feel good about myself, and then when I pick up the willow like that, it gives me a sense of direction. It gives me a sense of security. I feel secure in holding it and singing with that willow, holding that willow in rhythm with the music. Because otherwise I feel shy. It's not really big enough to hide behind, but it gives you a sense of security. That's the way I feel about it."

On one occasion Helene sang Sun Dance songs for me. Some she sang alone; some I initiated, and she chimed in with me.

HELENE: "Did you know that one I just sang?"

JUDY: "That sounds familiar to me. I thought you were starting onto another one."

HELENE: "I think I did start off two. But like I say, once one song comes to me, then two, three other songs—I kind of hitch them together, and then I kind of slowly unwind it. It's kind of like spaghetti. [*Helene then sang the Flag Song, the song Emily knows but does not sing, for it's just a World War II "newcomer."*] When I was a little girl, they never had flags. They just had cloths [usually blue and white tied to the top of the center pole]. It was during the wartime, I think, when it originated. A veteran has to put up the flag."

JUDY: "Do you know the Sunrise Ceremony Song?"

HELENE: "I used to know it right then and there. But I haven't been to the Sunrise service for I don't know how long. [*Helene and I sang the Sunrise Song.*] That's a pretty one. I like that. That's one thing I like to see, is the Sunrise services when they all get up and dance. I used to know the Morning Prayer Song, too."

JUDY: "When you say that do you mean those four sacred songs or the Morning Prayer Song [the song Angie's mother received]?"

HELENE: "All of them including that."

JUDY: "Are those four sacred songs as old as the Sun Dance?"

HELENE: "Yes. Probably no one will ever know how old they are unless they can say, well, that's the year the Sun Dance was first here. It just goes on and on, and you just don't know when it existed. The [four] morning songs almost sound like the same one. They make them sound so beautiful when everybody [all the Sun Dancers and the Sun Dance Chief] sings it. And you see them all lined up, sitting around like that. And they go back and forth like this [*gently sway*] you know. It's just so beautiful, gives you a good feeling. Really full of prayer, I think. I really enjoy seeing that."

JUDY: "Do you feel that those four Morning Prayer songs have a special power in them or that there's something different about them that sets them apart from the other songs?"

HELENE: "Like you have a special feeling for those songs. But if you never seen the Sun Dance and then heard those songs, would you feel the same?"

JUDY: "No, I don't know that I would if I had never seen the Sun Dance."

HELENE: "Well, that's the same here. I kind of grew up around it, you know, when my dad used to go in. They are special songs, and they do give you a good feeling, especially when you're there in the morning and they're all bowed down and all singing. It's just like going into church with a heavy burden on your shoulder and then go up to the altar and take communion. Or if you're Catholic, go into confession. You have this good feeling about yourself, like you're cleansed and you're looking forward to a new day. Like you throw off dirty socks and put on clean ones. That's the way it feels."

Years later when Helene read this last line, she wrote her concerns about it: "Judy, I hope no one feels like I'm making fun instead of explaining how it is and feels. Explaining to white people and trying to get them to understand is hard."

Peyote Songs

HELENE: "I used to listen to my dad sing Peyote songs in the morning and in the evening and outside working. I enjoyed listening to Peyote songs. That gives me a good feeling when I'm feeling bad. Any songs, to tell you the truth, really gives me kind of a lift listening to it, you know. The Peyote songs have a great deal of meaning to me. And that's how come I sing Peyote songs to myself when I'm driving on the highway. It's kind of private with me, you know. I guess maybe I still have that feeling that ladies do not, are not the top singers for Peyote and all that, you know, to sing along with it. I probably still have that feeling. It probably overrules my sense a little bit on that. Like G. asked me, 'Can you sing some?' And then I'd tell him no, 'cause I just feel I'm not adequate enough to sing to somebody that knows songs. I feel like I might make a mistake or something. And it's sacred, you know. I don't sing them publicly. And the oddest time that Peyote songs really come into my mind is when there's a big crowd or you got visitors, and I'm not going to just blurt out and sing these songs. So humming it, or whistling it, it just whirls around in my mind.

"Someone calls a meeting if there's sickness in the family or somebody pledged to have a meeting or say, birthday meeting or doctor meeting, whatever. It's up to the family or whoever's putting it up. They ask the [Peyote] Chief. There's just certain ones, too, that can be Chief who conduct the meeting. There's just a very few of that left among the Shoshone people, too. So you can ask them, and they can say yes or no. It's not just when someone's sick. Like M., she puts up meetings the week before Decoration Day because that's the way the old man, J., had wanted it. They've been putting up meetings for that purpose and for the purpose of keeping their people well, praying for everybody. It's just an open meeting, like somebody says, 'So and so's going to have a meeting there.' It just kind of spreads like wildfire. And whoever wants to come can come. It's not like a private party, it's just open for anybody [that believes in the Peyote ceremony]. Even a person that's sick can come, a person that's feeling bad can come, or just to help out can come. At the meetings men sing, and the ladies, they help sing, but they don't drum or hold the gourd [rattle].[6]

"One day I was either sitting out here or washing clothes, and I remembered that one song of my dad's; and it was just like it was flying, and it came to me and it just left again. We had a meeting one time a long time ago, and this fireplace was still there in front of the cabin, and the wood was still like that [both remained in place a long time after their use in the Peyote meeting]. There was a butterfly flying right on top of it, and it was humming this certain song. It was a real pretty song; my mother was asleep, and she started humming that same song that my dad was thinking about and he was seeing. You know, you can't visualize somebody seeing a song, but he did. He seen that song as well as it coming to his mind. This butterfly was fluttering around that song just like that song right over that fireplace. And he seen it. See, this is his dream, or he seen it, visualized it. All of a sudden he just woke up and started singing that song. And my mother was thinking about that same song."

HELENE'S MOTHER: "The old man was blessed with that song. Seen this butterfly singing and that's where he got that song. Today people sing it."

Helene comments as follows on the loving remembrances that link singers with Peyote songs: "Maybe a person has passed on, and they'll sing a song he used to sing. In the morning after breakfast, they'll talk about what happened in there that night. They'll say, 'The first song I sang belonged to a certain person. I sang it because I remembered him.' Or, 'I remember that certain time he sang it, or we did something together and he sang that song.' Just kind of little memories about that particular person, even though he's gone. Something nice is said about him. I find this a lot in Peyote meetings.

"I got Peyote tapes I listen to, and some of 'em are real beautiful. They're something I've grown up with and something you don't forget

6. McAllester's *Peyote Music,* based on research with the Comanche in Oklahoma, remains the classic study of this topic.

easy. They're special kind of songs, you know. But the songs in the meeting is so beautiful, right in it. It's so different when you sing it out, if you're just singing it, you know. Like if I think about a Peyote song while I'm doing something, it's not the same as listening and singing along with it in the meeting. It's so different, too. 'Cause the song itself gives you a different feeling when you're in there. And it gives you a different feeling at different times. It just depends. It could affect you in a real lonely way; you could just feel like crying. Or another time you could feel real happy, oh that's just so beautiful! And another time that same song wouldn't even phase you either way. So it just depends on how you are feeling that day. Or if you feel ill, you might hear that same song and think, well, I got to get well. This is really a nice song; I really like it."

JUDY: "Where do people get the Peyote songs here?"

HELENE: "I think a lot of 'em they have heard before, and they're just passed on to them. You know, people from some other tribe come in their [Native American Church] meeting, and then they pick it up. So I think it's nice. Sometimes they got what they call new songs. It's just like War Dance songs, you know, they get new songs. Some of the songs I'm familiar with, I'll sing along. But other times I'm just too glorified to even catch on to their song.

"Peyote songs used to have Shoshone words years ago, but a lot of them don't now. There's certain songs they use for Morning song and Midnight song and Water song, certain ones. I can't remember them until I'm in the meeting. Then when they start singing them I've got time, and then I know what's going to come on. [With or without Shoshone text, certain songs serve as markers during the course of the meeting.] Sometimes there's Shoshone words in songs, like *dave doih hiyena. Dave doih* means sun coming up; *nïmishuntai* means bless us. That kind of thing here and there. You hear that. Later on we'll play you a tape that has, I call it, Holy Jesus song. It's the Lord's Prayer in a Peyote song. English words in it. I think it's really great for certain people that don't understand a certain language. It's really nice to convert the Indian into English between lines. It's really understandable that way."

The Powwow: War Dance Songs

The powwows of Helene's youth evoke vivid and detailed memories. Her descriptions of the dancing she witnessed at these events follow: "The powwows I remember is when I started being interested in dancing. Before that time the powwows I remember weren't what they are today. What I remember of that is after Sun Dance, after the Shoshone Sun Dance, they had open dances, you know, outside they'd dance. Mostly it was men, too, that danced. You know, women [War Dancing] are just latest things now. These War Dances are from way back, when they had been to war. And then they celebrated their victory and so forth. That's the reason why it's named War Dance. And then the Wolf Dance is another terminology for the same thing, or War Dance.

"And I think the style of dancing is adopted from nature—the sage chicken. Have you ever seen a sage chicken dance? It's beautiful. There's one type of War Dancing—I forget what they call it now—it's one beat at a time, almost like a stomp, and it's a slow kind of War Dance. I guess it's similar to a Chicken Dance [of today]. That's the reason why it's called that because of the sage chickens. And if you happen to be around a place where the sage chickens are, like in March, and then before the sun is just beginning to come up, that's when you notice these. If you creep up on 'em, you see these sage chickens dancing. Every once in a while you'll hear, 'mphhh,' and then, 'boom.' Just like a regular Indian drum, you know, going, 'boomph, boomph.' And that's their whole chest bag. It comes out and then it hits and then the back end of their feathers spread out just like a bustle. Beautiful! And then when part of their feathers touch the ground, it makes that noise, just beautiful noise. And the mouth and everything they make is just according to the sound of their own drum. And they get fancy, their heads just go this way and that way. It's just beautiful. It just really makes you feel good to see it. I know a lot of these dances have been adopted from nature.[7]

"And then a lot of them have to do with war and enemies, too. You see them go like this, too, [Wolf Dancers] imitating that they're slowly creeping on to the enemy. Probably you could start to imagine what would be really going on. When I was a little girl, I used to really observe the dancers pretty good, and there's certain songs I remember from years back. [When I hear] a certain song or a particular beat, rhythm of it, then I kind of go back. I guess you would say I relive my childhood, sitting back on a chair and watching certain favorite dancers of mine and seeing them keep rhythm to it. Like this man, he was a big, heavyset guy. He really had an oversized tummy, and he wore beads over his tummy, bone breastplates. And he danced naked. All he had on was a pair of moccasins. They were

7. In his paper titled "Male Competition and Female Sexual Selection: An Ethnoethological Perspective on Dance," William Powers not only notes similarities of dance movement and costume between the dance of the male prairie chicken and that of the male War Dancers but even suggests parallel functions of courtship (Powers 1978).

plain with a little beadwork on there and just a little bit of fur around it, brown fur, probably from a white lady's coat. And then he had bells tied around his ankles, about three rows of medium-sized bells. And then he had huge, huge bells, the biggest I've ever seen at my time when I was a little girl. There was about four or five around his knees, under his knees. And then he had a whole string of medium-small bells running from his ankles all the way up to his waist. And he had a traditional Shoshone little bitty bustle, hawk or owl feathers shredded in a round ball and eagle or hawk feathers, like little horns sticking out of it and little hawk bells on the top. And then he was naked except for his breechcloth and his shorts. And then he would have braids, little skinny braids, and he had, you know, old men always have bangs sort of cut. And he would have a porcupine headdress way on his very head notch, up here where your hair divides, hanging up here and then it just goes down, just beautiful. He only had arm bands of brass, big, wide brass arm bands. Over here he had little braids coming down from his hair right front. They call it *mutsiwegwa* and that's little hair pipes. They're hair pipe bones, or they could be brass, anything that's a tube and hollow inside. They stick their little braids through it, and they call it *mutsiwegwa.* These are gone away with the old men. I'll probably never see it again. And he'd put red Indian paint all over his face. Dancing was his bag. He just loved to dance. And I think today if he lived in the eighties and saw these people dance for money and contests, I think he'd die all over again. So when I hear a certain rhythm of a drum or just the song in particular, I remember this old guy out there. It's just really amazing how a kid can visualize. And this is why I wish I was a real top artist, a straight-line drawer. I could probably do it. In my own mind I can just see it and it's painted, but if I was to do it on paper. . . . Like my mom always tells me, 'Don't just describe it, do your description on paper. Just sit down and doodle and maybe you'll get it.' Maybe she has something there. Maybe I might just try it someday." Note Helene's wish to represent her memory in a drawing and her mother's preference for a visual rather than verbal representation.

With respect to War Dance songs, Helene cannot say how many she knows. "That's pretty hard to number," she states. "So far this year I think I've heard only two new War Dance songs. We learn them whether we like them or not, just to be current, to be up with everyone else [*laugh*]. 'Cause there's a lot of songs that I don't care for, you know, but I learn them. Handgame songs are [the most] easy to learn, and I think second easy are War Dance songs. To me, that is. But I think Round Dance songs are a little bit harder for me to learn. They got a lot of up and downs and a lot of little close notes. But War Dance songs, they're just open, you know. You can let go and just really come on to it. A War Dance song will be popular about a couple of years, and if they're really pretty, you know, where everybody likes it and it's a good song and easy to dance to, then it just stays on for a good long time."

Helene's last comment expresses part of her underlying network of values and personal preferences. First and foremost Helene prizes the pure pleasure of War Dance singing and dancing, unalloyed with money and competition. "I think cash prizes has really ruined a lot of pleasure dancing," she asserts. "Nobody's going to dance for nothing anymore. Up in Canada they don't put on costumes like we do. Some of them dress in their Levi's, cowboy hat, and tennis shoes or cowboy boots. And that's what's so unique about them. They're just really into it, but they're not into it for show. They're into it because this is what they like to do and to heck with the audiences. It's what they can do and how they feel about doing it themselves. And that's why I mean they're not competing with their dresswear, their costumes. They're just in it. That's what's so inspiring to me about them dancers up there."

Helene not only values enjoyment and relaxation in and of themselves but considers these to be essential conditions for high quality performance. This came out as we reviewed a tape of her and Wayland singing War Dance songs.

JUDY: "If you want to, make comments on your performance — good or bad. 'Cause that was kind of like a practice session last night, you know; it wasn't a performance." [Note my biased opposition of practice versus "performance"; according to my prejudice practice sessions have errors, whereas formal public "performances" are more letter-perfect. To Helene this is upside-down.]

HELENE: "Well I think, Judy, that's about the best way you can tape it, more or less, practicing. You can get the best songs from there. And it's the same way when you dance. You notice (I do all the time) there's a lot of good dancers, and they're just doing their thing because they love to dance. And then when they say contest, they withdraw themselves. They're not going to get out there. And then a lot of times, too, they get out there and they're competing and they're uptight. They're just scared. So, they can't win because they're not doing their best thing out there. The time, I think, to judge people is when they're just cutting loose and enjoying themselves."

Helene and Wayland concur on what makes a good War Dance song. According to Wayland: "It depends on how many get up and dance to that song. If they like that song and if you like it, too, then it's more or less a pretty song." Helene expands on this theme: "Some of the War Dance songs that they sing, a real clear good song with a real good beat, will turn me on where I just want to get out there and groove to it, you know, just really cut out. And other songs will just turn me off where I just want to sit and I wish they'd hurry up and get it over with and sing a different song.

"Some of these old songs, you know, my ear kind of grabs 'em right away; my ears kind of stand out, you know, 'Hey!' you know. I don't know, it just has electricity about the old songs. They really grab me, and I can just about tell. And from what my dad used to tell me, way back, the shorter the song is the more beautiful it is. He said if you sing a song, sing it for a short length of time; and just when dancers get to be in the groove, end the song, and they'll want to dance more and they'll want you to sing another pretty song, or the same song. But nowadays, he said, these young groups sing on and on. They stretch the song where you just get bored to death with that song.[8] So that's the way it is nowadays, but way back they had it what they call short and sweet. And then old War Dance songs, they had all them curves, and that's what made them so pretty. But now, you know, they just straighten out the curves and angles in a song.

"And if you intend to sing through the powwow days, you better start with your own natural voice or the voice you are comfortable with and keep it at that level. Because that's where the beauty lies, is how you can hold your voice throughout the powwow, not demanding or outdoing each other. And a lot of times I see that. Even the best lady singer, man singer who tries to outdo one another like that is all shot, and their voice is no good for the best part of the powwow."

JUDY: "So stamina is part of your idea of a good powwow singer?"

HELENE: "I think so. I like a loud, well not real loud, but a clear voice, kind of medium high. And yet some guys have a real deep throat and yet they have a loud voice and yet they carry the music beautifully. So it just varies to me. Some singers appeal to me singing a certain song."

JUDY: "What about the person who has a good memory and knows lots of songs? Is that part of being a good singer?"

HELENE: "I don't think it matters how many songs you've got in your pockets.

"Wayland is a really fun person to sing with. He really helps you along

---

8. Hatton explained the increase in song length in his discussion of Northern Plains powwow performance. "Until about 1960," he reports, "Grass Dance songs lasted roughly five or six minutes. . . . Today, it is possible to observe songs lasting as long as half an hour. The change in length is due to the increased numbers of singing groups taking part in the music-making; their prolonging of the song is a matter of self-defense as they have quite a wait until their next turn" (Hatton 1974:128).

or relax. And when we're trying to sing together, he'll give you time to adjust to that song. We cover each other's mistake, you know, and some people don't realize this unless you know that song pretty well. We trade songs, and I get a chance to say, 'Well, what about this song, why don't we sing this?' It's my choice, and he says, 'OK,' if he knows it. And then same way with him, you know. Besides that, if there's a lot of other singers at our drum, he'll say, 'Go ahead, it's your turn.' He'll give the others a chance to do their thing, because they might have pretty songs, too. And it gives the shy person a chance to start off a song, and then he'll cover in for you. That's good. Our dad used to be that way when he was sitting at the drum. He welcomes people at the drum, no matter who they are, even from a different tribe. He'll give them a chance to share their song with him and the drum is open. After we get through singing we laugh because we might have fell off [the song] and somebody covered up for him, or we got onto a different song, maybe several songs. We laugh and tell jokes. And I guess a lot of times our drum is the noisiest. We're just doing this because it's fun for ourselves."

In her tribute to Wayland and her father, Helene summarizes her own ideals for the music-making process: fun, relaxing, supportive, welcoming, sharing, focusing on the congenial process rather than the "performance." Not only is the group music-making process fun, but it provides a basic norm in Helene's aesthetic. Helene sang a War Dance song by herself one time and then commented, "It sounds better when there's a group."

Among the first songs that Helene and Wayland sang for me in 1977 was a Flag song (not to be confused with the Sun Dance Flag Song, which is only used in the Sun Dance), a special song that opens the powwow and accompanies the ceremonial presentation of the United States flag (usually in consort with a state and local American Legion flag). Within the context of the powwow, the Flag song takes the place of "The Star-Spangled Banner." Men remove their hats, and everyone stands, as veterans carry the flags around the dancing area. Honoring, one of the most important virtues that Shoshones practice in public and private, extends here to flag, country, and the veterans who have defended both. There is an unspoken integration of past and present, a continuity that merges the Plains warrior of the past with his modern counterpart, the veteran. Even though Flag songs are distinct from War Dance songs, I include this Flag song with War Dance songs because of the close ties that join flag, warrior, and powwow.[9]

9. William Powers states: "My own interpretation of the effects of World War I and II and, to a lesser extent, the wars in Korea and Vietnam, is that they gave American Indians the opportunity to reinforce cultural institutions that might have become dysfunctional. Indian soldiers who participated were regarded as heroes by their people and, in accordance

Flag Song no. 1

with tribal custom, were publicly acknowledged through songs, dances, and giveaways"
(Powers 1980b:219).

HELENE: "We adopted the Cheyenne Flag song that we heard and learned in Lame Deer, Montana [the Northern Cheyenne reservation]. Just our family learned this song. Maybe next year you'll hear it. But years ago I understand the Shoshone people did have their own Flag song for their different dances and so forth. But it just died down with the other Indians and it was never passed on, and some of the younger generation wasn't interested in learning it until now. It's the 'in' thing now. They're trying desperately to grasp what they have lost. We just thought, well, people are interchanging their songs and modifying songs. And it's a nice thing to have, so this is what we have practiced and sang. And that's the song we sang for the Grand Entry, too. [For the Grand Entry all the dancers dance into and around the arena for the first time in single file.] It's one of the prettiest Flag songs I've heard since I've been around."

JUDY: "Is that an old song amongst the Cheyennes?"

HELENE: "I think so, because, you know, they really value that song."

JUDY: "What do you think about your performance of it?"

HELENE: "I think this tape that you have is probably on one of the best ones, because it was the beginning and we were doing our best then. But I don't think we could do it again. We've really gotten away from practicing, and we don't do too much anymore."

The slow, deliberate tempo of this Flag song is common to many Flag song performances. The drum accompaniment, which sets it apart from other War Dance songs, enhances the feeling of time slowed down. In place of a steady pulse of even drumbeats, the drum hits every other beat (♩ ♪ ♩ ♪) or every other beat with a faint tap on the intervening beat (♩ ♩ ♩ ♩). Still another distinctive feature of this song is its concluding drum (and voice) tremolo flourish. War Dance songs characteristically end with a decisive final drumbeat.

War Dance Song no. 6

HELENE: "I think that's a Canadian song. Sometimes, like next week [late in August], they're going to have a celebration in Poplar, Montana, and that's next to the Canadian borderline. We try to make it up there so we can get the songs from Canada. They are beautiful songs, you know. They're hard, but once you learn them it's really nice. They're all different, and that's what's so good about it. We get most of our songs at Lame Deer [Montana, the Northern Cheyenne reservation] during the Fourth of July when it's just being introduced to the new songs. Most of the new songs come from Canada, the pretty songs. They have good singers up there. So the Canadians bring them down to Lame Deer, and that's where we hear it first, Fourth of July. Then we pick it up from there. It takes me a while to pick up on a song I'm not familiar with."

JUDY: "When you get a new song, is it from Wayland sitting at a drum group or both of you standing behind a drum group and singing with them?"

HELENE: "We just get it from observing or just listening and standing further away from the drum group, behind. 'Cause a lot of times nowadays you can't drum hop, what they call drum hopping. You can't just plop down and sing with them, because a lot of them have restrictions now. So you got to be very careful.[10] We listen and sing with them. And then maybe later, coming home, well, we'd be singing it. One doesn't know it too well, the other grabs something that the other guy missed. So we kind of put it together, and we got it, pretty much."

JUDY: "If there's places that you're missing—say you kind of have it, but there's a little place here and there that you're missing—will you then sometimes kind of fix it your own way? Or don't you like to do that?"

HELENE: "We more or less like to keep it with the way we heard it. And if we didn't, well, it's too bad. 'Cause we'll just have our own way about that particular song."

Wayland begins the performance of War Dance song no. 6 at one tempo, ♩ = ca. 168, and after a couple of repetitions accelerates to a faster tempo, ♩ = ca. 184, for the last two repeats. Although in abbreviated form here, this parallels Helene's description of the old way of easing into a song: "When I was about ten the old guys, when they start singing, they sat

---

10. Hatton notes that "certain rules of etiquette must be observed by singers who 'sit in' with other than their own groups. At times, men move from drum to drum helping out in an effort to pass the time until their next turn. In such a case they are not helping out if they do not pay attention, cannot keep time, muscle in hard beats or song leads, continually sing the wrong song, or beat on the drum too hard or with an unprotected beater that could put a hole in the drum head. A serious breach of conduct is to travel to another drum while intoxicated" (Hatton 1974:136).

around the drum and they'd hit the edge of the drum. The head singer, whoever's going to lead that particular War Dance song, he would sing it to his group so everybody can grasp that song. Whereas now the drummer just goes ahead and starts pounding like that and comes out full force, even their voices full force. But back in them days, the old guys would sit at the drum, slightly beating on the edge of the drum or on the drum just very delicately, like as if they were hitting a chinaware or something. And then you could hear this muffling like, 'hmmmm,' just like a whole cluster of bees. And then they'd be still doing that and pretty soon the drumbeat got a little louder and then the singing got a little louder and pretty soon it'd go to where you didn't even notice how loud they got. And then the beat, they just went into it very delicately and came out, you know, singing forcefully. And everybody got the song. That's what I really observed about the old guys beating and singing their songs. They did it very carefully and very gently as if the songs are very precious to them as well as their drum and the beat of their rhythm. Everything about it. It's so different now. You just dive into it full force. Everybody takes it for granted that everybody knows that song. Now it's just something to outdo the next drum. I'm not trying to criticize the Indian people for what they're doing. What I'm trying to do is to compare. And like I say, you know, the way the old people did it is a lost thing now."

War Dance song no. 6 presents the typical War Dance drum accompaniment, a steady pulse with a short series of accents on every other beat, just after the beginning of the second main section (an incomplete repetition of the first). These accents are structural markers and often cue the dancers that the song is about to end.

When I arrived on the scene in 1977, War Dance song no. 6 was a very popular powwow song. It's popularity waxed in 1978. Or maybe it was just my excitement over returning to the reservation with a small repertoire of songs I could recognize, but it seemed like every other song was War Dance no. 6. Then in 1979 a new War Dance song became the rage (the song excerpted on p. 79); the intense popularity of War Dance song no. 6 was on the wane. By the summer of 1982 it was something of a has-been, crowded out by a bevy of younger favorites.

JUDY: "How many different War Dance songs do drum groups sing during the course of an evening?"

HELENE: "So far as I listened the other night, I would offhand say five popular ones that went around. They're five different songs, and each drum group had a different way of singing that same song, but it was the same song. If there's a new powwow song and we're introducing it, we sing it maybe six verses [repetitions], maybe even as far as eight, and then we quit. Later on we sing about three more songs, and then we bring that same song back again. It's more fun that way. And if the new song's a little hard to sing, then a lot of people don't like to sing it until they learn it good."

WAYLAND: "Until they smooth the curves out."

Helene's earlier comments about old War Dance songs having more curves and Wayland's comment here bring out some of the contradictions and countercurrents in the Shoshone musical scene. Angie maintains that the old War Dance songs were straight or without many curves, implying a contrast with more recent War Dance songs. Many Shoshones make the same assessment: there are more curves in today's songs. Although this may well be the case, Wayland notes that in the process of learning and performing a song, some of the curves are effaced, smoothed out, lost. At a subtler level Helene and Wayland may be responding and sensitive to the loss of curves in the learning process. Then, too, differences of opinion about the presence or absence of curves may arise from particular and different frames of reference for the "old" songs. (Also recall Alberta's comments on the abbreviation of Sun Dance cadences in contemporary performances through omission of the "little drop-downs," a viewpoint that similarly counters the general perception of more curves in contemporary song performances.)

War Dance Song no. 7 ("Amazing Grace")

HELENE: "Like I'd see a beauty in a song. It would be just like Indian paintbrush [a red wildflower, the state flower of Wyoming], maybe just one or two, way out in a field where there's no fence. Just the two, or just one. And it would be a brilliant color. It's the kind I would see with the beauty in a song. Like I would describe that particular kind of scenery to the 'Amazing Grace' [War Dance song]. Because that's so pretty when it's sung high. And when I heard 'Amazing Grace' as a white man's song, there's only certain singers in the white man's world that when they sing 'Amazing Grace' make it beautiful. And the others that come along, they don't have the beauty in that song. That's the way I see it.

"That [War Dance] song came from Albuquerque, New Mexico, someplace around there. These friends of ours brought it up. They had a little tape, you could barely hear it. And then we knew a little bit about 'Amazing Grace,' so we just kind of put it together and we practiced it up and worked on it. I would say that was two or three years ago [1976 or 1977]. It's not really that popular here. It probably is elsewhere. Usually after the first year of new songs, they're singing it down here. But it wasn't like that with that 'Amazing Grace.' It surprised me."

There is a timetable for the learning and dissemination of powwow songs, both on the Wind River reservation and between reservations. According to Helene: "If a person is a good song-learner, they can learn it that time [during a summer powwow], sing it at Christmas time [for the holiday dances]. And then everybody [on the reservation] learns it within that year's time. It's passed on. When it comes from Canada and hits Montana, then the Wyoming people pick it up, or Idaho pick it up. And then we pass it on and it goes down south, and then they're learning it. They might not be singing it this year in Utah or even around here until next year. And then it will be on the top list. See, it's just a year later or six months later they're singing it."

To my knowledge War Dance song no. 7 made its debut on the reservation during the 1978 powwow. Helene and her family drum group sang it the following year, 1979. They were prompted to sing it on that particular occasion because they saw a church bus parked at the powwow grounds and thought they might please those non-Indian visitors. In spite of these two learning opportunities, I wondered why the song never caught on.

HELENE: "I don't think anybody really likes to sing it. It's because they think they're singing a white man song, same as that 'Amazing Grace.' So you hardly hear the local people sing it, just visitors."

JUDY: "So when you sing it, you think most Shoshone people realize the song it's been made from?"

HELENE: "Yes."

Helene, who is bicultural and bimusical, attempted to use War Dance song no. 7 as a cultural bridge for Euro-Americans. We will see in her later discussion of older Shoshone dances that she was drawing on Shoshone traditions of musically welcoming visitors (see pp. 171, 173). The Big Wind Singers adopted this tradition to a new situation when they sang War Dance song no. 7, a musical hybrid. While Shoshones rejected it because of its mixed heritage, one wonders whether the Euro-American church visitors even made any connection between the two songs, parent and offspring. Certainly the substitution of vocables for the original text is an important difference between the two.

JUDY: "With the vocables, are there patterns that people use over and over again or are they all kind of different?"

HELENE: "To my hearing I would say they're all just very slightly different. You have to have a real sensitive ear for that kind of music. I guess, really, I don't pay too much attention to that, like you do in analyzing the songs. If it's on my tongue, that's fine with me, you know. That's where it's going to be."

JUDY: "It seems like there are some conventions which you follow. I've noticed that you wouldn't start off the song, 'wi,' you'll start with 'we.' "

HELENE: "More or less 'he ya' or 'we ya.' It's something that's in you, that's built, that's there and in your brain saying you don't go 'yo.' "

Hinton has pointed out the use of vocables in specific Havasupai song genres promoting and expressing social solidarity (Hinton 1980:294, 299). One sees further applications of this in powwow music. Despite differences between each tribe's vocable inventory as derived from their specific phonologies (Powers 1961c:159, 160; Powers 1979), there is a broadly shared framework on the Northern Plains. Vocables facilitate an easy transfer of songs between groups at the powwow. It is a special kind of Indian lingua franca for song, one that, like the powwow itself, expresses and promotes intertribal identity and solidarity.

If the vocable text did not obscure the recognition of "Amazing Grace" to Euro-American listeners, then the deletion of the entire middle section of the song and the restructuring of the melodic contour may have (see ex. 8). In place of an arch-shaped melody with the highest note and climax at the center, War Dance song no. 7 ("Amazing Grace") begins on the highest note (reversing the order of the first two notes in the hymn tune and raising them an octave) and descends through a series of melodic plateaus. Each section (call, response, main body of the song, and repeat of the main body

Example 8. General melodic contour of "Amazing Grace"

of the song) begins high and steps down. It is very likely that many or all of the church bus spectators missed the point of War Dance song no. 7, which for them bore no family resemblance to "Amazing Grace." Incognito, it remained an unrecognized stranger.

War Dance Song no. 8

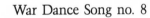

If War Dance song no. 8 were performed by an all-male drum group, the singing would be in unison. And if women were to join in, they would sing an octave above the men, entering after the call and response section.[11]

11. We have seen this same pattern in Shoshone Sun Dance song performance (see chart 1, p. 33). A review of historical evidence in charts 2A and B (pp. 44 and 45) shows that the musical participation of women in War Dance songs and its precursors has historical depth, both for Shoshones and other Plains tribes. Hatton and Powers document female musical roles in contemporary War Dance songs (Hatton 1974:135; Powers 1961b:128).

But when Helene sings War Dance song no. 8 at the drum, she combines two singing roles in addition to the male instrumental role. She sings the response to the opening solo call in unison with Wayland and then leaps up the octave to the "lady's" part. She is pragmatic about this, as one can see in the third repeat of the song: Helene continues in unison with Wayland well beyond the call and response before moving up the octave.

Helene comments on her role: "When we practice we talk about where I should come in high and where he should come in high — I'll come in high, and you come under me. You come in high, or I'll second you. [Helene uses "second" in two senses. It can refer to the repeat of the opening solo call and to the principal supporting singer who "seconds" the lead singer.] You second me, but you come in high. I can just reverse my voice to whichever suits me at the drum, and it's not difficult for me. I think that all started with me because I used to do a lot of mimicking of different things on radio and TV. When I like some singer, like Loretta Lynn, I can make my voice sound just like her, or if some man's talking, you know, I'll practice all this kind of stuff. I used to do that a lot when I was a kid, tease my mom and dad and come in the door with a different voice. If the song itself is sung high, then I come along in his tone [unison with Wayland], with whatever tone he's using, and then I get a chance someplace in the line where I think he needs the octave high, so I'll kind of turn my voice over where I can, where it's needed. When it's just the two of us, like he needs support each time to come in, if he can't get his breath, he'll look at me. That's the reason why we look at one another all the time, especially if it's a song that we're trying to learn and we're right on the dance floor; and he looks at me, and I know what he wants. That's why we have a lot of our special sign language at the drum. He'll make some kind of motion with his hands or his eyes or with his mouth.[12] You just have to learn these little tricks so that it's not noticeable to the whole crowd. So that's the reason a lot of singers look at their head, lead singer. So that's why I look at him or his beating, not because he's made any mistake or anything. Same as he does to me, because he'll want me to either come in as a second, because some songs take such tremendous breathing, you know, it takes a lot of breath out of him. He has to regain his breath, so he tells me to come in. So I'll stop [and catch a breath] before he ends it and then come in. You have to learn where to take a breath and when not to. It kind of takes a lot of work, your breathwise and all that. [For example, only Helene sings the final note at the cadence of verses 1–3 in War Dance

---

12. See Hatton for illustration of eight drumming signals used by Northern Plains powwow singers (Hatton 1974:134).

song no. 8; this allows Wayland to prepare for the long high first note that begins the song.]

"It's not the same as a Sun Dance song where the ladies come in all the time [at the same place]. We practice different voice levels [i.e., different starting notes] where we are more at ease and not straining our throat. And then we kind of tear the song apart and say, 'Why don't you come in high over here?' So it's not in the same areas. I never come in on the same areas [unison versus octave above] as you will find out in a lot of songs. As a matter of fact, I think in '76 we worked on a song where Wayland would sing his natural voice level and just quit. And then me and my sisters and my mom, we all come in on the high-note part. Somewhere along the line we heard it like that. The men sang the harder, the song part, and we just come in on the chorus, and then the men came in again [to begin the next repetition of the song].[13] And that's beautiful. We practiced it one summer, but we didn't sing it in the arena or on the dance floor. The reason why we didn't was because we all didn't get together, the ladies, you know. It was always myself and my mom, and my mom didn't care too much to be pushed out there and sing. So we did it at home; we practiced a lot at home but never out [in public]. It sounded real good."

While new, this experimental enlargement of the female singing part is not revolutionary. It fits in with a general "finishing" singing role for women found in the performance practice of a variety of tribes. A description of women ending Shoshone Sun Dance songs has already been discussed. Powers noted the extension of mid-cadences by female Sioux singers (Powers 1961b:128; Powers 1961a:98). In addition Hatton documented examples of Northern Plains women finishing most of the last section of the final repeat in powwow songs (Hatton 1974:135). According to Vennum, "It is the practice of some Ojibwa singing groups for the men to drop out completely once the women have begun their singing, to let them finish the particular musical phrase; the men reenter after a cadence is reached and begin the melody anew" (Vennum 1982:84, 85).

In private there is a lot of give and take between Helene and Wayland as they work up songs, even down to deciding which version to sing. "We compare songs," Helene states. "Sometimes Wayland learns a song from one group, the same song I learned or I've known a little bit longer than he

---

13. The term *chorus*, like *motet* in Western art music, has more than one meaning. Some scholars use it to refer to the song section that comes after the opening call and response (Powers 1961b:128). Shoshones may use this meaning or may refer to the second section of the song, the incomplete repetition, as the chorus. It is not completely clear in which sense Helene uses the term here.

has. Then I sing it my way and he sings it his way and then we compare it. And then we say I like it your way or I like it this way. Or we find out we got two different kinds of rhythms to it. We do that once in a while." But when the Big Wind Singers sing at a powwow or for my tape recorder, Wayland, as lead singer, is in control. "Wayland will do the song the way he wants," Helene adds, "the old way or new way. He has certain kinks in certain songs, and it's up to the whole drum group to try to follow through. And when I'm the only one helping Wayland, I know he depends on me. So if it's a song that he knows that I don't know, he expects me to be right there singing it with him, learning it. So I don't try to drag behind him; I try to keep up with him. A lot of his mouth movements tell me when to come in and when to curve off [i.e., a fading downward or portamento on final notes; see, for example, the last note of War Dance song no. 9, p. 168]. That's the reason why a lot of times I'm always looking at his mouth. And sometimes he just makes it into an oval shape and just rolls up his eyes, and that's when I get to laughing. And that's when we get comical there. I had to learn to do that a lot because I can't hear too well, and I learned to try to read lips a long time ago. So it's not too difficult for me to tag along on a song that I don't really know. I will just get right in there and hang in. And a lot of times I try not to outdo him because I know the song or love the song. I try to keep up with him even though I do an octave higher, but I won't try to really force myself to outdo him. Some ladies I hear try to outdo the singers."

JUDY: "So it's the lead singer who decides when you speed up and when you get softer or louder?"

HELENE: "Yes, usually. He's the one that's going to come off louder, or, when he goes like this, it means to go softer. He'll slow up or be going faster. And in the past when somebody started getting too fast for the rhythm, then the lead singer had the authority to tap his drumstick, and that meant you put your drumstick down until the next go-around. You couldn't hit again [until the next repeat of the song]. They try to do that now, but when they tap their hands they just take their hand and start in right after that again and get in. But way back he had the authority to rule the other singers. He was more stricter than what it is today."

JUDY: "How did you [any singer] get to be the lead singer?"

HELENE: "From what I gather in the past, you was just a born natural leader people looked up to."

JUDY: "And did the leader also know more songs than other people?"

HELENE: "Yes, definitely. They'd have to make up songs and stuff like that."

Although the lead singer has control over the singing group, the ultimate authority rests with the spectators and especially the dancers. They judge the songs and singing groups through their enthusiastic response and participation, and a good lead singer responds to their feedback and needs. "A lot of times when Wayland and I are singing," Helene notes, "and we look and there are some dancers that really like the song and they come over and they're really doing their thing, then we pick up a little bit speed and a little bit more push to it, force, and then we continue the song. But if we see that nobody is interested, we shorten our song. So I think it's a good thing, too; you look around to see what's going on in the arbor or on the dance floor. Because a lot of singers, they don't have consideration for the dancers. They just sing on and on and on, until you're dropping. A lot of dancers don't like to walk off the floor; they like to finish out. And it gets to be a boresome thing. And you look at your dancers, too; and a lot of them will be real elderly guys, and you don't want to have a traditional beat that's really fast for them people. How's that elderly guy going to do? And yet he might be the outstanding dancer of them all, too. So for the Traditional War Dance song, it's usually kind of slow where they can bend around. And then sometimes, too, you get some spectators that stand behind you, and they'll say [*spoken in an urgent whisper*], 'Sing that song you sang before.' In order to please everybody you sing that same song again."

A good lead singer, like a good song, fosters participation and enjoyment. A good powwow combines each of these parts into the larger whole. Appraising the 1978 Shoshone powwow, Helene states: "It was pretty good. We didn't have that many spectators [a minus], but we had a lot of dancers, so that was good. Everybody, to me, it looked like they enjoyed it."

War Dance song no. 8 typifies many aspects of Northern Plains musical style. If one listens to the last note of the first section (see bracket 1, p. 159), one hears pulsation, which frequently articulates long ending notes. (See Hatton 1986:205–8 for an analysis of the rhythmic patterns of vocal pulsation as a distinguishing element of Grass Dance musical style and area.) Another important characteristic of War Dance song no. 8 and of Northern Plains musical style comes from the complex relationship between the drum and vocal parts; they do not precisely coincide.[14] Several strategies achieve this result. On the one hand there is a common practice of delaying the vocal note a fraction of a second after each drumbeat, thus creating one

14. Because detailed analyses of individual songs and song genres are beyond the scope of this book, my musical transcriptions do not indicate the slight separation between vocal and drum attacks.

kind of asynchrony. (Honor Song for Bird Women, on pp. 224–25, exemplifies this practice.) But on the other hand singers may also do just the reverse. They sometimes enter "early" and anticipate melodic notes just before the drumbeat, thus leading one to perceive a consistent pattern of the voice being ever so slightly ahead of the drum. (War Dance song no. 8 illustrates this point.) This may be a measurable fraction of a note (for example, the sixteenth note tied to the whole note at bracket 1, p. 159), which, in turn, causes the placement of ensuing pulsations to be "early." Or it may be less easily quantified and more in the nature of a grace note or an even shorter duration. Finally, various rhythmic syncopations in the vocal line are another means of enhancing the separation and independence of vocal and drum parts (see bracket 2, p. 159).[15] As one male Shoshone singer expressed it, "What I try to do is get them a little behind the other."

War Dance Song no. 9

15. Scholars have analyzed the complex relationship between the voice and drum in various ways. William Powers noted the asynchronous relationship in Sioux music, stating that the drum slightly precedes the voice (Powers 1961b:133; Powers 1961a:104). Elsewhere I have also observed this particular relationship in Shoshone performance (Vander 1978:138). While the issue of which comes first — the voice or drum — may differ, the tempo for both is the same. In his analysis of Dakota music, Pantaleoni suggests that the fast metric unit of the singer's vibrato is the organizing key for the noncoincident drum and vocal rhythms (Pantaleoni 1987:39). Both Hatton and Vennum note the use of vocal syncopation as a means of achieving independence of parts (Hatton 1974:130; Vennum 1980:49). Germane to this point are the particular drum-vocal rhythmic patterns commonly heard in Round Dance songs (see pp. 38, 39) and the accents that mark phrase beginnings (see p. 42). Hatton's discussion of the rhythmic pulsations of the voice presents another facet of this strategy (Hatton 1986:206, 216). In contrast to these analyses, which imply one underlying rhythmic reference for the drum and voice, Densmore, McAllester, and Nettl have reported different tempos for the voice and drum (Densmore 1918:77; McAllester 1984:13; Nettl 1967:304).

HELENE: "Other tribes call it the Grass Dance, but it's the same thing as War Dance. This particular Grass Dance song they sang in Browning, Montana, a long time ago. All of us were just tiny guys then. I think my mom sees it, too, when we sing that song, and I see it, too, where one of her relatives, Blackfeet relatives, won a prize on that particular song. And this girl, she was a young lady, she had a buckskin dress on. Our grandpa was one of the chiefs up there. And then she happened to be dancing in the ladies' contest, and this is one of the songs they sang for her. She was dancing in a particular way that is kind of comical, and yet she won the prize. It's the one that we'll always remember with that person. That's what I was telling you about; each song reminds you of a certain person."

Midway through their performance of this Grass Dance song, Helene picked up a set of large bells (the type that War Dancers strap on under their knees) and began to shake them in time to the song. It was a brief reminder that the complete musical ensemble for War Dance songs should include the dancer, whose bells jingle with every rhythmic motion of the dance.

When singing for me, Wayland and Helene always try to follow older Shoshone customs. And so, even though they sing here what they believe to be a Blackfoot song, they add a short *nduah* at the end of it.

HELENE: "That's the traditional way of the Shoshones. They call it *nduah,* and it means son; that could be the son of the whole song. The song would be over with, and instead of just leaving it, they have a little pause and then they hit the drum again and then add just one short verse to it, like a chorus [see p. 168]. That's something I've seen as a little girl, and they don't do that anymore, Judy. And that's what's really bad. Most of the songs, they always had an *nduah."*

JUDY: "Is that what other tribes call a 'tail?' "

HELENE: "That's the same thing. But nowadays when they add it, it's the whole song all over again.

JUDY: "Let's say you went to a powwow and there were Shoshone singers. Would you recognize from their singing style that it was a Shoshone group?"

HELENE: "I think back about ten, fifteen years ago it would be real noticeable. I think it would be the beat of the drum, the song itself, and [the old way of easing into a song, moving] from the light and then going into the whole thing [at full force and speed]."

JUDY: "What would you have noticed about the drumbeat?"

HELENE: "I think it would be kind of modern type hitting, but there would be the *nduah* at the end. And they used to have the nice medium voice. Now either have the real heavy voice or they're tuned up [high] just like everybody else. So it's hard to say now. If it was nighttime and you couldn't see who was singing, I don't think I could tell."

Helene and other Shoshones are acutely sensitive to vocal quality and pitch level, which can distinguish not only old and new Shoshone singing styles but also other tribal styles. "I would know right away whether it's an Oklahoma drum or not," Helene asserts. "And I would know if it's from Canada, or even an older group of men. I would know. More or less the singing would give them away, not the type of song but the way they're holding their voices. An Oklahoma singer, they go just like the Forty-nine [song]. They start off with a Forty-nine kind of tune or beat, rhythm [♪ ↱ ♪ ♪ ↱ ♪], while the Sioux go, you know, like coyotes with that high pitch. And then the older group would have their moderate kind of a slow type of beat with the everyday kind of voice. And then the Montana or the Canadian would have that pretty kind of tone. More operatic type of voice."[16]

JUDY: "Would you say Wayland is more that kind of singer?"

HELENE: "I would say he'd be between the Canadian and the Sioux. So he feels more at ease with the high-tone, high-pitched voices than the lower ones."

Vocal quality and pitch levels relate not only to tribal or regional styles but also to different types of song. Wayland summarizes the male singer's perspective: "High voice, usually War Dance. Medium voice is Peyote songs. You can use medium and low for Handgame songs and then lowest is your Sun Dance songs. You have to sing with your heavy voice."

Helene elaborated on the various aspects of vocal quality as they relate to types of songs and singing situations from the female point of view: "On War Dance songs the men are doing all the voice straining, while the ladies that are singing come up with the higher pitch in the back, you know. So they don't have to strain their throats, and they can use their ladylike tones in that situation there. But on the Handgame songs, especially if you're the leader, you just want to blurt out and, you know, use your big heavy voice. And then Sun Dance song you use your ladylike voice, too, on that. 'Cause, you know, you just bring up the end on that. A lot of times I like to start off on a War Dance song on my original voice, and then I gradually change it on to the higher pitch at certain places."

JUDY: "Do you gradually get into that stronger voice as you get going?"

HELENE: "Sometimes. It all depends on what kind of song it is. If it's a *good* song that I really enjoy or like, I'll go into it full blast. If it's

---

16. It is interesting to compare Helene's vocal analysis and terminology with Hatton's (Hatton 1986:204).

	Helene	Hatton
Sioux singers	coyote	"pinched throat technique," AVF setting — adduction of the vocal folds
Montana, Canadian singers	operatic	"warbling sound," MPC setting — manipulation of the pharyngeal cavity

something that I'm not too familiar with, I'll just kind of use a softer tone until I learn it or get with it."

JUDY: "What about Round Dance? Do you sing that in the softer voice?"

HELENE: "Yes. If you're with ladies singing with a drum group, well, you use your ladylike voice. It just all depends on what kind of song you're singing. You have to adjust your voice according to that."

Because there is sensitivity to all the varying shades of vocal quality that combine with different pitch and volume levels, this becomes a factor in the perception of a song. "Like the Sioux," Helene notes, "they got this high-pitch voice, really high. So their songs sound either beautiful or they sound off-key to certain other groups that sing. And somebody from Idaho sings it and they got a real heavy voice and they sing it — the same song — but it all sound different. So it depends on your voice and the group. Like the Spearfish Singers [from Washington], they've been singing the songs, about four-year-ago songs. So those songs are quite old. And the type of voices they have make it sound new."

All powwow singers, including Helene and her family drum group, have favorite remedies to protect their voices during the powwow, for, in addition to singing for several hours, they must also contend with the fine clouds of dust that dancers beat from the dry summer powwow grounds. "The dust dries up your throat," Helene remarks. "Before you know it you've got a cold the next day. We use raw lemon juice, and coffee does pretty good, too. A lot of times we don't try anything that's sweet, because sugar seems to settle in the throat, and it doesn't do you any good. Candy is really bad on your throat. But something that has a little bit of salt is really good."

Round Dance Songs

HELENE: "My dad really liked Round Dance songs. He used to sing them all the time. He said they had an old community hall, and then they had one round hall right below the cemetery someplace [see plate 9 following p. 46]. And I guess, from what I can gather, they did have good dances. And that's before my times. And my dad said they had a song for each thing. They had the Welcome song, Traditional Welcome song. And like they're going to just start their dancing, they had a song for that, the song, Getting Ready to Round Dance. That means all the ladies shed their babies they had on their backs and get out there and Round Dance. They just about knew each thing that was going to go on without the song being announced. And then every two or three War Dances they had a Round

Dance song or a Rabbit Dance or a Two-Step [all dances for men and women] or Owl Dance [sometimes called the Indian Waltz], which some people call Push Dance. Every two or three songs they have that so the ladies can stretch up and enjoy themselves. And then on the very last, just before they were going to wrap up their dances, they'd have that Goodnight Sweetheart, Goodnight song [see p. 71]. That was to wrap up everything. So the ladies that had babies and kids, they knew, when they start singing that song, that it was time to get their babies all ready, bundled up, and start putting their babies on their backs and rolling them up to take home. That's the signal for goodnight." (Unable to sing this Goodnight song by herself, Helene recognized Angie's taped performance of it.)

JUDY: "Was the Round Dance done in partners at that time?"

HELENE: "Yes, it was. And years ago it was kind of tough, in a way, 'cause it meant expense for the man. It didn't matter whether the man was young or old, what mattered was if he had money. That's the way the Indians do it. The women get up and ask the man, where at white dances a man asks a lady. Our situation here is women will get up and go ask the man. And they can't refuse; they got to dance. Where today you can be refused and be embarrassed. But in that time, when somebody asked you to dance, you get up and dance or you pay a fine. See, if you refuse, you pay a fine, and also when you dance around, you pay. The man pays the lady. And so the women know which old man has a lot of money. They're going to grab, maybe fight over him, not really fight over him, but, you know, kind of want him to dance with them. And then if the man didn't have any money, he'd look around for his cousins or his sisters. He'd look around, and these cousins and sisters would kind of hide, 'cause they know they have to pay his fine. They have to pay for him. I guess it was a lot of fun in those days, from what I hear."

Helene remembers bits and snatches of old Round Dance songs her dad sang, songs that were part of the dances before her time. "And then that Prisoner song I was telling you about," she recalls, "that's a nice one, too. If people could even learn it, you know, and revise it, it would be really nice. I don't know who made it up or what, but my dad used to sing it. He had learned that song from his dad. Here around the house he would sing it, and it's got white man words in it, like,

Prisoner Song (Fragment)

You know that Prisoner song—he was in prison and dreaming about his girlfriend—well, it's the same thing. It goes like this:

Prisoner Song as Round Dance Song no. 9

we ya   he   ya he yai ya he   yo   we ya   he   ya he yo   ya he_____

It's much more beautiful when my dad used to sing it."

JUDY: "So the actual tune was from a folksong?"

HELENE: "Uh-huh. And then that Welcome song, I can't think of it offhand. It's kind of a greeting song, too."

JUDY: "Is it an American folk tune or an Indian?"

HELENE: "Well, it has both I think. If I can think of it, I'll give you a verse of it. These old songs I get kind of all tangled up, too, you know."

Later in the summer Helene was able to recall the following tantalizing fragment from a Welcoming or Greeting Round Dance song (notice how "hello" repeats and functions like a vocable such as "he yo"):

Welcoming Round Dance Song no. 10 (Fragment)

I'm glad   to   see   you hel-lo   hel-lo   hel-lo   hel-lo__ hai__   ya

HELENE: "A lot of the old Round Dance songs like that, they fit their English words into it. My dad used to sing quite a few of those. He used to sing a verse and then skip onto a different one. It was kind of hard to grasp. See, a lot of them that have words in them *are* probably what you would call Shoshone songs—probably composed by the Shoshone old guys from here. And then they put the English language into it. A lot of these songs, they're originally from here."

[July 10, 1978. "Helene talked of symbolism of feathers on the head. The women used to wear a headband and feathers: one feather = single, two feathers = married. She thought if the feathers were cut it meant husband had died, and maybe a 'v' cut in feathers meant a man had been wounded."] These are some of the little bits and pieces that Helene carefully preserves from her grandfather's and father's days. Sights and sounds from the dances of her own childhood remain vividly imprinted on the "video-tape" of her mind. "When they had Round Dances," she recollects, "the ladies were all sleeked up. They had beautiful dresses, whether it's cotton, calico, or silk, or satin and velvet. It's still pretty, decorated with beautiful wide, beaded belts and maybe cowrie shells. It's just the way they dress up, the beauty of dancing. And all the old ladies would get up, and one would walk onto the floor. The others would shed off their Pendleton blankets, their scarves [see the scarf Angie wears in plate 10 following p. 58], they just pull it back down and let it hang and kind of moistened their hair by a little bit of spit, matten their hair down. And all the old ladies would get out there, and they'd all be about the same height [probably the same stature as Helene's mom, under five feet tall and stocky]. It was so beautiful, Judy, it's beyond description." (For a picture of a 1910 Shoshone Women's Dance, see plate 7 following p. 46.)

Round Dance Song no. 11

Wayland and Helene sing this song at a leisurely pace, ♩. = ca. 77. Helene comments that she likes "the slow, smooth kind of beat. A lot of times some of these guys that sing the Round Dance songs, they go so fast, they just pound away. You notice a lot of times they go [♩.= 132] ♪ ♪ ᵞ ♪ ♪ ᵞ ♪ ♪ . Golly, they don't give the ladies enough time. They don't give enough consideration to the ladies' movement. It may be a beautiful song, but the drumming is poor. That's what I would call poor, because some of the older ladies, like my mom or somebody else in her age level that likes the song, wants to get up and stretch their legs and dance—how are they going to dance with that kind of rhythm? It's really hard. It's what you would call *biŏnʒoginï'këp*, where everything just kind of shakes. I don't think that I approve of that kind of thing.

"And I approve 100 percent when they do the Round Dance songs, and I would like to see it year after year done with the hand drums, or squaw drums. Because that's what it's made for, and that's our tradition and our culture, the Shoshone people. But we've gotten away from it, and I think very few people here have hand drums. Before, when I was a kid, the guys that had hand drums brought them to the dances and let the singers use 'em. That's what it was made for, and that's why they let everybody enjoy it. They brought it, and whoever wanted to sing Squaw songs, well, they up and use it. I would really like to see it revised again.

"The different tones of each squaw drum and the tune or tone of each individual that's singing it — that's the beauty of a song right there, instead of five to ten people sitting around a big war drum [bass drum], all trying to beat the Round Dance. They've lost it right there. The war drum itself doesn't have the tone for the nice ——. It should be a lady tone, a ladylike tone, for the ladies. And that's why I say they've really gone away from it, no respect in that field there. But I think that's where the secret lies, is the tones of each squaw drum and the tone of each individual man that's singing."

Another conversation explored the matter further.

HELENE: "A real pretty Round Dance song, not only by singing it but by looking at it, would be — I would have to go back and say the Round Dance drums. That makes a great deal of difference in the tone of the singing. Because they have a lighter tone than the bass drum, it makes a better sound, and it helps the singer's voice. I've seen it and I've heard it and I've observed it, and it looks good. Not only it looks good, but it makes people feel good, too; well, they went through all this trouble to bring their hand drums and get out there and sing, so I'm going to get out there. I'm going to look my best, and I'm going to dress up. It gives you the incentive to dress up and get out there and dance. That's my feeling about it. And it looks good."

JUDY: "If they use the Round Dance drum, do they sing in a little bit lighter voice than if they were singing at the bass drum?"

HELENE: "I think they do. The singers themselves might not know it, but I think it helps the tone of their voices. It doesn't wear out as fast. And I notice when they beat the bass drum, it's just straight through, boom, boom. And when you beat the hand drums the beat goes tong, tong [the tone getting softer as it trails down after the initial strike], and like that two times, and then [*softly*] boom, boom, boom, tong, tong, tong, like that. Instead of that bass drum — you just have to hit it [*low and heavy*] BOOM, BOOM, BOOM, like that. So that really makes a difference. You haven't seen a regular Squaw Dance, have you, with the small drums? I wish there were some way in my power to have you see some of these things. You'd get a good feeling about it, and I think everybody else would. And I think it'd be a good observation for the younger people, and I think maybe give a good feeling to everybody else. We'd be going back and saying, 'Hey, we're going back to our own way.' And it would give the older men a chance to get up and do their thing, sing. The younger guys can sit at the [bass] drum. And the older guys would stand and sing in the middle [of the dancing area] and be teaching the younger guys. 'Hey, this is the way we hit the drum, and this is the way we used to do it.' "

The physical environment also makes a difference in the sound and impact of the Round Dance drum. This may well be a factor in the declining use of hand drums over the last decades. Comparing the indoor versus outdoor use of hand drums, Helene believes that "the Round Dance drum has a better sound inside of a building than if it's in the arbor, an open area. I think all the sound would blow away. My dad used to talk about a round building, and they used to have dances here. That's as far back as I can remember." Helene describes the special conditions needed for an effective outdoor performance using hand drums: "Up at Lame Deer they used round squaw drums. It sounded pretty good, but, of course, it wasn't blowing. It was very still and very hot, and they had two microphones right close to them."

On the proper positioning of singers and drummers in the Round Dance, Helene comments as follows: "You notice a lot of these opera singers, they don't set down and sing. For the best singing they stand up and let all the breath in and out. I think the old men [who sang Round Dance songs] found that out, see? So in those days they had certain people to sing Round Dance song, and then certain guys sat around the big drum and did their thing."

JUDY: "When several men stood and sang the Squaw Dance songs, would one man be the lead singer?"

HELENE: "Yes, he starts it off. I've seen it real pretty several times with the squaw drums there. I've seen five guys standing in a semicircle and two guys facing them. That's beautiful. And I've seen maybe seven men standing in a straight row like that and maybe two, three ladies standing behind, way behind. And I seen beauty in that, and it's no longer that way."

Round Dance Song no. 12

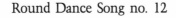

we ya hai ya ya ha__ ya hai ya ya he__ ya hai

ya___ ya he___ ye___ya hai ya   ya he___ ya hai ya   ya he___

___ ye___ya hai ya   ya hai___ya   hai ya   we ya hai_____ ya

hai   e   he hai ya   ya hai___ ya hai   ya___ ya he___ ya

hai ya   ya he___ e_____ ya hai ya   ya he___ ya hai ya

Note: Like the fragments of other old Round Dance songs that Helene sang (see p. 173), the song does not start on the highest note as is generally the case for War Dance songs. Instead it begins at mid-level and leaps up to the highest note.

HELENE: "My dad used to sing that. I don't know where it came from. That's an old song that he used to sing."

JUDY: "Do you hear that song today?"

HELENE: "No, I hardly hear any Round Dance songs, Judy. You have to either request it or be in the mood for it, you know. Like I tell Wayland, too, when we go sing. I tell him, 'Well, let's flip on a Round Dance song.' Every now and then we try, you know, and we get a good response. But the dance itself is kind of fading out. There's too much jealousy. You cannot dance with somebody else's husband 'cause they'll get jealous. Back in the old days brother-in-laws would have a real bad teasing [relationship] with their sister-in-laws, that kind of thing. If you were a jealous person, you just had to get over it. But today it's just all too modern. That's what killed off a lot of fun in everything, socialization."

I. (Helene's brother): "Everybody wants to get into the contests [which carry large cash prizes]. There's no time for other stuff."

HELENE: "No time for fun and games. It's all work [*hardy laughter*]! You know, dollar signs!"

Fighting against this trend, Helene's father tried to revive interest in the Round Dance. "My dad organized certain people to sing Round Dance songs. They'd get up and Round Dance every three or four songs to let the men relax and let the ladies get up. He tried to revive that, and he made a lot of Round Dance drums. He had about seven or eight of them." In the end it was a losing battle.

Plate 18. Helene posed for this picture in the summer of 1980. She and some other friends had joined my husband and me for brunch just before our departure from Wyoming. Photograph by Arthur Vander.

Plate 19. Crowheart powwow about 1980. Helene dancing in what she playfully calls her "monkey suit." Photograph by Ken Timbana.

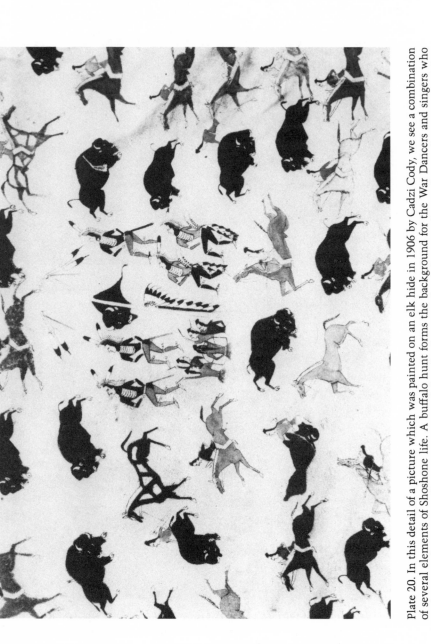

Plate 20. In this detail of a picture which was painted on an elk hide in 1906 by Cadzi Cody, we see a combination of several elements of Shoshone life. A buffalo hunt forms the background for the War Dancers and singers who perform in the center. This picture exemplifies the linear style of drawing that Helene refers to on p. 129, a style common to many tribes on the Plains. Courtesy of the Archives — American Heritage Center, University of Wyoming, Laramie, Wyoming, no. 0266.

Plate 21. Helene and her brother Wayland singing around the drum in August 1981. Photograph by the author.

Plate 22. During the 1982 Crowheart powwow, Helene and her family had a Giveaway in honor of her family's participation in the powwow (her sister was powwow announcer, her brother worked on the Entertainment Committee). In this photograph Helene has just given a tote bag to an out-of-state visitor. Photograph by the author.

Handgame Songs

According to Helene the Handgame is experiencing a fate similar to that of the Round Dance. "The Handgame is kind of dying off too," she states. "There's very few of us that really enjoy Handgame and like to play it. I think I would like to see that revised again. The old people that used to play Handgame, most of 'em are all gone. I think in about 1975, '76, we were getting these younger kids, ten-, twelve-year-olds interested in Handgame. They were really sitting down, really taking interest. And they'd be betting quarter, fifty cents, maybe a dollar. They were good players, fresh players, you know. These old guys didn't know which way to guess young players. They were getting good. And then what happened? BIA steps in. They step in, and the feds step in and say, 'You guys are betting, this is gambling. You cannot initiate gambling onto these kids. They're all under eighteen. So this is gambling.' And we fought 'em and we told 'em, 'No, this may look like gambling, but it's a tradition and it's a culture.' They just say, 'Well, if we catch any young kids here gambling or sitting down playing, we're going to close you guys up.' And then, what do the old guys do? They lose interest. If that's the way the police and the BIA are going to create a fuss, well, that's it.

"It's an Indian game, and it's been passed on from year to year, so I would have stood on my two feet and went down fighting for it, 'cause I feel this is part of tradition. And the kids, when they get twelve years old, should learn all this stuff. I think they should get involved. I just don't think it's right that they can't. It's just like saying, well, your kid at twelve years old cannot go out on the street and sell newspapers. That's making money. This other way is just for pleasure and fun and games. They're enjoying, learning songs, and learning the tradition or culture.

"Handgame songs are the only ones I can think of that have kind of humor in it. You can put your own words in it if you feel like it. My dad talked about people around here who were all dressed up, fancied up, and then they'd be singing cute songs, like,

Handgame Song no. 6

Gǐ-dǐ-ki yò-ri-kin gǐ-dǐ-ki yò-ri-kin gǐ-dǐ-ki yò-ri-ki yò-ri-kin gǐ-dǐ-ki yò-ri-kin

Gǐdǐki is cat and yòriki is flying. That's just all of it. The same thing over and over and over. And the other one they'd sing was:

Handgame Song no. 7

Bĭ - mi - pŭn - du   wai - gi - nĕ bĭ - mi - pŭn - du   wai - gin

Just like that clear through. *Bĭmipŭndu* means backwards, and *waiyĭn* is go down. So it probably means walking backwards down. That's just what they'd sing at some of these Handgames they'd have."

Helene also describes a song her "uncle used to sing about the old roan horse. In Indian, *a·via viotsogĭn*":

Handgame Song no. 8

A - vi - a   vi - ot - so - gĭn   a - vi - a   vi -

ot - so - gĭn   a - vi - a_____   vi - ot - so - gĭn

"It means that your roan horse is barely plugging along, and you're trying to make it go faster. My uncle used to sing that a lot. That's his favorite song, you know."

JUDY: "Do they still sing that one?"

HELENE: "Oh yeah. But it don't have the *a·via viotsogĭn;* just once in a great while you can throw that in to throw the other people off. I can't think about the regular song on that one [with vocables]. You just go into your melody like that, just keep a-going, but it's prettier. I can't never remember that one. You know, in singing fashion, it's got to be somebody that sings it right away, then I can continue. But that's the parts that I remember. I think they had more words years ago, but we come into where it's rhythm kind of songs now [with vocables]. And I think now it's going back again; like B., he's kind of recapturing it. He listens to the rhythm and then puts words in there and kind of makes you laugh. I think Handgame songs are kind of fun to play around with."

Handgame Song no. 9

ho   hai   ya   he   yo   hai   ya   ho   hai   ya   he

HELENE: "Some people get really gross on it; they go, 'Ho' [*accented with a low heavy sound*], like that, really jumpy. On that [song] people do a lot of motions. I see people sit on their knee and kind of beg like a little puppy dog with their bones in their hands. It's a cute song, but it wears your throat out if you're still hanging in the game and they just take their time in pointing on the other side. They just do that to you 'cause it's a song that can wear your throat out. I imagine you heard that a lot, 'cause that's a popular song. People mostly come out with that."

There is playfulness in the music and vocables, too. Just as we saw in Handgame song no. 2, a song that went round and round, so Handgame song no. 9 circles around as it confounds one's sense of beginnings and endings. First, the melody inscribes a tiny circle around C, now above it, on D, and now below it, on A. The vocable text then adds to the feeling of seamless circular movement by beginning with the vowel sound "o," usually reserved for song endings. (We will see this again in Handgame songs nos. 10 and 11.) Also, "he yo," the common ending vocable pattern, actually occurs just *before* each cadence on "hai ya." Like blue jeans pinned on a clothesline, the beginning "ho" and concluding "he yo hai ya" hang inside out and upside down.

Handgame Song no. 10

HELENE: "That's 'Isle of Catri.' I can't remember when I learned it, but I first heard it from some people from Idaho. They were over here, I think it was after Sun Dance time. We were having a Handgame. They sang it, and then I kind of hummed along; and then when I was coming home I kind of practiced a little bit. I knew the other one, the white man's song, the music part.[17] Then I just kept going. I didn't know if I was doing

17. Helene is referring to the Euro-American popular song from which Handgame song no. 10 was derived, "Isle of Capri," first published in 1934. She explains the substitution of "Catri" for "Capri" in the Handgame song title: "Somebody just told me 'Isle of Catri,' or whatever. Maybe it was my misunderstanding, too, because they weren't very good in

it right, but as long as I got the music part of it, the swing on it, then I was OK. I don't think anybody really likes to sing it. You don't hear it now. Maybe it's that they think they're singing a white song or something."[18]

Helene sang Handgame song no. 10 for me with no rhythmic accompaniment. During an actual game she would have hit a stick on a log or beat on a hand drum (similar to the Round Dance drum, but even smaller). She notes that her father "made these little ones just for the Handgame, *naiyawhe witua,* 'Handgame drum.' "

"I think the time I can remember Handgame songs right off," she adds, "is when I get down and start pounding on my stick. And usually it takes me a while, but after thinking about one song, then I can think of about a dozen more at the same time."

Handgame Song no. 11

(1st verse)

♩ = ca. 104

ho hai ya he yo— hai ya hai ye— hai ya he yo— hai ya

ya e ya hai ya he yo— hai ya yo we e—— he yo hai ya

HELENE: "I would say that runs back quite a ways. My understanding on that particular song is that some tribes sing it when they only have one stick left. [If they lose their one remaining stick, they have lost the game.] It's kind of a good luck song. That's the song to sing when you've got just one stick left."

Helene says that she just hums along with some of the other Handgame songs. "I try to grasp from some others, like them Utes. Maybe someplace I'll really grab the tune. Other times I just completely lose it, and because I'm involved with a game, concentrating on—I wonder where it is, that kind of thing. I don't have time to really listen to their song or carry a tape recorder and tape 'em. So all I can do is kind of recall, or try to, anyway."

English. [And in the past] some Indians might know the tune but not the name of the song."

18. Shoshones easily recognize the Euro-American derivation of Handgame song no. 10, just as they did of War Dance song no. 7. I doubt that most Euro-Americans would register any relationship between the two songs, estranged by the vocable text, reduction of the major scale to four pitches, and rhythmic alterations. (For the published score of "Isle of Capri," see pp. 184–85.)

JUDY: "Do you ever make up Handgame songs?"

HELENE: "Yeah, try to put two and two together, or page number 1 with page 21."

JUDY: "Does it come out?"

HELENE: "Not as I would just making up a white man's song, just putting it together. On a white man's song you can jazz it up or you can countrify it or make it a more spiritual type if you want to. You can put whatever your thoughts are into it. But on Indian music it's kind of different. You have to really have the same kind of beat, more or less. They're more one kind of beat; like Handgame's one kind of beat and the War Dance one kind of beat and the Round Dance. It's kind of more difficult than the white man's song, I think."

Handgame Song no. 12

HELENE: "I like fast ones. I think the faster rhythm song you sing, the faster your hiders go and make motions and they enjoy it better. It's a lively song where it makes you have a good feeling. But if you sing a draggy song, you know, it kind of puts weight on your hiders, and then they're just going to barely whip along. So I try to whip them out as fast as I can and sing them as fast as I can.

"My dad sang that [Handgame song no. 12]. He learned that song up at Crow Fair [Montana] among the Crow Indians. Matter of fact, he had four songs that he brought back. But he used to sing two of them quite often, and they almost sound alike. They're real pretty ones. And he used to tell me how the Crows used to play it and how he visualized it—the colorful way they did their Handgame and all that. We never recorded them songs, but we kept it in our mind. Sometimes it scares me because I think I lost the songs. But then you give yourself a trial basis where you think, well, if it's not recorded you really have to learn it and keep it in mind, way in the back. Someday it will come back to your mind, no matter where it is. It may not be at a Handgame or anything. Anywhere, you know, walking or

ISLE OF CAPRI

Words by
JIMMY KENNEDY

Music by
WILL GROSZ

like a lot of times when I wash dishes or going to work, I flip out these songs and I think that's my best time, you know. Just really cut loose.

"And there's one or two songs that are almost like that [Handgame song no. 12]. They're pretty if you sing it right and all the people sing it with you. But a lot of people don't know these songs, then it's kind of difficult. So you really have to boom it out if you're going to make it sound good. I try to get all the ladies to help me sing, but they're scared to sing. They just sound like a jar of bees. Here I am just really screeching my lungs out, and then when I stop everybody stops. And they all look at me, like, 'Why did you stop for?' And here they are just like a closed-in wad of bees. They're barely going, 'Hmmm,' like that. I know they have voices, but I don't know whether they're afraid to use it, or what? I feel like if you've got a good voice or a loud voice, use it.

"And I notice a lot of it, too, they cut out the little, the curves in it. They like to straighten it out, but the beauty in a song is every curve in a song, instead of cutting it out, shorten it out, smoothing it out. The beauty is there with edges and the dips and the pauses, or whatever comes in the song. And that's where the beauty lays. And I think the old people really knew about things like that. We're so civilized now that we want to hurry, hurry, hurry. So we just cut things short. Like I'm saying, I said I felt kind of uneasy, you know, without really having a team, recording by myself; and I just felt at ease with two verses, more or less. If I was just messing around [by myself], I'd probably sing it for a whole session."

Helene talks about Handgame song no. 12 as if it were a journey, attending to topographical considerations—the dips and curves and edges—and time factors—the length of the journey and the pauses interspersing it.[19] Her focus is on the journey itself and not the destination. Thus, she dislikes the shortcuts that abbreviate and straighten the way to the final cadence, omitting part of the route and its varied terrain.

Handgame Song no. 13

(2d and abridged 3d verse)

we yo__ hai ya we a__ hai yo__ hai ya we ya o hai yo__ hai ya we

19. It is interesting to relate Helene's comment here and other Shoshone descriptions of music with Robertson's discussion of *tayil* performance among the Mapuche of Argentina. According to Robertson: "The Mapuche assert that people do not think in words; rather, they think in 'pictures.' Images prefacing *tayil* performances usually include lines which 'rise, twist, and fall.' Stick-on-ground illustrations of these visualized lines or paths follow the melodic contour of each *tayil* phrase" (Robertson 1979:412).

ya o hai   yo   hai   yo   hai   ya   we a o hai   ya we ai hai   ya   we ai yo hai

ya   we ya o hai   ya   we a o hai   yo__ hai   ya   we o   hai   yo   hai   yo   hai

JUDY: "Is that popular around here?"

HELENE: "No, I haven't heard it around here. Somewhere along the line I either heard it from a Washington group or from Montana. I can't remember which one. But I hear so many, you know, like the Arlee bunch [Flathead] from Montana or the White Swan [reservation], them Washington people. They got so many songs that they whip out. It's just really amazing. We try to learn other songs so that people can just pick it up around here."

Helene and other Shoshone singers gather songs on their visits to other reservations and from visitors to the Shoshone reservation. In this way, for each song genre, the Shoshone larder is always replenished and full. Each genre has its own links with a constellation of tribes, and within this system individuals such as Helene collect songs according to their personal background, experience, and taste. For example, there are two principal sources of War Dance songs on the reservation. Most emanate from tribes in Montana or Canada (Cree and so on) and come south by way of the Montana reservations. A smaller number travel west from the Sioux of North and South Dakota. Within this particular configuration, Helene looks to the north for War Dance songs. As we shall see later, Lenore gathers more War Dance songs from the Sioux than Helene does, as well as from the Ute reservation in Utah, where Lenore has relatives. As already noted, the Idaho Shoshones, Utes, and Crows, who learned the Sun Dance from the Wind River Shoshones, attend the Shoshone Sun Dance and sometimes introduce their Sun Dance songs. Because the Sun Dance always winds down with socializing and Handgaming, these same visiting tribes bring Handgame songs. Notice that Helene learned Handgame song no. 10 from Idaho Shoshones; her father learned Handgame song no. 12 from Crows. Washington tribes, state neighbors to the Idaho Shoshones and well known for their love of Handgaming, sit at the outer edge of the Wind River Shoshone Handgame constellation. Within Helene's repertoire we see her conjecture that she might have learned Handgame song no. 13 from Washington singers. Peyote songs, discussed earlier, offer still another example of intertribal song dispersal.

Shoshone Ceremonial Songs

HELENE: "Chokecherry, Giveaway, and all them special songs—I know them but I just can't flip 'em out. I'm just like all the singers; somebody else sings it, then I can remember it. Even the War Bonnet songs, I helped sing with the ladies in the back. I helped them ladies do it. I didn't volunteer to do that myself. My aunt—she's gone now—she used to kind of be the head lady to get people. She'd go around asking certain old ladies to dance the War Bonnet Dance, and they were all older ladies. But now, recently, maybe the last time four years ago, I seen young girls dance. In my days that was a no-no for that age. Only the old ladies, the senior ladies are the ones to do it. And then a certain lady heads that. So she'll go and ask them to come. And the old ladies that dance it, they know who they are. And same with the ladies that sing in the back. They're the ladies that are more or less appointed. So my aunt said to me, 'I think maybe you could sing in the back with them.' And that was a good feeling to me because I would just sit back and watch and not run out there with the other ladies on the War Bonnet Dance. 'Cause to me you have to work for it or be a party of the men that went to combat. That's my observation of it. I don't know what the real detail is or the story behind it. But that's my own thinking about it. Like today, if they had one, I think that the younger girls would all get up. I hate to say it, but it just doesn't look as nice as having the senior ladies, the old ladies do it. I feel the younger girls ruin it instead of making it beautiful. But like now you see most senior citizens that are alive today hardly ever dance. They don't take part in it, so then who's left? Just the young girls. But they should be told the meaning and the purpose of it before they do let them dance.

"The way I understand it is that they put that dance on when they came back from the war. And then the ladies joined in. Now, when they say they're going to have a War Bonnet Dance, people bring in the war bonnets and just set it down. Then when they line 'em up, all the ladies get the war bonnets. It's really colorful. When I was a kid there were four to six women who sang in back of the drum. They'd just keep it to that number. But I don't think there's any restrictions to the ladies that stand back there anymore. And they used to pick out older ladies to sing. Now, whoever wants to sing can probably go over there and join in. On one Christmas there was scads of us, a double row of us standing behind. Nowadays it's changed where they go and get visitors, any male visitor, and stand him between the ladies. It wasn't like that when I seen it a long time ago. Just the ladies danced [for the third and final song]. To me it's kind of scaring the visitors because they don't know what it's all about. And it's not really a social dance."

In 1977 I taped Helene and Wayland singing the third and final War Bonnet song. At the time, Helene simply identified it as an old Round Dance song. (It was not until 1982 and after I had transcribed two earlier recordings of the War Bonnet songs that I recognized the song's special identity.) "I like that one," Helene remarked at the time. "That's a real old, old Shoshone Round Dance song. I think some of the older ladies would remember it, but the younger people might think it was a new song. My dad used to sing that a lot. That's one of the ones we never recorded from my dad, so that's one of the ones that we rake up from the back of our brain. I really don't know which one—like the *Ohamupes* [Yellow Bangs Society]—is the ones that sang these songs. I don't think anybody can really remember, but my dad used to sing that a lot."

JUDY: "Was he a member of one of the societies?"

HELENE: "No, they were before his time.

"A lot of times these old songs, like I was just saying, they're beautiful. The old songs are really pretty. I think I do put them in the top 10, is the old songs. I don't think I'd want to revise them in any way, because they are pretty. If they're let laying for a couple of years and then sang again, then they really have the beauty in it then."

Songs on the Musical Periphery

HELENE: "My mom used to sing some songs for kids when they're little. I don't know what you would call it, when she'd put babies to sleep she'd go:

Lullaby Fragment no. 2

And babies, they really like that. They get so sleepy, and their little eyes just kind of close; and they really enjoy music, especially the tone of the mother. She'd rock them and go, 'Hmmmm,' like that. I don't know what you would call it, lullaby? I can remember it with my mom with little Wayland and Deeatrice."

Lucy's lullaby and body movement fit together like hand in glove.

Each tiny fragment of this song breaks in half and mirrors Lucy's back-and-forth rocking motion, a final accent marking the reverse movement.

forward ┆ back   forward ┆ back

JUDY: "Do you know any Forty-nine songs?"

HELENE: "Oh, I used to know a few, but I don't think right off the bat I can sing any. Like Montana and Oklahoma, they really go in for this Forty-nine. But on our reservation they're kind of more strict on that than they are in several other places. I'm not too sure, but I would guess it's probably because there's a conduct problem. People get too rowdy and out of line, so they'd rather not let you do the Forty-nine. When I was younger I wasn't interested in any of this sort of thing, really, just the War Dance part and the Handgame part and the Sun Dance part. So when I was growing up already the Forty-nine wasn't a popular thing here.

"Forty-nine songs are similar to Round Dance songs and they have words, English words and some have Indian words. The beat is faster, but then some of them are slow. Like in Montana, after Sun Dance, they have Forty-nine going from one tepee to the other. They have really beautiful ones. It's a lot of fun. It's a fun kind of social dance if you make it that way, if you keep in line and everybody else keeps in line. I would say it's kind of a fishing song, you know, when another guy's looking around for a girl and the girl's looking around. That kind of thing, you know." (Shoshones humorously refer to this as "snagging.")

Non-Indian Music

Although Helene and I did not devote a great deal of time exploring her non-Indian, Euro-American repertoire, it is, by her own admission, third largest only after War Dance and Handgame songs. All her life Helene has "really enjoyed singing, whether it was Indian or white man's songs. When I've been in school, like in Dubois, I joined the glee club and the chorus; and when I went away to school, I joined the choir down there. I just really enjoy any kind of song, even white man song. I like classics, I like folk music, country, I like western, and I like soul music, jazz. I like the instrumental music if it's good. I used to know a lot of old songs, old cowboy songs or western songs. I even used to practice yodeling. My dad used to do a few yodelings, and then I used to try it. I used to work with horses a lot, ride horses, and I'd try my yodeling. It didn't come out right, so I gave that up. I did a lot of white man singing, like some of the western songs that I heard on the radio before."

"Humpty-Dumpty Heart"

I've got a hump-ty-dump-ty heart. You dropped it and broke it a-part. All the king's hors-es, all the king's men could-n't put to-geth-er a-gain. I gave to you my heart. You said that we must part. My heart went boom, my heart went boom. I've got a hump-ty-dump-ty heart.

HELENE: "That's an old Hank Williams song. It's just one of my favorites. That's an old, old song. Some people will say, 'Gee, I never heard of 'em.' Makes me feel ancient or something. I know quite a few of those."

"Bluebird"

There's a blue-bird on my win-dow-sill, there's a rain-bow in your sky, There are hap-py thoughts your heart to feel near e-nough to make you cry.

HELENE: "That's just the chorus. Some of those old songs, they're more beautiful. I used to really like 'Old Black Joe,' and 'My Old Kentucky Home,' and 'God Bless America,' the regular famous songs like that. I'm always singing 'You Are My Sunshine' to my [Head Start] kids. It's just my favorite, you know. I used to be a big fan of Buck Owens and tried to learn all his songs. I used to have albums. It was the thing for me; every time I got paid, I'd run into town and buy one album at least of Buck Owens. I'd go into it. I've forgotten about all his songs.

"And I like children's songs. When I was a kid I didn't learn very many kids' songs except "Jack and Jill," "Baa Baa Black Sheep," and little Christmas songs. Nothing like what I've learned at the Head Start workshops recently, like "Go Tell Aunt Rhody." I experiment with white man's songs, the little songs like "Humpty-Dumpty Sat on a Wall." So instead of doing that where it's just so blah, I think why can't I have it a little jazzier? Like,

"Humpty-Dumpty" Experiments

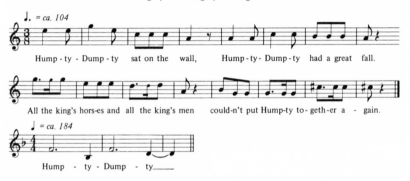

Just experiment. Then I get to thinking, why can't I put this Handgame song with this Handgame song? Before I know it, I'm not doing it properly. I've just got one song going, and I already forgot the other one. Mostly I kind of tear up the white man's songs to my own liking, I guess you'd say."

JUDY: "But you have a harder time with the Indian songs."

HELENE: "Right. Isn't that strange? I guess, you know, to me, I still feel that I shouldn't be tearing up the good old songs."

Vocal quality, a topic that cropped up frequently in our conversations about Indian songs, inevitably came up with respect to white man songs.

HELENE: "I usually use my loud voice for Handgame songs, 'cause if you just try to sing tenderly, you can't hear yourself with the beating of the sticks. So you just have to use your big throat."

JUDY: "When do you use your tender throat?"

HELENE: "On my white songs [*lots of laughter*]."

JUDY: "The secret's out!"

HELENE: "Right [*more laughter*]."

Helene's Musical Roles

"Janus (jä'nəs). *Mythology.* An ancient Roman god of gates and doorways, depicted with two faces looking in opposite directions" (*American Heritage Dictionary* 1973:700). Helene has moved in and out of a series of gates and doorways, boundary points separating cultures, gender, and periods of life. Her songprint reflects this, containing both Native American and Euro-American songs. The two Indian songs based on Euro-American songs and unique to Helene's songprint (War Dance song no. 7 and Handgame song no. 10) best symbolize her bicultural, bimusical knowledge and experience.

Within her own culture Helene's singing, drumming, and dancing roles place her at the gateway between male-female musical roles. As a child she began War Dancing in her buckskin dress, an innovation her family supported. As a young woman she went one step further, performing the Fancy War Dance in male costume. While this was strongly encouraged by her father, at a later point, discouraged by her brother's chiding, Helene set aside her Fancy War Dance costume and dance. But her example along with other influences of the time played their part at the beginning stages

Songprint 4: Helene Furlong

Sample Size: 80	
Naraya	1
Sun Dance	5
Peyote	◑
Round Dance	6
Forty-nine	◑
Flag	1
War Dance	37
Handgame	24
Giveaway	◐
Chokecherry	◐
War Bonnet	1 (no. 3)
Lullaby	1
Euro-American	4

Key: ◐ knows but does not sing

◑ sings, but not represented in sample

of female War Dancing, both the Traditional and what came to be known as the Fancy Shawl Dance. As a young woman, again with strong family backing, Helene crossed musical gender boundaries when she drummed and sang a combination of male and female parts for powwow songs. Her example opened up new musical roles for women and, as we shall see when we discuss Lenore Shoyo, lead singer for her family drum group, brought about change on the reservation. All of these experiences took place when Helene was a youth and a young woman. They left their mark on the community but were themselves subject to change as Helene moved through the door of her life, leading to mature adulthood. Still experimenting with costume and dance, Helene's adaptation of a fringed outfit (see plate 19 following p. 178) and her way of dancing in it were, in modified form, more in the style and manner of the male Traditional War Dancer. But sometime in the early 1980s Helene lost this dancing outfit. Never replacing it, she shed the experiments of her youth as naturally and effortlessly as an insect molts during its lifespan. She returned to wearing the traditional woman's outfit: cloth print dress, shawl, and high-topped moccasins. Because Helene, Wayland, and other family members are now too busy to practice around the drum, their drum group is, at least for the moment, in retirement. Thus, in singing as in dancing, Helene — no longer the young iconoclast — reverts to the traditional "lady's" part behind the powwow drum. As she moves through the gates of her life, she passes through gates of experimental innovation and arrives at traditional, conservative ground. [August 19, 1981. "Saw Helene. At lunch she said she thought people should be proud of their own culture. She noted that the Shoshone girls have started wearing the cape top of the male Fancy War Dancers. She noted S. N. did this. Will she [S. N.] tell her grandchildren this is the Shoshone way? She thought that it would be alright if she wore it once during the powwow, but that's all."] Musically, Helene has stood at all the gates looking in all directions: male-female, Indian–Euro-American, past-future, experimental-conservative.

Lenore Shoyo

"I guess I surprised myself. Like right now, how old
I am, that I'm — I think about it sometimes — how did
I ever end up being the leader of the drum group?"

— Lenore Shoyo

August 25, 1959. Almost a half century separates Lenore's birthday from Emily's. And yet, despite striking differences in personality, age, and song-print, there are some unexpected resonances between the two lives. It is as if time bends back on itself, circling back even as it spirals forward. Lenore was born into a very traditional Shoshone household. No doubt within the first few weeks of life, her family placed her detached umbilical cord on an anthill. Lenore explains: " 'Cause those ants are hard workers. You see them carrying little sticks and everything else. Well, we put ours on the anthill so the baby can be a hard worker when he grows up." (Emily tells how her grandfather's cousin carried out this Shoshone custom when she was an infant.) Traditional to the core, both women nevertheless crossed gender boundaries: Emily, when she supported herself on the land after she permanently separated from husband and marriage, and Lenore, when she became lead singer for what eventually became an all-female family drum group.

Within her large and closely knit family of six sisters and three brothers, Lenore is next to the youngest. Her father is Shoshone, her mother, Ute. This double heritage as well as the inclusion of a Ute relative and Oglala Sioux girl within the growing family had an impact on Lenore's songprint, as we shall see.

As with all the other women in this book, Lenore has a wealth of happy childhood memories. In large part they stem from the boons of childhood in a rural, farm-ranch setting, with an abundance of space and of time spent in the outdoors. She enjoyed horseback riding and racing; ducks, geese, and a pig were her pets. In warm weather the family swam in the Little Wind River, which runs through their land. Lenore played

195

with homemade stuffed animals in preference to dolls. "My parents never believed in buying games," she relates, " 'cause we could always find something to play with out around the house, they'd tell us. They just didn't care on spending the money on anything but food."

In the house Lenore's father told Shoshone stories: "He used to tell these stories about a long time ago—jokes and things. And we used to sit and laugh. Then, one day in high school, they asked us to write old Indian stories, so I wrote about rheumatism and how they say that disease came out the first time, and all that." There were other storytellers as well. "We always had a TV when we were little," Lenore recalls. "They used to play that *Wizard of Oz.* We used to always watch that, so I remember that movie pretty good [*lots of laughter*]. That's one game we used to play, you know, running around outside the house, one of us would be the Lion and Tin Man." Emily, Angie, Alberta, and Helene all have televisions today, but only Lenore, like her non-Indian peers, grew up with it. It is her window into non-Indian America, where the range and extent of her experience remain limited.

Indian singing and dancing have always played a large role in Lenore's family. "My mom just used to always dress us up," she says, and, dressed for dancing, the children danced. Her oldest sister, like Helene, experimented dancing the male Fancy War Dance in costume. She danced alongside her brother Chuck, the critical person in Lenore's life until his untimely death. Lenore danced too. "I used to do just the regular little girl's dance. I never really did care for contests very much when I was a little girl. Not until I got a little older."

As for singing, Lenore recalls how her father "used to sing with Roy and Ben [Lenore's uncles]. That's all I remember is those two and, I think, Frank and Chuck [Lenore's older brothers] when they used to sing down at the old house [the original family home; today, several houses and trailer homes shelter the growing extended family of spouses and grandchildren]. I remember them when they used to sing and I'd be bothering them about the drum and they'd be telling me to go play [*laughter*]. Anyway, I was young yet, small—in '63, somewhere around there [Lenore would have been about four years old]. My brother Chuck taught me how to sing. There was me and Chuck, Frank, Andrew, and my dad."

JUDY: "At four, you were both singing and drumming?"

LENORE: "Both. I wasn't that good, but I was trying."

Music—although in this case not Indian music—contributed to Lenore's smooth transition to elementary schooling on the reservation.

JUDY: "Did you like to sing the songs you learned in school?"

LENORE: "I think that's where I really got interested in school. That's why I lost my Shoshone language. I was told I spoke Shoshone until I got into school. I spoke a little bit of English but most of the time (I guess being around my mom and dad, that's all they did talk) Shoshone. And then I slowly drifted off from my language."

Parallel with her formal schooling Lenore received a rich variety of experience in several religious traditions. Churchgoing, for example, was an important part of her youth: "It was always when I was in elementary school I used to go to church a lot [the Wind River Church, a Protestant church]. Like after school was over there'd be a bus there to pick us up. I don't think I've ever missed—not even two days, maybe." Although when she was very young Lenore did not actually attend Native American Church meetings, she nevertheless had contact with the religion, for her parents often sponsored meetings. Even in her earliest remembrances of her father, uncles, and brothers singing around the drum, Lenore noted the types of songs they practiced: "Either they'd be singing Native American Church songs or War Dance songs." In addition to involvement with the Native American Church, Lenore and her family have always attended the Shoshone Sun Dance. In the natural way of children, Lenore and her sisters "played" Sun Dance. She remembers how "right after the Sun Dance was over, us girls would all get together down in front of the old house, in the front yard. We'd sit. They had these twigs, you know, the type you shake. We used to cut those down [willow branches] and pretend we was singing and Sun Dancing. It was crazy. That's when we used to listen to a lot of Sun Dance songs. We'd sing 'em. My brother would come out there and get after us because he'd say you're not supposed to be playing that. He told us. Then we'd be right back over there when he turns his back."

Lenore's religious training continued as she advanced through childhood and her schooling. The transition from grammar to high school was not an easy one.

LENORE: "Yeah, I was scared to go to high school. I went down to this Wyoming Indian High School [established on the reservation in 1972]."

JUDY: "Did it work out pretty well with the Arapahoe kids and Shoshone kids all mixed in?"

LENORE: "Well, at first it didn't 'cause that school was supposed to be built by the hot springs down here." (The hot springs mark an unofficial boundary between the Shoshone and Arapahoe communities. Shoshones were displeased when the high school was built at Ethete, the Arapahoe side of this landmark.)

JUDY: "But the kids got along pretty well?"

LENORE: "Yeah, I had a lot of friends in high school. And learning some of my language was really neat. I took both Shoshone language and the beading — arts and crafts. I really got along with those teachers.

"Well, I guess most of the time the only thing I like about high school was basketball practice [*laughs*]. I never started playing till I was fourteen, I think. The time I started singing. I went into it when I was a freshman. I was on the high school team."

JUDY: "Had Marita and some of your other sisters been basketball players before you?"

LENORE: "Yeah, they've always been basketball players. We always had a basketball hoop at home. Before I had ever gone to high school, they [Lenore's sisters] used to have a team. My mom, she was the coach then. They'd been champions for, I don't know how long."

JUDY: "You play in an independent league?"

LENORE: "It's just usually called All-Indian Basketball, Women's or Men's Tournament. We have our tournaments every year in March and April. We used to travel with my mother's team, mostly to Idaho and Utah."

Lenore, four of her sisters, and three nonfamily members make up a basketball team that covers a wide range of ages, from Linda, the youngest in the family, to Marita, the oldest of eight. This is also true of other teams in the league. Linda notes, for example, that "there's old ladies that play too; forty-year-old ladies play, and they're fast." Shades of the old Shinny games: enlisting women of different ages, full of admiration for the swift older women. For all her wins and trophies, Lenore recounted to me details of a hard-fought championship game that her team lost, and in which she suffered an injury and had to be hospitalized. Will this game stay with her through the years, like the game that remains green and fresh in Emily's memory, a triumph of Shoshone girls against a taller non-Indian high school team from neighboring Lander, Wyoming?

Lenore's high school experience was not all fun and games, however. "It was alright, I guess, except I messed up myself, you know, just fooled around too much in my last year. And I didn't get to graduate. But I want to get my GED, though, General Education Degree. I should have went out to school in the first place. Maybe I would have graduated."

JUDY: "So if you had to do it over again, where would you have gone?"

LENORE: "I would probably go off to [boarding] school or to Lander [Valley High School], 'cause they have a lot of tutors and they have help there."

After the demise of the reservation's boarding high school, which Emily attended, Shoshone children had two options for further education: attendance at non-Indian high schools off the reservation or out-of-state Indian boarding schools. Angie and Alberta never received high school educations; Helene took both options, attending non-Indian Dubois High School and Haskell Institute in Kansas. Wyoming Indian High School, which opened after Helene's high school years, provided a third option. Thus only Lenore and Emily received their elementary and secondary education on the reservation. Despite this similarity there are many significant contrasts between their schooling: Emily attended a boarding school, Lenore a day school; Emily had predominantly positive feelings toward the quality of her education and experience at school, Lenore's were mixed; Emily was punished for speaking Shoshone at school, Lenore took it as a subject — she and others who had "drifted off" from their native language. But what they shared is more important than these differences. Both had the continuity of Shoshone-Arapahoe peers throughout their schooling and a certain singularity and insularity of experience, since the reservation is a world unto itself, an island surrounded by a non-Indian sea.

Shoshone reservation life shaped Lenore's approach to health and menstruation. Commenting on her attitude toward medicine, Lenore states: "Well, most of the time I'm traditional. I don't really care to take medicine from the clinic because it just seems to get worse. On the prescription, maybe I don't know how to take it. But usually I just take traditional, like boiled sage, and then we'd drink the juice. I usually use the bitterroot when I'm going to sing or if I get a sore throat, 'cause it numbs my throat up then. If somebody, in some cases, thinks bad about you, trying to hurt you . . ."

JUDY: "That protects you from that, too?"

LENORE: "Uh-huh. I chew on it. It's just like chewing on gum.

"When we come down with a cold or are on our period we usually chew on sage, too, if we want something like gum to chew on. That's one thing we can't have either [during menstruation]. It's because of your teeth. We can't pick at our teeth 'cause your teeth is soft when you're having your period. It'll split your teeth easy, too, 'cause it just seems like your teeth is just thin. We can't eat any kind of game meat then. Because if we do our brothers or whoever killed that meat won't be able to kill another one again. We wait like three days after it, before we touch meat. And we can't touch the gum. We can't drink cold water. It could form blood clots in you and get you cramped up. We can't scratch our face or any part of our body with our hands. We got to use a stick or something, because they say when you use your own fingernails you're only tearing your skin, giving yourself stretch marks [and wrinkles]. We don't scratch our hair either. [This precaution is felt to avoid grey hair.] We can't sit down all the time. We just have to work around so it won't become our habit."

JUDY: "To be lazy, you mean?"

LENORE: "Yeah."

If I had closed my eyes, it could have been Emily speaking.

Shoshone reservation life likewise shaped Lenore's daily diet and food preferences. "When we were little," she recollects, "we used to have a garden and grow turnips and things like that. We used to eat that. We were raised on goat milk. The main thing we really like, though, is tripe. They call it the guts. That's what we really like to eat, our family. Everybody does, I think. It looks like foam, a bunch of holes. And there's one [part] that looks like it's got pages. They call it the Bible. When you get it right from the cow, it's still got the flavor, but when you buy it from the store, its flavor is all washed out. They just don't care to buy it from the store. You wash it up, then you cook it for how long you want to cook it. We usually cook it till it's really soft. You just chew it; it really tastes good. We really like to eat that." Pounded meat and the traditional chokecherry *gotsap,* "gravy," were other family favorites.

Beadwork, too, is a Shoshone legacy Lenore learned at home and in high school. She learned first at home through observation and then through direct instruction. "I used to sit and watch Frank and his wife when they were sitting at the table. They'd be beading buckles and things like that, you know, to sell. Or he'd be working on his outfit. So I'd sit and watch. And I asked him one day to show me how to make buckles, 'cause I wanted to make my own. So they showed me."

Lenore's comments on women, both old and those yet to come, integrate many of the above experiences and lessons of her life on the reservation.

JUDY: "What was it you admired in the older women as you were growing up?"

LENORE: "The way they took care of themselves. You know, they're older, but they didn't look that old. They didn't have that much wrinkles or anything like that. Mostly the way they would talk the Shoshone language. I'd just sit and watch."

JUDY: "If and when you have children, especially girls, what are some of the goals or things that you would want to teach and show them?"

LENORE: "I'd say probably cooking and doing things and mostly bead-work, I'd say. Because that way they don't have to depend on somebody else—making this thing or that thing for them. They could just do it on their own instead of buying it from somebody else, where it's going to cost a lot more money. Then they could say it's their own."

In sum, Lenore admires women who respect their bodies by observing traditional menstrual practices, know Shoshone, can cook, do beadwork, and who are industrious, independent, and frugal: in short, a list of traditional Shoshone values for women.

Two family accidents mark Lenore's life. They are part of the answer to her opening query and puzzlement: "How did I ever end up being the leader of the drum group?" The first serious accident involved her father: "We never really used to travel that much when I was very young. Because, see, most of the time we'd stay home. My dad, he used to farm. He used to run those machines out there till that accident happened and, I guess, we lost everything. And before that happened we had a lot of cattle. I don't know how many head, but we had a lot. We had like almost fifty head of horses first time. I remember we used to ride on the tractor with him, me and Linda. That was when he was still walking. I don't remember how the accident happened [a tractor fell over on him], but I just remember they were gone for a long time, my mom and dad. My older sisters and brothers, see, they stayed home and watched us. I never really knew where my mom and dad went. I guess all that time they were gone he was in the hospital in Cheyenne. They were operating on him." Lenore's father returned home from the hospital but never regained his ability to walk.

Responsibility within the family shifted. Lenore relates how her brothers "had to take time learning how to take over things, you know. 'Cause they used to help him. Then they got me to ride horses, and I used to help take the horses clear up to the mountains. There's a place up there I think I could show you from here. There's mountain lions there we found out later. That's how we lost most of our horses. They started getting our colts.[1]

1. What follows is a free translation of a *Naraya* song text that Emily sings (Vander 1986:45–48):

> Our Father's mountain lion walks down
>   the mountainside, yowling, *wainda,*
> Our Father's mountain lion walks down
>   the mountainside, yowling, *wainda.*
> Our dear Father's game animals, sitting
>   all, sweet young and old, *wainda,*
> Our dear Father's game animals, sitting
>   all, sweet young and old, *wainda.*

In ways reminiscent of Blake's "Tyger Tyger, burning bright" (Blake 1982:24), this *Naraya* text expresses admiration and wonder for the mountain lion and all of God's creatures, predator and prey. How different the meaning of mountain lion in this context compared to the hard realities of Lenore's experience.

In the wintertime, right before it starts to snow, we'd take them up, like in the fall. Then we'd bring them back down summertimes. We'd ride 'em all summer."

JUDY: "You kept this up for a little while after your dad's accident, but then the . . . "

LENORE: "No, for I think a long time, till we lost Chuck."

After his father's accident Chuck took on a special position of responsibility within the family. "He really kept our family in line," Lenore states, "even though he was younger than my [other] brothers. They were married. He'd talk F. into straightening himself up because he's got a family now; you know, it's time to grow up when you're married. You know, when we were younger we'd forget to do the dishes because Mom, she had a lot of things on her hands. And he'd remind us. He said, 'Later on in years this is going to be your work for the rest of your life, washing dishes, cleaning house. You're going to be married one of these days, you know.' Things like that. That we'd have to stay up with the lady's job. But then I would always be outside with them."

Again we see the inside-outside dichotomy: inside is the woman's realm, outside the man's. As a young child, when the boundaries between genders are still fluid, Lenore mostly played with boys. Within her family she became especially attached to Chuck, who assumed many roles to her — companion, teacher, parent, and role model. "I used to help him when he used to fix his car," Lenore recalls. "I started learning quite a few things about fixing cars. I used to go hunting with him, too. I used to do everything with him. He's the one that taught me how to shoot a gun. We used to go back there where there's a lot of prairie dog holes. We used to sit back there. There's where he first started learning me how to shoot. . . . And we used to shoot at prairie dogs. We used to always eat them."

JUDY: "Would he take you hunting for deer or larger animals?"

LENORE: "Yeah. Usually we'd park the pickup. Then we'd walk clear down into or on top of the hill. It'd be a lot of walking, and when we'd kill something, we'd carry it all the way back. We used to go camping in the mountains, too, our whole family. Chuck and Andrew would take horses and go up hunting. Then we'd go up on, like the last day when they're going to come down, to help pack things back down. That's what they'd do every fall. And we'd hold the legs for them when they'd butcher it. Things like that. We'd bring the hides back down 'cause our sister-in-law used to tan hides all winter."

In music, too, Chuck was Lenore's teacher and role model. There were several stages in the evolution of the Big Mountain Singers, as the Shoyo drum group was to be called later on. Recall that at first Lenore watched her father, uncles, and brothers sing around the drum. Then, as a very young child, she joined her father and brothers around the drum. We now pick up the story when there was only one generation around the drum, Lenore and her siblings. "When we first started our drum group," Lenore recounts, "it was Chuck and me, Randy, our first cousin, Andrew, Frank. That's just us guys then. (As they say, 'one of the boys.') I must have been about fourteen. Then it was Chuck and me and Andrew and Coleen [Lenore's sister]. Just us four."

JUDY: "How did it end up being all girls around the drum?"

LENORE: "I was first till my brother Chuck passed away, and then I started teaching them [her sisters] how to drum."

Chuck's death in 1973 was a crushing blow to Lenore and her family. Lenore describes the tragedy: "It was a car accident just on the other side of the hill. My mom and dad told everybody to stay home when they were going to go to the accident. But I went and snuck into the back seat of the car and went over with them. I wanted to see what was happening. Two ladies were dragging his body clear up back on top of the hill. They were drunk, those ladies, whoever they were. If they didn't move him, he would still be alive.

"Then after he passed away, Mom said, 'Well, I got a vest that used to be Chuck's.' My mom and dad gave it to me. It's hanging over at the green house."

JUDY: "And then they gave that to you with the idea that you would sort of step into what he had started out, started off there?"

LENORE: "Uh-huh. I just thought back to how my brother drummed and all that. Then I started up again."

JUDY: "So then Coleen was at the drum. When did JoAnn and Linda come around?"

LENORE: "Somewhere around 1973, all of them together."

JUDY: "Did you pick up how to be a lead singer from being around the drum with Chuck?"

LENORE: "Yeah, I guess I just picked it up from him. I just used to copy him. Chuck's the one that learned us to sing. Then from after what happened to him I just kind of took over from there. Went on with what he wanted us to do. And right now today we're still singing."

The name for the Shoyo drum group, the Big Mountain Singers, is another legacy from Chuck. It pays homage to the familiar presence of the Wind River Mountains, special mountains for the Shoshones not only for their plant and animal life but also for their associational significance in Shoshone history and mythology (Shimkin 1947c:332).[2]

Continuing the story of her family drum group, Lenore recounts the following: "When we started singing, Mark Dewey, he's an Arapahoe, he gave that drum to us. He's been friends with my mom and dad. I can't remember what year it was. That was when we first started singing, anyway. And an old man, Ben Goggles, he prayed for our drum: that we'd be able to use it in a good way, not to use it for like ways as Forty-nine — you know, where they drink and all that. He wanted us to go on using it in a good way. He prayed in his Arapahoe language.

"We never used to travel. We used to stay home and take care of the land, things like that. And then after Chuck passed away, we never traveled no place for about a year, maybe even longer. And then we finally started traveling. After that happened to him, we traveled, 'cause my mom and dad really missed him. They just didn't care to stay around, you know, they wanted something to do." What began as a response to grief eventually settled into a new pattern of life for the family. Their drum group became part of a far-flung powwow circuit, an Indian network of people, places, songs, and dances.

"When we first started off," Lenore continues, "we traveled out of state to South Dakota [to the Sioux reservation at Pine Ridge]. They donated us a lot of money. We got a lot of Giveaway stuff. They helped us out a lot because we used most of it for our gas, you know."

JUDY: "Did most people pretty well accept you, or was there some feeling against girls?"

LENORE: "At first, where we traveled to, they kind of didn't like it 'cause we're all girls, a drum group. They thought we weren't any good for singing contests or anything like that. We had to prove to them that we could be just the same."

JUDY: "When you formed your drum group, had you heard of other all-girl drum groups?"

LENORE: "Yes, there's one from Canada." (Recall that Canadian women also served as musical models for Helene.)

JUDY: "Now when you go to powwows is it pretty well accepted that there's an all-girls' drum group? Will they give you the contest songs?"

2. *Naraya* songs nos. 2 and 3 make special reference to these mountains. In his 1879 *Annual Report*, Colonel Brackett wrote: "The Wind River Mountains are supposed by the Indians [Shoshones] to be the home of the spirits. . . . When an old man is dying he finds himself near the top of a high hill on the Wind River Mountains, and as the breath leaves his body, he reaches the top of it, and there, in front of him, the whole magnificent landscape of eternity is spread out" (Brackett 1879:330).

LENORE: "Yes, they do. Everybody knows our drum group now— Montana, Idaho, down in South Dakota, we're well known."

Overcoming initial prejudice, the Big Mountain Singers have gone on to win prizes in drum group competitions at Pine Ridge, South Dakota, and Ft. Duchesne, Utah.

The yearly round of powwows and Sun Dances, which she also attends, structures Lenore's life, defining the seasons of her year as clearly as weather and calendar. She is at home for the two Shoshone powwows in late spring and early summer, then out to other powwows, home for the Sun Dance in late July, and out to other Sun Dances and more powwows. In late summer, mindful of the land and season, Lenore and her family take time out from their migrations to pick berries, an activity vestigial to their ancient Shoshone past. "If we see chokecherries, we just stop right there. We got I don't know how many bucketfulls when we came from Crow Fair this year." The summer season draws to a close. Nieces and nephews return to school and, as Lenore notes: "In the wintertime we don't really travel that much. That's when I really get down to my beading then. Right now [in September] I'm making a whole outfit a lady wants me to make for her. I should have it done in November to take over for the Thanksgiving dance that they're going to have."

Wintertime, in late December, Shoshones celebrate the holiday season with community dances. A Round Dance traditionally brings in the New Year, the new calendar year, that is. The new powwow year begins much later, after the snows flee to the mountain tops. Still, to Lenore it now "just seems like we just travel, and we just don't know how to stay home no more."

Although Lenore and her family travel extensively, to attend Indian League basketball games, Sun Dances, and powwows, they keep within reservation borders or at least within an Indian context. This is Lenore's second home: an intertribal, multicultural, but exclusively Indian world. The powwow is a subunit within this intertribal world, an institution that honors both men and women. Whereas men win the highest cash prizes for their dancing, women figuratively rule over the powwow. Borrowing titles of court, they serve as powwow queens, princesses, and royal attendants. Lenore has been the Shoshone powwow queen and queen's attendant on several occasions. As queen she represented the Shoshone tribe at the home powwow and at all powwows she attended for the year of her "reign." (An identifying ribbon pinned across the queen's outfit always indicates her title, the powwow or tribe, and date.)

Something of Lenore's symbolic role within the Indian powwow carries over to her relationship to non-Indian society. For example, the Big Mountain Singers performed at the 1980 ceremonial unveiling of a large statue of Sacajawea at the Plains Indian Museum in Cody, Wyoming.[3] As it happened, Lenore was the Eastern Shoshone Indian Days queen at that time, and as such she wore her powwow outfit and sat up front facing the invited audience, flanked by the sculptor of the statue, museum dignitaries, and a senator from Wyoming. Each, in turn, spoke to the audience, including Lenore, who represented the Shoshone tribe. Three years later the museum hosted a weekend seminar entitled "Of Beauty and Power: The Plains Indian Woman." I presented a lecture-demonstration on Indian music that also included performances by Lenore and her sisters. Once again, within a Euro-American context, Lenore was a representative presence for Native American women and song. Both Helene and Lenore have traveled to many places, but herein lies a critical difference between their non-Indian experience. When Helene attended Head Start workshops off the reservation, her own Shoshone background was irrelevant. She was simply a teacher learning with other teachers. As already noted, Lenore's travel has been predominantly to Indian reservations. But on important occasions when she has taken part in the non-Indian world, she has stood apart, a symbol of her own separate Indian background and traditions.

In 1980 Lenore's purchase and addition of her own trailerhouse to the family compound was a milestone; it marked her transition to adult status. Grown to maturity, she continues to follow in Chuck's footsteps, becoming, in turn, a teacher and role model for her nieces and nephews. Recently she has been singing with them around the drum, grooming the next generation of Big Mountain Singers. "They're singing with us now," she states proudly. "We're learning them so that way later on years, when maybe we'd decide not to sing at all, they could go ahead and take over. The way I told them — don't be scared to come out loud, 'cause there's going to be more people, maybe, when you have your own drum group. People's going to come around your drum and just stand there and watch you. You can't be ashamed, I told them. You just got to sing I told 'em. 'Cause I used to be ashamed, you know, but then I'd forget about them after I really got into my singing, I'd forget about people around the drum. Just go on singing. But the longer I've sang I've, you know, to myself, I just think I don't care what people think, you know. I'm just singing because I want to help out, so I sing."

3. Sacajawea, female Shoshone guide who contributed to the success of the Lewis and Clark expedition, continues to capture the romantic imagination of non-Indian America. Differing accounts challenging the assertion that she spent her later years and was buried on the Wind River reservation remain contested and unresolved in scholarly and fictional writings.

Lenore's Songs

As lead singer for her sisters around the drum, Lenore completely assumes—at least for powwow music—what had formerly and exclusively been male singing and drumming roles. She and her sisters are a female counterpart to the male drum group; Lenore sings the solo call, and her sisters respond in unison. Only Lenore's mother, who sometimes performs with her daughters, sings the "lady's" part an octave above after the opening call and response.

While unusual, Lenore's position as leader of her family's drum group following the death of her brother Chuck was not out of step with the times; winds of change were already in the air. Helene was beginning to sing and drum with her family drum group. Lenore also knew of women who had joined family members at the drum in Canada and the Ft. Hall reservation in Idaho. And of these exceptional few, some, like Lenore, served as lead singers.

The ninety-three songs I have recorded of Lenore, both solo and with her sisters, represent only a small portion of an ever-expanding repertoire. This, as we shall see, is the consequence of Lenore's role as lead singer of a powwow drum group. My sampling includes fifty-nine War Dance, eighteen Round Dance, five Sun Dance, five Handgame, and two Forty-nine songs; one Flag, one Honor, and one Crow Hop song; and the Shoshone Giveaway song. Peyote songs are not included, although Lenore attends Native American Church meetings and will sometimes perform these songs along with the men. Also, five Sun Dance songs do not proportionally represent the extent of this genre in her repertoire. Because Lenore has always recorded for me at the drum, and because it is still taboo for a woman to play the drum for Sun Dance songs, Lenore has never performed them by herself for me. I was able to record her singing Sun Dance songs only on one occasion when her uncle drummed and sang with her. Lenore provided the traditional lady's part. In practice she attends the Sun Dance every summer and joins the women's chorus to sing the full repertoire of Sun Dance songs.

First and foremost Lenore is a powwow singer. The size of her repertoire, the turnover rate within it, and musical genres represented all serve the needs and musical conventions of the powwow. As she herself notes: "It just seems that we, you know, we just sing what they're singing this year. Then next year we'll be singing next year's songs. It just goes on and on. We don't really stick to one song."

JUDY: "Do you ever sometimes go through your tapes to listen to some old songs?"

LENORE: "Yeah. We don't sing them though."

JUDY: "Would you say that most groups don't make their own songs?"

LENORE: "They usually—well, probably like us—we get our songs from other drum groups at powwows."

Although the Big Mountain Singers can perform at any powwow they attend, the need for new songs each year draws them to the larger powwows where the newly minted songs are put into circulation. According to Lenore, at small powwows "you can't really get no music. . . . The drum groups that just hit the small powwows just have the same songs. They're just having a dance. The people that hit the big powwows, they're to make themselves noticed—who they are. Because they've got these new songs they're going to try out at the powwows that got drum [group] contests. I go to the Fourth of July, Ft. Duchesne [Ute reservation in Utah]. It's pretty big now. And Ft. Hall Festival [Shoshone-Bannock reservation in Idaho], Crow Agency [Crow reservation in Montana], and Bismarck, North Dakota [Sioux reservation]; they have one in June, then they have one in September up there. Rocky Boy Celebration [Chippewa-Cree reservation in Montana] is the end of July and beginning of August. They have mostly Round Dances, and I guess that's where you really get pretty Round Dance songs. That's why I like to go just to go record."

The amount of time a song remains in circulation varies. As Lenore notes: "Some peeter out. Some last a long time." But characteristically there is a run on new songs every year. Thus, Lenore and her family travel extensively to powwows each summer, performing, gathering, and learning the season's new songs. The quest for new powwow songs, in turn, intensifies Lenore's use and reliance on the tape recorder, which functions as an external memory bank, taking deposits (recording songs) and giving withdrawals (replay for song learning and recall)—a musical savings and loan account for powwow currency.

Before describing how she uses tapes for learning songs, Lenore made an interesting distinction between performances on commercial tapes and those she records live at the powwow, expressing a clear preference for the latter.

JUDY: "Do you sometimes learn off of the commercial tapes?"

LENORE: "Yes, but I'd rather record from a powwow. It's more better. They really put all their effort into singing that song, and it really brings that music out—the way they want to sing it."[4]

JUDY: "When you learn a song, you learn it off of the tape?"

---

4. This judgment that the best, most energetic performances occur spontaneously during an occasion and not isolated from it in a special setting is similar to Helene's opinions discussed on p. 145.

LENORE: "Yeah, sometimes. Well, most of the time the way I learn the songs is to, you know, when that drum group's singing that song I just sing along with them, you know, think about it. Then if I like that song I go ahead and sing "lady." You know, just go ahead and sing on top of them, right along with them. That's how I learn most of my songs."

JUDY: "When you do that, do you also tape them at the same time?"

LENORE: "Yeah. That way, if I'm going to sing with my drum group, when I listen to the tape then I know how low or how I have to use my vocal cords. You know, how high and things like that."

Lenore also described how she learns from tapes: "When I want to learn a song, I'll just sit and listen to it, the tape, for quite a while."

JUDY: "Just backtracking, hearing that same song?"

LENORE: "No, just let it run and when it comes on again, listen to it over again."

JUDY: "Do you sing with the tape?"

LENORE: "Yeah, I sing with the tape; then I turn the tape off and try it without the tape. Then I'm not listening to it. Then I try to remember it without the tape, without hearing it over again."

Because Lenore and her sisters want to sing the new songs that come out during the powwow season, they must learn them quickly. "It doesn't take me long to learn a song," Lenore asserts. "I could just learn it the same night. If I can't catch on to it right away, it takes me quite a while to get it—maybe a day or so. I sing it to them [her sisters]. It wouldn't take them that long, 'cause the backups just have to follow right along with the head singer. If we're traveling to another powwow and we want to sing a song that they don't know, then we sing it on the way. We sing 'em [the new songs] when we travel to different states. Pick up some songs at one powwow, then we hit another powwow the next weekend and sing 'em that following weekend."

In this fast-paced musical scene, Lenore must learn new songs and be able to lead her sisters in public performance of them. Here, too, the tape recorder is an indispensable aid.

JUDY: "Now as far as trying to recall a song, you pretty much use the tape recorder? Is that the main way?"

LENORE: "Yes, most of the time I listen to the song before I sing it. Except for some of the old songs that I know."

JUDY: "Do you do that at the powwow?"

LENORE: "Yeah, most of the time, like for Round Dance songs. But then some of the powwow songs [i.e., War Dance songs] I could just sing. This year [1981] we haven't sung that much, so most of the time I have to listen to the recorder." (See plate 29 following p. 266.)

A review of the use and emotional response to the tape recorder by all five women reveals a broad range of similarities and contrasts. Emily has taped herself singing *Naraya,* Sun Dance, and Round Dance songs, a large Shoshone repertoire. These tapes as well as some made during the Shoshone Sun Dance constitute her homemade collection. Its sole use is for private listening pleasure, a complement to singing. In recent years when Emily finds it harder and harder to sing, the tapes have taken the place of singing. But at some indefinable emotional level, Emily views the tape recorder as a hostile other. Songs taped out of your throat may be irretrievably gone. Too much use of the recorder ruins a person's ability to listen and remember; it replaces what should be the internal tape recorder of the mind and throat. Angie straddles the fence. She wanted very much to record her father singing, but his decidedly negative response to being taped left her with ambivalent feelings toward recording. Other older notions that songs should not be taped and could, in themselves, avoid being taped, fed this negative response. Still, Angie has made many homemade tapes over the years and thoroughly enjoys listening to them as well as to many commercial recordings. Tapes are also an integral part of Alberta's life. Homemade tapes of Peyote and Sun Dance songs are her constant companions. But in contrast to Angie's father, Alberta's father wanted to record the special four Morning Sun Dance Prayer songs for the family so that they would be properly sung and preserved. There is no inner dissonance. Helene, too, enjoys her large supply of homemade and commercial tapes. Nevertheless, she sees the recorder as a mixed blessing. Helene expresses her negative feelings in strictly rational, cause-and-effect terms: overdependence on the tape recorder leads to mental laziness and memory decline. These are also Emily's sentiments, but minus the deeper emotional hostility and fear. Lenore, as lead singer of a powwow drum group, could barely function without the tape recorder. In several regards she and Emily sit at opposite ends of the spectrum. Emily records herself and Shoshones on the Wind River reservation singing Shoshone songs, principally religious songs. Lenore never records herself (her folks do) but mostly tapes singers from other tribes on other reservations. Her prodigious collection contains principally Northern Plains powwow songs. The tape recorder is invaluable to her for collecting, learning, and recalling songs. It helps keep her afloat in a swift musical current.

Naraya *Songs*

JUDY: "Do you know any Ghost Dance songs, *Naraya huvia*?"
LENORE: "No. The only time we used to hear them was when Ben

[Lenore's uncle] used to tell us stories when we were little girls. But now he don't do that no more. We don't really know them. Haven't heard any of those songs for a while."

JUDY: "Did you ever attend a Ghost Dance?"

LENORE: "No, I don't think I ever did."

This is an empty category in Lenore's repertoire.

Sun Dance Songs

LENORE: "If they're sick or they got something wrong or things like that, that's what the Sun Dancers go in for. Or either because they dreamed about being in the Sun Dance is the only time they say you could go into the Sun Dance."

JUDY: "What about the spectators, or if you're singing in back of the drum with the women—can some of that [healing] come to those people too?"

LENORE: "Yeah, uh-huh. 'Cause when you sing a song in the Sun Dance, as you would in a Peyote meeting, you'd have to just like, you know, mean what you're singing. So that they, too, will, you know—what they're in there for, asking for help—it'll help them."

JUDY: "Have you seen changes in the Sun Dance from when you used to go as a young child?"

LENORE: "A lot of changes. They were usually not real young guys like there is today. It was mostly the ones that have age. Now all you see is just young boys in there. And then they don't dance. They used to dance all the time when I used to go watch down there all the time. 'Cause I'd go early morning for sunrise in order to take the damp rag you're supposed to take to the Sun Dancers. My brother Chuck used to go in all the time, so I used to always go down there and give it to him. But now that he's gone we don't really go down there in the mornings. Just in the afternoons, we just watch."

The Sun Dance is one of the important calendar markers for Lenore and her family.

LENORE: "We always stay home for our Sun Dance."

JUDY: "But do you sometimes travel to places just for the Sun Dance, too?"

LENORE: "Yeah. We used to go down to my mom's reservation for Sun Dance, the U & O Uintah reservation. And we used to go to Colorado [to the Southern Ute reservation]; we went down when my grandma, Jennie Nick, used to be a Sun Dance Chief."

JUDY: "Oh, they have women Sun Dancing there?"

LENORE: "Yeah, but they don't no more since she passed away. She was a real old lady, my mom's mom."

At home or away Lenore observes Sun Dance taboos for women.

LENORE: "We don't go near the lodge — pregnant or having a period. Because if you're pregnant and you go there or are on your period, you could hurt somebody that's in there that's got medicine, like one of the medicine men."

JUDY: "In what way would you hurt someone? You mean physically?"

LENORE: "They'd get dry fast. See, 'cause when you're having your period it'll be like water running. And the Sun Dancers will know it 'cause they're dry; they've been without water a couple of days."

JUDY: "Do a lot of young women observe these things?"

LENORE: "Well, most of them don't. Like I've got a few friends, and when they're having their period, you know girls, they tell you. And they're at the concession stand at the Sun Dance grounds, and they'll tell you about it. They just hang around those places. I usually tell my friends anyway that you shouldn't be around here because you'll only hurt somebody if you do things like that."

In 1973 when she was fourteen, Lenore began singing with the women for the Sun Dance. The willow branches she and her sisters had waved as part of their pretend Sun Dance game now serve a purpose. "The way I see it," Lenore says, "it provides shade for you while you're singing." Lenore sees no significant changes in the Sun Dance songs and their performance during her lifetime. Changes that the other older women point out, such as song shortening and faster tempos, occurred before her time.

Lenore's musical experience with the Sun Dance is strictly limited to the event itself, and she is content to limit her participation to yearly ceremonial performances.

LENORE: "My mom and dad say they don't allow women to be at the drum on that. We [Lenore and her sisters] just don't sing them. The only time we'd sing them is if we'd have our Sun Dance or we'd go someplace else for Sun Dance."

JUDY: "Do you sometimes tape and listen to Sun Dance songs?"

LENORE: "No, we don't record. The way they told us, you're not supposed to have tape recorders inside the Sun Dance Lodge. [The Sun Dance drum and the women who sit close behind the male drummers occupy part of the southeast section of the lodge.] So we don't record from there."

The Sun Dance Flag Song is among the five Sun Dance songs Lenore has sung for me with her uncle. She does not find it too "young" to sing, as Emily does. I have also recorded her singing the Sun Dance Prayer Song, the song received by Angie's mother one early morning. In her performance of Sun Dance songs, Lenore sings the customary lady's part (see chart 1, p. 33).

In 1979 I observed Lenore step just beyond the usual women's Sun Dance role to help the lead singer who had suffered a momentary memory lapse in the middle of the Sunrise Ceremony Song. Lenore sang out from the side and kept the song going until the lead singer quickly recovered his lead. It all happened in a flash, and no one commented about it afterward. Lenore's spontaneous response and power to act highlighted her own special musical status among the Shoshones and contrasts with Alberta's views of Sun Dance musical etiquette for women (see pp. 107–8).

Peyote Songs

LENORE: "I think I was about sixteen or so when I started going to those [Native American Church meetings]. When I go to Peyote meetings, my mom and dad always tell me not to be laughing around in there or giggling around and telling jokes. That's only supposed to be done after you get out of the Peyote meeting. Not while you're in there or even if you're having breakfast [the morning after the all-night meeting], you shouldn't be laughing because they'll be telling—maybe one of the elder people will be telling you something good and you're just sitting there laughing and not listening. You shouldn't be laughing in there, because it will become your habit, doing things like that.[5]

"I have faith in it [the use of peyote]. I was down with a cold, and my uncle went to a meeting with my brother-in-law. Then they brought some back for me. And I didn't feel good. It was like my head was really thick and I couldn't think. Then I took that that night. The next morning

5. Lenore's words vibrate sympathetically with a fable Emily tells: "Old people used to tell stories a long time ago, Indian stories, something like fairy stories. This eagle was a chief of all the birds. He was telling them how to make nests for the eggs. And these two birds, that *waiyavo* (some kind of nighthawk) and that little dove, these two—when all these different kinds of birds listened to the eagle telling them how to fix their nests— these two busy laughing, laughing. They didn't listen to him what he was telling the different birds. These two didn't listen, so they don't have nests. That other bird [dove] just has two, three sticks on the branches, tree branches like that. Have their eggs like that. When the wind blows then eggs fall out. Them *waiyavos* lay eggs in the rocks just because they didn't listen. Some people like that, see. Some people when somebody's telling some-thing, what's right and wrong, some people's busy laughing and talking about something else. That's what happened to those two birds. And now they don't know how to fix their nests. That's what the story is, old-timer's story."

I woke up, it was like I never did have a cold. But, you know, some people tell bad things about it, but it's the Indian people's way. It's their church, Native American Church. Just like the white man has his own church. And, you know, like they have their own medicine. We have our own medicine."

JUDY: "Does your family call for a Peyote meeting fairly frequently?"

LENORE: "Well, birthdays, or if somebody's sick in the family, or if they want to help somebody out. If somebody needs help they'll put it up for them."

JUDY: "When you give it for a happy occasion like a birthday, are you making prayers or blessings for that birthday person?"

LENORE: "I would say they're praying for that person that they're having a birthday meeting for. Pray for them for the future, you know, look up to the future, that they'll grow up in a good way. Not turn to this liquor and things like that. It's just like church, I guess you would say. There's singing, and they take time out to pray for that person or this person or what they're there for." (In 1984 Lenore asked her family's help to sponsor a birthday meeting marking her twenty-fifth birthday.)

JUDY: "Do many young people believe in the Peyote way here?"

LENORE: "I think just a few because all summer last year I been going to nothing but Peyote meetings, and I didn't see that many young people there."

JUDY: "Are there many meetings to attend? Like could you go almost every week?"

LENORE: "Yeah, uh-huh. But then sometimes it seems like everything just stops, then it starts up again and just starts going—having meetings."

Lenore has grown up with the Native American Church. Its music was part of her early childhood memories.

LENORE: "My mom sings. She used to sing Native American Church songs."

JUDY: "Do you sing Peyote songs?"

LENORE: "Once in a while. Most of the time is when I go to the Peyote meeting. I just sing along with the men."

JUDY: "When you're by yourself, do you ever sometimes start singing a Peyote song?"

LENORE: "Sometimes a song that I really like. I try to learn it, and then I go over and over on it, 'cause I can't get it right."

JUDY: "Do you find them hard?"

LENORE: "Sometimes. Well, I'm used to singing these War Dance songs. Sometimes I get mixed up."

JUDY: "Do the words get you mixed up or is it the actual tune?"

LENORE: "It's the tune, I think. With the War Dance songs you could just—they're just straight, you know. But then the Peyote songs, it's like you use all your vocal cords. Is that what it's called?"

JUDY: "You mean your range? Your lowest notes to your highest notes?"

LENORE: "Yeah. Just jumps back and forth sometimes."

In 1980 Lenore and I drove together down to Cody, Wyoming. She and her family were singing at the Plains Indian Museum for the unveiling of a statue of Sacajawea. En route Lenore put on a commercial tape of Sioux singers performing Peyote songs. We had both been up late the night before, and the music was relaxing. She commented that she likes to listen to Peyote tapes when she does beadwork. This particular use of Peyote tapes is also true of the other women, with the exception of Emily, who neither beads nor listens to Peyote songs. The meaning of Peyote songs to Lenore is private and, within the context of the ceremony, efficacious. In this regard she puts Peyote and Sun Dance songs together (see Lenore's statement to this effect on p. 211).

The Powwow[6] and Powwow Music

Over the years and generations of women represented in this book, we can trace an expanding role for women within the powwow, as singers, dancers, and drummers. Of equal significance to the increased participation of women is the relatively young age of those now taking part. We have seen this not only within the context of the powwow but even in ceremonial performance such as the War Bonnet Dance. A comparison of the comments

6. According to Young: "*Pawwaw* was a term listed by Roger Williams (1827) [*sic*] as meaning 'priest' among the New England Algonquian tribes. It also referred to the healing ceremonies these priests, who would have been called medicine men by later white settlers, held. Since large crowds gathered for curing ceremonies, especially ones like the rites of the Midewiwin, the term came to mean, in American English, a gathering. It was one of many New England Algonquian words such as Squaw, papoose, tomahawk, wampum, and wigwam which came into general use in English. By the 1800's, powwow was used in literature to mean a gathering of any number of people to make a decision. Among the Algonquian tribes themselves, pow wow continued to refer to healing ceremonies and was used by the Menomini in reference to the Drum Dance. The spelling powwow probably came about later as a newspaper expediency" (Young 1981:192). Young traces the history of the modern powwow to its origins in Oklahoma in this century and notes that "the Plains style as a symbol of Indianness had already been accepted by both Indians and non-Indians by the time the powwow crystallized in its modern form in the 1920's" (Young 1981:340). Wind River Shoshones hosted their first powwow in 1957, calling it Eastern Shoshone Indian Days. This has become an annual event. Since the mid-1970s an additional Shoshone powwow is sometimes sponsored on the reservation at Crowheart.

by four of the five women about the process and criteria for selecting Shoshone powwow queens documents another example of this evolutionary trend. (I have no comments from Emily, who sees powwow queens as just one more non-Shoshone importation.) We begin with Lenore, who has been both powwow queen and attendant on several occasions. Even within the limitations of her young age, she registers some of the subtle variants and changes in recent years.

JUDY: "How do they choose the queen now?"

LENORE: "Mostly by dancing, appearance, personality. The Entertainment Committee picks their own queen."

JUDY: "Does the queen represent the people here wherever she goes?"

LENORE: "Yeah, sometimes she could, when she travels throughout the states and to different powwows, she could go up to the announcer's stand and maybe say a few words on behalf of who she's representing. That's what I used to do, you know, if I felt like it."

JUDY: "Has it always been young women?"

LENORE: "No, it never was. It used to be eighteen years old to twenty-five years old. Now it's clear down the age limit. It's just really young. What I think is that they—the age limit should be where the person knows she's carrying responsibility on behalf of the people, instead of running around behind the arbor and outside from where she should be. She should be inside representing our tribe."

JUDY: "And should she dance most of the evening?"

LENORE: "Yeah. I used to dance from when the Grand Entry started clear until the dance ended. Then I had to [come back to the Shoyo drum group and] sing at the same time, back and forth. I can't do that no more."

The queens are now very young, and on one occasion, while serving in that capacity, Lenore even helped select the next year's queen. For a society that prizes the judgment of elders, this was standing things on its head.

LENORE: "When I got through reigning over my year [in 1978], they asked me to judge for the following year's queen."

JUDY: "How did you decide?"

LENORE: "On the movement of the girl, the way she dances. And I guess the personality, somebody that gets along with everybody and, you know, not afraid to stand up for her people. Go out to powwows. Somebody that dances a lot that I see travels to powwows. I never really judge by the outfit they wear. I usually judge by their dancing mostly."

Lenore adds that in other years judges have been picked from the audience of a dance held before the powwow. Other judges used different criteria for selection. Lenore's sister J. A., for example, related to Lenore why the latter lost one year: "Mostly she beat you because of her traditional outfit. She had roses." Rose motifs, long popular in Shoshone beadwork, are felt to be a traditional and distinctively Shoshone design (see plate 17 following p. 114).[7]

Compare Lenore's perspective with Helene's.

JUDY: "Now I'm curious what you think about the powwow queen, because that has importance. Or doesn't it have importance?"

HELENE: "All depends on which angle you look at it from. I'm kind of an oldy-goldy, so I probably give my idea on what I seen and all that years ago and what I've heard from the old people. Going way back in my mother's days, as a young lady, they said that when they chose the queen it was not what it is now, where you have to be unmarried. Years ago they chose them on poise and just ordinary beauty, on how they looked from their dresswear, and how they held themselves. And a lot of ladies, what I mean ladies, they weren't young girls, they were probably thirty and on up. I would say the youngest was thirty or more. They rode in front of the grandstand, maybe five, eight ladies, all mounted in their full regalia on their horse. They lined them up in front of the grandstand; they just looked them over and they looked them over from a distance, and they were chosen from that angle. And they only had one queen; there were no attendants. My cousin M. D. got to be chosen as a queen, and she wasn't a young girl. She was already in her middle age. That's how they chose them. I wouldn't actually say on beauty or horsemanship. It was just their outfits and their appearance. And they didn't get paid like they do now, $150. No way, you know, back then they just got it as an honor. And it was an honor to these ladies. And they weren't single. They were married, so it's definitely different. And then you come along and you get into the age group where my sister R. got in on the contests, and that was already when it started changing. And they didn't get very much money. I don't even know whether they got paid or not. And the Entertainment Committee at that time come beating the bushes, asking girls whether they wanted to run for queen or not. And, you know, it's an honor for the girls if there's a lot of them running, competing against each other. In R.'s time, when she ran for queen, it was horsemanship then. And then the Lander Chamber of Commerce [Lander is a nearby non-Indian town] came out, and they judged the Indian queens on horsemanship. You didn't have to be in your

7. Shimkin states that "the floral design was borrowed in the 19th century from Northeast and Plains Indians" (Shimkin 1986:313).

regalia or anything. It just depends on how good of a rider you are. R. was chosen an attendant and D. [another sister] a queen in, I think, 1972."

JUDY: "Now is it sometime in May that the girls compete?"

HELENE: "Yeah, after the high school kids from [Indian] boarding school come home. They put up one night's dance just to pick the queen out. It just depends on how the Entertainment [Committee] wants to work it, really. It's no set way I don't think."

Alberta's two daughters have competed and been chosen attendants to the queen. She gives her recollections and viewpoint.

ALBERTA: "Well, just lately they been choosing these queens — not in the earlier days. And then I guess out-of-state people had queens, so then we started. They were a little older then. See, like now they can't be over twenty, but then they can be queens at any age."

JUDY: "How do you get to be chosen a powwow queen?"

ALBERTA: "Well, just like maybe how you're dressed and how you think you're going to represent your people. They have to make a speech. But recently I don't hardly hear them give a speech out like that. Just once in a while they do. Now they set a date to select the queen so all the girls can be there dressed. So then they pick out judges and have 'em dance. When V. [Alberta's daughter] was attendant, it was how they dress and how they speak. How they want to talk and represent the tribe. In V.'s time that's what they used to do. But nowadays they choose maybe just a small twelve-year-old. They should pick an older person, older girl. Really, when I see those powwows, they [Shoshone queens] don't even represent the tribe. They don't talk for us. But like when I see other people, other tribes, they really represent their tribes, how they should carry on this Indian heritage, traditions. They'll be on the stage for a long time and talk, and I think that's good. But here we don't."

Angie adds her observations: "The powwow queens a long time ago used to be just anybody. Like, they ride horses — them older women, like J. B.'s wife, J., she was a queen. They were about [in their] thirties, forties. That's different. You don't have to be single girls either. It's got to be your horsemanship, you know, they could ride. They don't have to select one queen. Then, they could just go ahead and have many queens. They really used to love that long line of them queens. [See plate 25 following p. 266.]

"I was one of those judges once. There's about four or five of them girls [competing]. The way I figured that out was she [Angie's choice] got an Indian language, [speaks the] Shoshone language, and she knows how to talk English. And she knows more about the people, and she dances. And then, besides that, she's got a good, you know, she's good to people —

talks to anyone. She could go up and talk for herself in her Indian, Shoshone language and then in white man. She's good to talk to a lot of people. That's the way I judged that once. And she was queen then. It doesn't have to be her looks, you know, fat and all that. No. She's got to have a personality, good towards people, not ashamed to go up and talk. But I didn't put in, say she's well educated. No, that don't include that. That's white man way."

There are constants in all of these comments. A powwow queen wears Indian dress, has confidence to speak before people, and has a friendly personality. Interwoven with these constants are changes in form. Young unmarried women have supplanted mature married women. Skill in War Dancing, a relatively recent phenomenon for Shoshone women, replaces skill in horsemanship as a contest criterion. Cash prizes and their steady increase over the years are also new. Multiple queens, consistent with Shoshone reticence to place undue attention on an individual (a possible source of jealousy and social disharmony), have given way to a hierarchy of one queen and two attendants.

Shoshones did not originate the idea for a powwow queen. Emily is right; it is another example of intertribal borrowing.[8] There are non-Indian influences as well. The very notion of a powwow queen, the competitive process for her selection, and cash prizes for the winner reflect input from Euro-American culture (see pp. 56–57). The recent prominence of younger women within the powwow may also bear relationship to Euro-American culture, which stresses the importance of youth, youthful looks, and, in recent times, the status and rights of women. But whatever the case may be as to Euro-American influences, these in no way change Shoshone perception of the powwow and all that takes place within its borders as being unalterably Indian. Certainly, traditions of public honoring are old and ingrained with the Shoshones and other North American Indian cultures. Powwow queens are new manifestations that embody these traditions. The selection of a powwow queen sets in motion another old ceremony, the

8. Young traces the beginning of powwow queens and princesses to the late 1920s: "The 1929 Cheyenne and Arapaho Fair at Watonga included an Indian maiden contest. In 1926, an Indian princess or queen had been selected for the Round-up at Pendleton, Oregon. . . . In November, 1926, the International Petroleum Congress and Exposition in Tulsa had a princess representing the Osage tribe (*American Indian* 1(2):3). This was apparently the beginning of the selection of Oklahoma tribal and powwow princesses" (Young 1981:283–84). Powers describes the selection process in Oklahoma in more recent times (since approximately the 1960s): "At each of the larger pan-Indian powwows, a Powwow Princess representing her tribe and/or the celebration itself is chosen. Here prerequisites match those of most other non-Indian beauty contests with the exception that: 1) she must have a certain percentage of Indian blood; and 2) she must be dressed in the traditional costume of her tribe" (Powers 1968:363).

Giveaway. The circle is completed: A Giveaway, held in honor of the powwow queen by her family, in turn honors the community and powwow visitors with generous distributions of gifts. It leaves in its wake good feeling and renewed communal relations. Thus, while the age of the powwow queen and the outward signs of her Indian identity may take many forms— horsemanship, fluency in Shoshone, skill in War Dancing, etc. —unchang- ing Indian values of honoring, generosity, and harmonious group context continue to flow beneath the surface. These inform the whole.

JUDY: "What makes a good, successful powwow?"

LENORE: "The singers, the drummers. Because without them there's no way you could have a powwow. They're the ones that's giving you the music to dance to."

JUDY: "Do you measure whether it's been a good powwow by how many people come and how many people dance?"

LENORE: "Yeah, dance. Mostly the dancers, you know, nowadays they go for the money competition. It depends on how high it is, and they'll be a lot of dancers. That's what really pulls the dancers in towards the powwow."

JUDY: "Do you think that's been a good thing or a bad thing?"

LENORE: "Well, I'd say it's a good thing. Because you go up there, you compete against other dancers. You know, it really gives you a chance to show that just 'cause they got a name for themselves, you're not scared of them. And you're out there trying your best. It's really something because you get to see a lot of people. You meet new friends."

Lenore also addresses aspects of powwow music. About the Flag song, for example, she states: "Our [Shoshone] Flag song, it's just like it's being held back. Nobody knows it. But then I've heard that two persons are still alive that know that song, but they won't pass it. And that's going to be bad for our tribe, you know. In a few more years they might pass away, too, and nobody will know the Flag song, so we could learn it and pass it on to the next generation. Because it's just that we're losing out on that one. It really would be something to hear that the Shoshone got their own Flag song instead of having to sing somebody else's Flag song.

"There's all types of Flag songs that we sing. There's the song that most of the drum groups sing. The Parker Singers from Rocky Boy, Montana [Chippewa-Cree reservation], that's the Flag song they use, too. There's the Flag song that Chinicky Lake Singers sing. And the Sioux got their own Sioux Anthem song. We know those people that sing that song. She takes my mother as her sister."

JUDY: "So if you're called upon you'll sing one of those?"

LENORE: "Yeah. But when we travel to a powwow, you know, just because we're a girls' drum group, they might think that we don't know the Flag song. And they'll give it to the men's [drum group]. They won't call upon us because they think we're girls and we don't really know that much."

At home on the reservation Lenore's musical ability and knowledge are known. "Like we're asked to sing," she comments. "Were you here when L. A. [a veteran] passed away? We were asked to sing the Honor song for L. A.'s flag over at the cemetery. We just sang the Flag song, the Sioux Flag song. They wanted us to sing that song so we went ahead and did. I think there was B. [male singer who is Lenore's cousin], B. [Lenore's uncle], C. [Lenore's sister], and A. [Lenore's brother], D. [her brother-in-law's brother], and me. But I sang 'lady' in the background." The occasion, a veteran's burial, dictated Lenore's female musical role. That she was capable of leading the song was both irrelevant and inappropriate. However, it was acceptable and accepted for Lenore and her sister to drum with the men.

Flag Song no. 2

LENORE: "That was the one that Rocky Boy Singers sing."

JUDY: "How would you say a Flag song is different from a powwow War Dance song?"

LENORE: "Well, they usually go around like four 'push-ups,' four verses [or repetitions of the song].[9] Some hit their Flag songs different. See, there's different ways of doing these Flag songs. They got different beats. Some are almost like the Round Dance song [♪ ⅄ ♪ ♪ ⅄ ♪]. And some are just straight [♩ ♩ ♩ ♩]. It's much slower, and it's just like you got a meaning to it, a Flag song."

9. The term *push-ups* is a recent powwow expression denoting the number of repeats in a song performance. William Powers documents its older Sioux origins and several meanings. According to Sioux terminology the repeat of the opening solo call in a song is the "*pawankiye*, to push the voice upwards." Powers adds that since 1974 the Sioux use the English translation, push-ups, to refer not only to this particular section of the song but, in a more general sense, to the number of song repetitions (Powers 1980a:31). Shoshones use the term *push-ups* in this sense. I first heard this expression on the Wind River reservation in the early 1980s.

JUDY: "Is that true of your Grand Entry song [the song accompanying the initial single file entry of dancers into the dancing arena]?"

LENORE: "Grand Entry song is just like intertribal [War Dance song], 'cause you're bringing the dancers in behind the flag."

JUDY: "So that's not special in the way that you're talking about this . . . "

LENORE: "Well it is, sort of, because the flag's coming in front of the dancers. And they're dancing behind the flag in respect. And the people are standing in respect of the flag."

JUDY: "So anytime, you mean, that you're singing for the flag, the flag is involved, that's kind of a . . ."

LENORE: "Yeah. It's just the same way as you would have respect for the eagle feather. Because the eagle flies above us and watches over us. That's why they have this Feather Dance when anyone drops any eagle plume. [Because the eagle is held sacred, many tribes have a special song and ceremonial way to pick up eagle feathers that accidentally drop off of a dancer's outfit.] They usually have a veteran [pick up the dropped eagle feather and] come on up and pray for the feather and owner. He also prays in all four directions and talks about his experience in war. And the drummers hit the drum when, you know, he talks about that, after he finished the sentence."

Further information provided by Helene suggests that the drum punctuation is a symbolic reference to warfare. [June 12, 1982. "Helene talked of eagle feathers—traditional ways to pick it up—some have dance and song, others have veteran tell war exploits and then throw the feather onto the drum—like a blow."] Scholarly writings strengthen this point. Lowie documents direct connections between War Dance songs and actual gunshots, stating that "war songs were chanted and guns were discharged as the [Comanche war] party came back" (Lowie 1915:811). (It is unclear whether one alternated with the other or overlapped or both.) Powers comments on the symbolic preservation of this connection in contemporary War Dance songs: "In the war songs, loud accented beats interspersed between steady beats imitated gunshots" (Powers 1973:171).

The flag and eagle are respected and honored in the powwow, and it is interesting to see how Lenore intertwines the two in her thoughts. People, however, are the primary focus of honoring: the veteran in connection with the flag. In the 1980s a new fashion of honoring based on older name-giving customs has become popular among the Shoshones. Families of a daughter chosen to be a powwow or rodeo queen see the powwow as the opportune time and place to bestow publicly an Indian name on her (still another variant of our theme—an expanding role for women, especially young women). A special Honor song marks the occasion.

LENORE: "Honor songs are mostly made by the person that they've asked to sing. Like this past summer we were asked to sing a song for Ruby McGill for when she was given an Indian name. Bird Woman [*Huchu waipë?*] was what they called her."

JUDY: "Do you have an Indian name?"

LENORE: "Yeah, my mom and dad named me, but in a different way. They told me not to mention it."

JUDY: "But this was different where it was done at the powwow, where it's kind of a public thing?"

LENORE: "Yeah."

JUDY: "Can you sing that song for me, or should I go ask her parents and make some donation?"

LENORE: "I think it would be best if you asked Ruby McGill's parents, because that way, if they happened to somehow hear about what we're doing here, they won't have any kind of feelings against me. That song was only given to Ruby."

JUDY: "It's like . . . "

LENORE: "Her own song."

I went to see the McGills, who received me in a warm and friendly manner. Observing custom and proper etiquette, I donated money and received permission to record the following Honor song as part of my research.[10]

Honor Song for Bird Woman

(4th and final verse)

10. In my interview with the McGills, they explained that the name Bird Woman was chosen because their daughter was going all around, here and there, just like a bird. As part of the name-giving ceremony, Ruby received prayers for spiritual blessing, an eagle plume, and red paint to protect her. The protective use of red paint has long precedence with the Shoshones and many other tribes. It had great use in the Ghost Dance. According to Mooney, "It is believed to ward off sickness, to contribute to long life" (Mooney [1896] 1965:21). A picture drawn by Emily's sister shows that in this century Shoshone women who attended Ghost Dances sometimes applied red paint to the part in their hair (Vander 1986:9).

* Note clear example of the voice slightly following the drum.

The McGills explained that they had, themselves, paid for the song. They had bought it from Lenore, and the song was now exclusively their daughter's. Lenore notes that "if a different drum group sings that song as a regular War Dance song at a different powwow, the mother or father is supposed to charge that drum for singing that song that was given to their daughter. They're [Ruby's parents] supposed to record it the day that song was given to her. It was her own song. But I guess they didn't, because we heard a drum group sing it down at Ethete. And we thought they were going to do something about it. We only sang that song to be given to her. We can't do anything about it, 'cause that's the mother and father's."

JUDY: "Now you'll never sing that song again."

LENORE: "No, that was given to her."

JUDY: "So that other drum group did wrong in what they did?"

LENORE: "Right. Or they're supposed to donate money to that girl.

"They've never really done that on this reservation I don't think for a long time — ask somebody to give them a song."

JUDY: "And then don't you think it was an honor that they asked you to sing that song?"

LENORE: "Yeah, because usually always, you know, they ask the men-folks to sing for them. But it's the girl, they said, that wanted us to sing for her, 'cause we're her aunts. They asked her who she wanted, so she picked us. It's kind of funny, too, because usually they pick the men to drum because they think that just because we're all girls we don't know anything about singing.

"Well, they didn't tell us till the morning of when they were going to have that doings for that girl. It was short notice. We were trying to find out what her Indian name was. We asked our dad who was going to name her, so that way we'd find out what the Indian name was going to be and put her Indian name in the song. But we couldn't find them, so we just sang it straight [all vocables]."

JUDY: "When you were trying to make it up, how did you go about doing it?"

LENORE: "I don't know; to me it kind of sounds like one of the old songs so many years ago. You know, when somebody else sings a song that's sung by somebody that's got a lower voice, it sounds different." (Again, we see great sensitivity to individual vocal timbre and where a song is pitched.)

JUDY: "Do you think because you were singing it slower, does that make it sound older?"

LENORE: "No, it's not anything like that. It's just that the tune, I've sung so many songs and I — it kind of reminds me of another song. I can't remember it though."

JUDY: "Did it come to you in one piece, or did you kind of get the beginning . . ."

LENORE: "Yeah, I had to work at it. So I sat home all day thinking of a song. And I keep getting mixed up. I had a hard time, but I finally got it together. [On another occasion when I asked Lenore how she made this song, she replied, "I don't know, it just seemed to pop into my head."] I just kept practicing it over and over till I thought about the way I was really going to sing it, you know, the whole verse. Then I had my recorder ready so I recorded myself, so I wouldn't forget it. So I'd, you know, kind of tune it up myself and sing it. Then I sing it to the girls. About 4:00 P.M. I went over and sang it for them. We practiced about an hour. And then they couldn't quite catch on. Then I told them, I said, 'Well, you're going to catch on anyway when we start singing it if you'll think of it.' So they practiced it all day, and then they must have caught on because they just came right on out and sang right behind me when I sang that song. We sing all the way through straight, and then at the end we hit it [drum accents] three times and then we ended it."

JUDY: "Is there a certain number of times you sing the song?"

LENORE: "You know, when you sing an Honor song, people's got to see who they're honoring. So we sing it for how many times it takes [for Ruby McGill, followed by her parents and friends] to go all the way around the [powwow] arbor. When we come to the end, we kind of go fast on the last verse."

Song length, tempo changes, and drum accents cue and are cued by the movement of the honored person and entourage.

War Dance Songs

War Dance Song no. 10

Singers: Big Mountain Singers (Lenore, Coleen, JoAnn, and Linda Shoyo)

I recorded War Dance song no. 10 during the 1978 Eastern Shoshone Indian Days. The performance captured on tape catches some of the noisy ambience of the powwow setting. Talking after the song has already started, the announcer invites everyone to dance: "It's intertribal time" (as opposed to contest time, which is restricted only to competitors). The jingle of bells grows louder as more and more dancers get up to dance. The dynamic burst of bells near the end coincides with a sharp increase in the song tempo. Throughout, onlookers chat and visit with one another. The public-address system and microphones that amplify the music at times add distortions and random electronic sounds.

Lenore's verbal assessment of her War Dance song repertoire and my recorded sample of it over the years yield a very consistent picture of size and acquisition.

JUDY (July 1978): "How many powwow [i.e., War Dance] songs do you think you know?"

LENORE: "Between fifty and sixty songs."

JUDY: "This year, how many new songs will you learn in a summer?"

LENORE: "Eight."

JUDY (June 1979): "Since I saw you last, about how many new songs have you learned?"

LENORE: "About twenty since we went up to Canada and we came back down this way."

JUDY (September 1981): "How many War Dance songs did you learn this year or this summer?"

LENORE: "I'd say a lot. There's a lot of different ones. Some were changed."

JUDY: "So it might be ten or fifteen?"

LENORE: "Yeah, somewhere around there. If you notice the Northern songs are — [Northern Plains singers] they wait for a few songs to come out, new ones. But the Oklahoma [Southern Plains songs] just go on and on."

Chart 3 shows the year I recorded Lenore's War Dance songs, the number of duplicate performances for each year, and the recording contexts: public (for powwows and a museum lecture-demonstration) and private (for my research). Most of the tapes from 1978, 1979, and 1980 were made during three evenings of the Eastern Shoshone Indian Days. Comparing these three years, only four songs overlap between 1978 and 1979 (including War Dance song no. 10) and only two between 1979 and 1980. While most of the recordings are admittedly from only one powwow, nevertheless, the fifteen to seventeen songs for each of these three years match Lenore's reckoning of the number of War Dance songs she performs during a year and her contention that she sings primarily a new batch of songs each season. The data of the entire recording period from 1977 to 1984 strengthen and cor-

CHART 3
War Dance Song Recordings of Lenore Shoyo and the Big Mountain Singers

1977	1978	1979	1980	1981	1982	1983	1984
Private	Powwow	Powwow			None		Private
1***	1**	1					1
2							
3		Private					
	4***	4					
	5**						
	6						
	7						
	8						
	9						
	10***						
	Private	Powwow					
	11	11					
	12						
	13						
	14						
	15						
	16		Powwow				
	17	17	17				
		18					
		19					
		20					
		21					
		22					
		23	23				
		24					
		25					
		26****					
		27**					
		28**					

29

30**
31**
32**

33**
34
35
36
37
38**
39
40**
41
42
43
44
Museum
45**

Private
46
47**
48
49
50
51
52
53

Museum
54
55
56
57
58

59

Total	3	15	15	19	15	8	0	5	2

* indicates the number of recorded performances.
The numbers in this chart are chronological and do not correspond to the song numbers in the book.

roborate the fast turnover for War Dance songs. As for the old Shoshone Wolf Dance songs of Emily and Angie's youth, these are unknown to Lenore.

Late in the summer of 1978 Lenore and I reviewed some of the War Dance songs that, like War Dance song no. 10, she had sung earlier during the Shoshone powwow. Her comments document at the smallest level individual pieces in the large mosaic of song diffusion. She identifies songs by the lead singer or the singing group. For example, William C'Hair, Jr., an Arapahoe singer who performs with the Community Singers on the Wind River reservation, sings War Dance song no. 4 (this and all the song numbers that follow refer to the enumeration given in chart 3). Lenore learned this song from him in 1978. It was a new song. She learned song no. 5 from Verlin Gould and the Snake River Singers (Shoshone-Bannock singers from the Ft. Hall reservation in Idaho). Song no. 6 she learned from William C'Hair, Jr. Lenore often remembers where she first heard a song. For example, she first heard song no. 48, performed by the Chinicky Lake Singers (Chippewa-Cree singers from Alberta, Canada) at the 1981 Ft. Hall Festival in Idaho. Furthermore she recognizes her own role in the diffusion process on the reservation: "When it comes winter we go down to this [American] Legion dance that we have every Christmas. We just sing the songs that we picked up at the powwows that we traveled to [in the summer]. Then that way the drum groups that don't travel that much, they could get those songs that we bring down then."

War Dance Song no. 11

Singers: Big Mountain Singers (Lottie, Lenore, Coleen, JoAnn, and Linda Shoyo)

JUDY: "Can you guess whether this will be popular for a long time, or just come and go?"

LENORE: "Sometimes they stay for so long, you know. If a drum group really likes a song, they'll just go ahead and sing it, like three times in one night."

JUDY: "And some of the songs will last for several seasons, too?"

LENORE: "Yeah."

JUDY: "What makes a song stick around and stay popular?"

LENORE: "I guess it'd be the dancers. You know, 'cause if they think it's a real pretty song and good song to dance to, they'll get right out there without waiting for other people to go out into the center and dance. They'll just be right out there all at once. I guess it's just if it attracts the dancers it'll just stay.

"Some of the new songs start at the first part of the powwow season.

The drum groups with the new songs, they want to be, you know, noticed. So they're going to make their own songs. Like they'll maybe practice all winter long and make songs. Then when powwow season starts they'll bring them out. The singers that want to make themselves noticed hit the big powwows, the powwows that got drum contests. Because they've got these new songs they're going to try out there, then."

JUDY: "Do you try to sing different songs at different powwows?"

LENORE: "Yeah."

JUDY: "Do you mostly sing the new songs?"

LENORE: "Well, most of the time if you go to a powwow that's going to go four nights [warm-up night, along with three nights of contests], we start off with the old songs first, from the years back. Then we go on to the newer ones and new ones and then the new[est] ones."

The order to the songs that Lenore and her sisters sing parallels and amplifies the crescendo form of the dance contests and accompanying cash prizes. The latest songs are reserved for the peak.

Throughout most of War Dance song no. 11, one can clearly hear Lenore's mother, Lottie, singing the lady's part an octave above her daughters.

JUDY: "For the lady's part, do you wait till after the men sing the opening solo part and the repeat of it?"

LENORE: "Yeah. They do that part, then I come in right in the middle of the verse, the first verse [section of the song] and [continue singing] all the way through.[11]

There is appreciation for the addition of the lady's part to a drum ensemble and for the female vocal quality per se. A middle-aged Shoshone man who is a well-known lead singer himself, expressed it this way: "You know how girls really scream—that's the way they sing. Really makes a song pretty." In War Dance singing, vocal style is an important distinguishing characteristic between male and female singers. Women sing with a "steady, flat, somewhat reedy tone . . . which largely omits pulsation" (Nettl 1967:303). This contrasts with male vocal style in which pulsation is prominent (Hatton 1986:215). In her delayed entrance, octave placement above the male singing part, and vocal quality, Lottie performs the traditional women's singing role. (Her performance in Round Dance song no. 17, which appears on the cassette

11. William Powers has analyzed War Dance songs, including the musical part for women. There is only one small point of variance between his schematic outline and Lenore's brief statement and Lottie's performance. Powers notes that at the cadence of the first large section of the song, "Women's voices trail off a few beats longer than the men by extending the final vocable" (Powers 1961b:128). This is another example of a "finishing" role for women. However, with respect to Shoshone women, Lenore does not mention this, nor does her mother extend any of the cadences in War Dance song no. 11.

accompanying this book, illustrates all of these points.) Hatton observes that women "smooth out the texture of the ensemble sound after the heavily pulsated male vocal introduction. In performances of the mixed [male-female] drum groups we find women drumming and singing in styles derived from various combinations of the traditional female and male styles" (Hatton 1986:215). This is true for Helene. Lenore and her sisters more closely approximate male singing roles and style.

War Dance Song no. 12 (Traditional)

LENORE: "There's two songs that we know that are Traditional songs. One I know myself; I don't have to listen to the tape. But another one we listen off of the tape [War Dance song no. 12]. That's an old Sioux song. We first heard that down in Rosebud, South Dakota, in 1975, I think it was.

"The way I see it, is the prize money in the Traditional Men's Dance and Women's is way up above the Fancy.[12] I heard from a friend that there was a lot of Traditional Dancers at Ft. Belknap [Montana]."

JUDY: "Is it part of a trend that people just want to get back to traditional ways?"

LENORE: "I think so. I think that even if they're older than I am and they're getting old, they got grandparents, you know, elderly people. They're turning to them more now. Because they're getting older, and we don't know for how long they'll be on earth with us. They'll be going on, and I think they want to learn their traditional ways from them before anything happens. That way when they have children, they could pass it on to their children."

Returning to traditions is no simple matter within the context of the powwow. Old traditions vary from tribe to tribe, as do their forms and vitality. An older tradition may be revived, changed in the process, and then enter the intertribal powwow scene where it gains popularity. Contests and cash prizes are an important factor here.

With respect to the Traditional Dance for women, Lenore and her sister Linda, both dancers, can attest to recent changes that are part of the

12. In an effort to strengthen participation in the Traditional War Dance, the Shoshones have recently experimented making the cash prize for this category greater than for the Fancy Dance. In 1978 the winner of the Men's Fancy Dance received $400 compared with $200 for the Men's Traditional. In 1979 the winner of the Men's Traditional received $300 compared with $200 for the Men's Fancy Dance.

trend toward "tradition." To understand the popular new traditional dance step for women, some Oglala Sioux background is necessary. Powers wrote in 1968:

> There is some indication that women, at least at the smaller functions, are dancing "old-time," that is, simply bobbing in place around the outer perimeter of the dance area. This was the old Oglala style of dance which was disrupted by the Oklahoma influence in the mid-fifties and which permitted women to dance in the same area as the men. At the larger functions the Oglala women dance clockwise around the men performing the typical "walking" step of the Oklahoma women. (Powers 1968:368)

A variant on the older "bobbing" style has emerged recently, and young Shoshones identify it as an old Sioux tradition. The dancer bobs up and down four times in one direction and then pivots 45°, bobs up and down four times in that direction and then pivots 45°, and so on. Slowly revolving and holding an eagle-feather fan in one hand, she dances to the four directions. Stylized hand motions coordinate the raising and lowering of the fan with the drum accents in the song.[13] Lenore, too, recognizes the dance's connection to an older Sioux tradition: "At first when we went to South Dakota, we noted that when you dance, you know, like you have your own Traditional Dance, they say the Shoshone ladies just dance round, you know. But I guess you'd have to know their way [Sioux] of dancing in order to get in top with them [and win contests]."

In 1979 Linda Shoyo competed in the Women's Traditional contest at the Eastern Shoshone Indian Days. I asked her some questions about style and origins.

JUDY: "And what about that style where you are in one place pivoting, have you been doing that for a while?"

LINDA: "Where you stand in one place like that? That's the Sioux way. That's the traditional way now."

JUDY: "How long have you been doing that?"

LINDA: "For two and a half years. 'Cause see, we been down in South Dakota all the time. Women that go into Traditional [Dancing], they don't go around. They just stand in one place."

JUDY: "Is that where you learned to dance it, in South Dakota?"

LINDA: "Yeah. That man's wife told us that next time we come down there we should dance that way."

---

13. Bobbing up and down in place was also done by Shoshone women in the past. Older Shoshone women remember this; Lowie noted it in his study of Shoshone music and dance (Lowie 1915:820). However, there is never any mention of the pivoting to the four directions nor of accompanying hand motions.

The Shoyos and other Shoshones who travel to other powwows bring home songs and dances—old, new, and renewed. By 1982 a large fraction of young women competing in the Women's Traditional contest on the Wind River reservation danced in place, the Sioux way.

War Dance song no. 12 would be appropriate for either the Men's or Women's Traditional Dance. Within the Men's Traditional Dance category, however, there is a special dance, the Sneak-Up Dance, that has its own distinct steps and musical accompaniment.

JUDY: "Could you use War Dance song no. 12 for a Sneak-Up Dance, or do you have to sing a different song?"

LENORE: "It would be the original Sneak-Up song. That's a Sioux song. I know it, but I have to listen to it [on the tape recorder for recall]. Usually, if a drum group doesn't know the Sneak-Up song, they just sing a song that they know, but for four verses they'd do that [unmeasured tremolo] beat [during the first section of the song]; they then go into the regular beat, kind of medium pace. Then on the fifth verse they go straight on through [with the regular beat for the last complete song repetition]."[14]

Within the Fancy War Dance category, there is an analogous song and dance to the Sneak-Up Dance, the Shake Dance, which also may be used for contests. Lenore's only musical distinction between the two is the faster tempo in the second section of the Shake Dance song. The next song, War Dance no. 13, a Shake Dance song, illustrates the musical characteristics of both Shake Dance and Sneak-Up Dance songs.

War Dance Song no. 13 (Shake Dance)

14. William Powers describes and analyzes the Sioux Sneak-Up Dance, which the Sioux call *Tonweya Wacipi,* "Scout Dance." The two musical sections that Lenore describes accompany the dancer's pantomime of warfare. Imitating a war scout, the dancer crouches, quivers, and looks around for the first part of the song, the "sneak-up section." The second part is the "advance," during which the dancer moves forward to the regular drumbeat. According to Powers the Sioux repeat the song six times together with a tail rather than five times, as described by Lenore (Powers 1962:168–69).

hai ya e hai_ ya e ha ya e ai ya e hai ya he yo

mp ——— *mf*

LENORE: "First time we heard it was when Lloyd Top Sky, Billy Runs Above sang it down to the Wyoming Indian High School powwow, May 29th and 30th, '81. Traditional Dance has to have a slower beat to their dancing than the Fancy."

JUDY: "Could you sing the same song for both but do it slower for the one?"

LENORE: "No, there's a Traditional song. There's some old songs, like, you know, the songs from Montana, that you can sing for that [Traditional War Dance]. And then the Fancy Dance you sing the song they sing now, like today."

JUDY: "Could you just take an intertribal song and speed it up for a Fancy War Dance contest?"

LENORE: "Uh-huh."

JUDY: "Do you sometimes do that?"

LENORE: "Most of the time. 'Cause most of the time [Fancy] dancers like to dance fast. They'll dance like two verses slow, and you make it faster, then maybe even faster."

JUDY: "Is there such a thing as a Fancy War Dance song that's separate from your intertribal War Dance songs which you would only use for contests?"

LENORE: "Yeah, I know one now that we use mostly for Fancy Dance contests. They just call it the Shake Dance now [War Dance song no. 13]. And if it's for the Traditional Dancers, they usually call it the Sneak-Up Dance."

JUDY: "When you learn a song [like War Dance song no. 13], do you try as much as possible to sing it just the way that person sang it?"

LENORE: "Yeah, 'cause it sounds much better if you sing it the way that drum group sang it. You try to change it, it doesn't sound too good, 'cause they're the ones that made that song and they know the way it should be sung. Other drum groups should try to sing it the same instead of trying to change the whole thing. 'Cause it just don't sound right."

War Dance Song no. 14

Lenore sang this song in 1981 whenever called upon to sing for either the men's or women's Fancy Dance contests.

LENORE: "When we first heard that [song], it was from the Snake River Singers, from Ft. Hall, Idaho."

JUDY: "Is that an older song?"

LENORE: "Yeah, sounds like it. I think it sounds different because they're younger and the tune on their voices changes that song."

At issue again is Lenore's emphasis on vocal timbre, here colored by the age of the singers. Over time Lenore has noticed a change in her own voice.

JUDY: "Did your voice change and get heavier as you got more used to the singing and taking the lead part?"

LENORE: "Yeah. My voice, seems like it's lower."

War Dance Song no. 15

Singers: Big Mountain Singers (Lenore, Coleen, JoAnn, and Linda Shoyo)

I recorded Lenore and her sisters when they sang this song for a Fancy War Dance contest during the 1980 Eastern Shoshone Indian Days. This dictated its length, four repetitions or push-ups.

LENORE: "We mostly end up singing the men's Fancy Dance songs [for the contests]."

JUDY: "Are those songs different from intertribal songs?"

LENORE: "Yeah, because they're faster. The songs that we sing, we have to bring it out much faster, and the words are kind of shortlike so they sound fast. Intertribal songs, it'd be you just take your time singing those. It just goes on and on."

Before moving on to Lenore's participation as a dancer, I wish to summarize and bring into focus some of the distinctions between intertribal and contest War Dance songs that have come up in her comments about War Dance songs nos. 13–15. Earlier (p. 241) Lenore noted that the appropriate song for a Traditional War Dance contest is a Traditional War Dance song. It should be an old song, a special song for a particular situation. The relatively slow tempo frequently used for Traditional War Dance contests (in comparison with Fancy War Dance competitions) is often a distinguishing musical characteristic. But the simple application of a slower tempo to any War Dance song will not make it a proper Traditional War Dance song. The song itself and its history and associations make it appropriate. On the other hand, the fast tempo of a Fancy War Dance contest song is perhaps the distinctive difference between it and an intertribal War Dance song. Lenore could choose any of the new songs she learns each season, "bring it out much faster," and it would be appropriate for a Fancy War Dance contest. (War Dance song no. 13, which accompanies a special type of Fancy War Dance, is an exception to this.) Finally, the length of a song performance is different for contest and intertribal dances. The number of repeats for a contest song is predetermined by the announcer or person in charge rather than by the lead singer, as is the case for intertribal songs. In practice contest song performance is short, four or five repeats. Lenore contrasts this with intertribal singing, which "goes on and on."

Youngest of the five women in the book, Lenore has seen and participated in the most recent developments for girls and young women, for example, the Fancy Shawl Dance, the female equivalent of the Fancy War Dance.

JUDY: "When did you start dancing in contests?"

LENORE: "Must have been when I was maybe sixteen [in 1975]."

JUDY: "When you first started dancing in the contests, did they have the Fancy Shawl Dance then?"

LENORE: "Yeah, they just had it like Cloth Dance and Shawl Dance; it was two divisions. One was you had to wear cloth dress and the other one shawl."

JUDY: "Where did buckskin dresses fit in?"

LENORE: "There were three divisions right there: Shawl, Buckskin, and Cloth."

JUDY: "Did they then have a difference between the Fancy type of step and the Traditional?"

LENORE: "No, they used to just dance two steps [on each foot, a light feint and then full step] and, you know, move the top. [The upper torso is relaxed.] They never used to bounce off the feet, off the ground like they're doing nowadays. The girls nowadays, they just jump all over and throw their arms all over, spin around. They never used to do that. [One can almost hear Emily's concern about change in Lenore's comments.]

JUDY: "So there was really [and formerly] just one [dancing] style?"

LENORE: "Uh-huh."

JUDY: "This year [1979] you competed for the Fancy Shawl contest. Was this year your first time doing that?"

LENORE: "No, I've been into Fancy Shawl for quite a while now. I used to be into Buckskin [and the Traditional Dance] but my buckskin dress got too small, so I'm working on it. So I'm just in Fancy Shawl for I don't know how long; till I finish my other outfit."

In addition to dance contests, many powwows have competitions for the drum groups. The Big Mountain Singers have won or placed in several contests, including one at Pine Ridge, South Dakota, and Ft. Duchesne, Utah. But for Lenore these are not a major motivating factor. "The powwows in Wyoming," she states, "they don't have no drum contests. But states around us, they do. They have a lot of money for it, too. But we don't go out to compete against other drum groups. We go sing at powwows because we like to sing. Because when we go sing like where they're having a drum contest, we don't care if we don't win or place. We just go because we like to sing. We want to participate in a powwow and help them out."

The presence of many drum groups at a powwow is always deeply appreciated by the host tribe. To attract singers the tribe often pays drum groups to help defray their expenses of food and gas on the road. There are other rewards as well: the ties woven of friendship and gifts. As Lenore relates: "We went to Red Pheasant Reserve in Saskatchewan. We got paid something like $120 for one night. And then we left after that next day. We went to Ft. Belknap [for a powwow in Montana] and met up with the S. R. family. And we met them at another powwow. They said that when we left they were calling upon us. They were having big Giveaways.

"My mom met a lady up at Crow Agency [Montana]. She said it's her friend now, I guess. So she invited us up [for Crow Fair]. She's going to have her sons build us a shade house so that my dad won't get too hot, you know, from the weather."

War Dance Song no. 16

Lenore sang this song for me in 1979 as part of my private lesson with her. To help me hear the vocables more clearly, she sang through it one time with a very soft drumbeat. (Lenore and her sister did not previously use the term *vocable* until I defined it for them during an interview.)

J. A. (Lenore's older sister): "[Singing the vocables,] that's like jumping from one note to another on a scale again."

Implied in this comment is, first, the predominance of syllabic text setting for most songs Shoshones sing and, second, a metaphor between vocables (a linguistic stock for texts) and "scales" (a pitch stock for melodies).

JUDY: "When you learn a song, do you try real hard to get the words the way the group sings it?"

LENORE: "Yeah, 'cause it sounds much better from the ones that made that song."

JUDY: "Does that sometimes give you difficulty, hearing the vocables?"

LENORE: "Yeah."

While it is often difficult to tell the origins of many powwow songs, song texts can be indicative. "The Sioux," as Lenore points out, "got their own type of song. Mostly they have [Sioux] words [rather than vocables] in them." Although this poses a problem for singers from other tribes, it is not always insurmountable. "There's one song," Lenore goes on to say, "but I don't really know the words to it. But it sounds like it's saying 'cockadoo.' The Badland Singers [Sioux] sang it at Ft. Duchesne, Fourth of July. I don't know what that means. Quite a few drum groups I've heard that aren't part of the [Sioux] tribe are singing that song around at the powwows."

War Dance Song no. 17

JUDY: "How shall I start to learn this?"

LENORE: "Drum on the edge, like that."

J. A.: "Probably tap at the edge, not the whole arm."

LENORE: "Just the wrist part, this part has got to bend. You just gotta listen real carefully.

L. A. (Lenore's younger sister): "Get it in your head."

J. A.: "Maybe hum along."

LENORE: "We'll sing two verses, then you could . . ."

J. A.: "Be caught on. Then you could try it."

Just Lenore and I sang War Dance song no. 17 together during another song-learning session. Given my own Western musical background, I tried to break the song into parts and repeat small segments after Lenore. This approach was entirely foreign to her and led to confusion. We immediately switched to the usual way of learning a song just quoted above by Lenore and her sisters. After several repetitions Lenore silently mentioned that I should take the lead. The above transcription is of the fifth and final repeat of the song.

JUDY: "The first part, the thing that you sing by yourself?"

LENORE: "We call it starter, that's all."

J. A.: "We say she firsts it, and then we second it."

JUDY: "You [the lead singer] do the whole first part by yourself?"

LENORE: "Not exactly the whole first part."

JUDY: "They break in sooner, don't they?"

LENORE: "Yeah."

One can clearly hear the overlapped early entrance of Lenore as the "seconder" in War Dance song no. 17. This is the rule in War Dance songs (Powers 1961b:128). The juxtaposition of our two voices contrasts my stylistic mistakes—synchronization of drum and vocal part and lack of pulsation on long notes (more hangover from my own musical training)—with Lenore's culture-perfect performance.

War Dance Song no. 18

Singers: Big Mountain Singers (Lenore, Coleen, JoAnn, and Linda Shoyo)

In 1978 Lenore learned this song from Verlin Gould, lead singer of the Snake River Singers. She categorizes it as being "pretty new."

Overlapping, joining parts in a way that obscures the boundary, is an important aspect of War Dance song performance. We saw this between the opening solo call and its repeat in War Dance song no. 17, and we encounter it in the repetitions of War Dance song no. 18. Typically, Lenore begins the solo call of the next repeat before the final cadential note is completed. (See Hatton 1974:127; Powers 1961b:131; and Young 1981:330.)

JUDY: "Do you know ahead of time how many times you're going to go through the song?"

J. A.: "We have to watch her good. Sometimes she signals and sometimes she don't."

LENORE: "When I want us to stop, I go like [*flat palm motion above the drum* ⏚ ; see Hatton 1974:134], or just one [*finger raised for one more repeat*] or two more. When they're singing, the drum group's got to watch really the head singer, so they'll know how they're going to go about on their trick song or any kind of song they're singing. They need to watch the dancers in order to see if they're beating their drum right."

JUDY: "When you're singing for a contest, do you keep an eye on the dancers?"

LENORE: "Yeah. That's why I think most of the time the head singers are sitting towards the dancers."

JUDY: "What is it that you're looking for as you're singing?"

LENORE: "The movements, I'd say. I watch how the dancers go into the beat of your drum. To see that you're not messing up your drumbeat, mixing everything up. So they'll know what they're dancing to, your beat. When we're drumming, if our drumbeat kind of gets out of beat—one's going too fast or something—I tell 'em, keep our drumming together."

JUDY: "Do you always do these heavy beats [drum accents] at the end of the War Dance?"

LENORE: "Yeah, to [let the dancers] know that it's going to stop."

The circle is complete. Singers watch the lead singer, the lead singer watches the dancers, the dancers listen for the tempo of the drumbeat and drum accents, which, in turn, cue the end of song and dance.

Like the overlapping of vocal parts, the six or seven drum accents on every other beat in War Dance song no. 18 do not coincide with the beginning of the second section. They are placed roughly in the middle. "When we hit that hard part [accents]," Lenore states, "then we go low and then we bring our drums back up." These accents invariably occur during the last repetition of a song. At other times they may be omitted, for example, during the first few repetitions or in a repetition that changes to a faster tempo (see the fourth repetition of War Dance song no. 18). The last few beats of a performance often build to a final definitive beat. Lenore and her sisters perform drum accents two ways. Either they all play an accented beat followed by one that is unaccented (or by a rest) or the sisters continue to play a steady unaccented beat as Lenore lifts her drumstick very high and hits the drum with considerable force every other beat. (See plate 28 following p. 266 for a picture of Lenore preparing to hit the accented beat.)[15]

15. As already mentioned, Powers suggests that War Dance drum accents originated as imitations of gun shots (Powers 1973:171). In another article he discusses their functional origins: "In the series of steady beats that makes up the rhythm of the war dance, there appears several groups of accented beats. These accented beats appear in definite places in

According to Hatton, "A facet of the group sound that might easily be overlooked is the sound of all of the drum beaters together. The coordination . . . produces a bouncy or 'boing' sound" (Hatton 1974:131). One hears this rather indefinable quality in the performance of War Dance song no. 18. Also, the sound of each bass drum used for War Dance songs varies according to its size and type of drumhead. In 1978 when I taped War Dance song no. 18, the Shoyo drum had a commercial bass drumhead. In 1983 the same drum had a different deer rawhide head.

War Dance Song No. 19

the song. Their origin seems to have been that they were developed to keep the dancers dancing on the right beats of the drum, but now simply appear as a traditional part of the drumming" (Powers 1961b:133; see Powers 1961b:133 for additional comments on drum tempo, accent, and volume). Within Hatton's analysis of drum accents in War Dance songs, the Big Mountain Singers observe the traditional method rather than the "Hot Five" method, ♪ ♪ ♪ ♪ ♪ ♪ ♪ ♪ ♪ ♪ (Hatton 1974:129–30).

we ya ha___ we___ ya we___ hai ya he___ yo

we ya ha___ we___ ya we___ hai ya he___ yo

we ya ha___ we___ ya we___ hai ya he___ yo

Singers: Big Mountain Singers (Lenore, Coleen, JoAnn, Linda, and (?)Lottie Shoyo)

The Big Mountain Singers performed this song for an intertribal dance during the 1980 Eastern Shoshone Indian Days. Although War Dance song no. 19 was not the starting point for the following conversation with Lenore, the tenor of her comments about curves in songs relates directly to this song and, indeed, to all of her repertoire.

JUDY: "When you think about songs, do you think about the curves in them?"

LENORE: "Yeah, about the curves in it. I don't really remember when I was younger, because I didn't pay that much attention then, but it seems to me that they got more curves in their songs now, Round Dance songs, War Dance songs, any kind."

JUDY: "And when you hear a song, is that what you're noticing—the curves to it?"

LENORE: "Yeah. That's how I most of the time I remember a song like that."

Then, describing how she teaches songs to her sisters, Lenore adds: "I usually sing it to them the way I'm going to sing it. And they sing that same verse over the way I sing it. I tell them if they sing it right or not. Sometimes I correct them if they can't get some certain parts of a song."

JUDY: "What sorts of things might they do a mistake on?"

LENORE: "You know, just the curves on the song they use. Sometimes they would just try to make it go straight through."

Lenore's remarks about curves bring to mind those of Helene and Wayland (see, for example, pp. 128–29, 154).

War Dance Song no. 20 (A and B)

JUDY: "Do you sometimes make up a new song by reworking old songs?"

LENORE: "Yeah, there's some. Most of the songs that people sing nowadays, they think they're new songs; but they're old ones, and they just change a verse or two or just change in between."

JUDY: "Could you give me an example of an old song, of the way it originally was and then the way you might change it?"

LENORE: "Let's see if I could get it. There's one that's changed. It goes:

[*Lenore sang War Dance song no. 20A*]. But then this verse at the end's changed. It's got like another part to it: [*Lenore sang War Dance song no. 20B*]. It's kind of changed right there. See, they just put in another verse or maybe jump to a higher note, and sometimes they bring it back down."[16]

JUDY: "Did you do that to the song or did somebody else?"

LENORE: "Somebody else did. Once in a while we do, but most of the time we just get it from somebody else."

Reworked versions of older songs have additional sections and other minor melodic changes. As a consequence there are slightly different and often more curves. In contrast the small omissions that may occur in performance often straighten and remove curves. These contrary forces shape the melodic contour, a central focus in Shoshone musical experience. Although the links between older and newer versions of songs are not necessarily lost, relatively small changes in melodic contour may cross a fine dividing line and establish the independent identity of a song. A renewed song may become just that, made new again.

Round Dance, Crow Hop, and Forty-nine Dance Songs

JUDY: "Do you like Round Dance songs as much as War Dance songs?"

LENORE: "Yeah, 'cause they're, they sound much prettier."

JUDY: "Can you guess how many Round Dance songs you might know?"

LENORE: "About maybe around seven is all. I'd have to get them off the tapes [for recall], like I usually do."

JUDY: "Do you try to learn several new Round Dance songs every year?"

LENORE: "Uh-huh."

JUDY: "Would the six Round Dance songs that you sang this afternoon cover the songs you learned and sang this past summer [of 1981]?"

LENORE: "Yeah, this is the group we picked up, except for that song the Parker Singers sang at Browning. That's a song from '78, and the second song I sang [is not a new song]."

JUDY: "So when you were asked to sing a Round Dance, you'd sing one of these?"

LENORE: "Yeah."

JUDY: "Are there other old favorites that you sing every year?"

16. Bracket 1 on the transcription illustrates a higher starting note, bracket 2, a lower cadential note. At bracket 3 the insertion of a new closing phrase concludes on f, the original cadential note of the section and song.

LENORE: "No."

JUDY: "How about from last year's [1980] Round Dance songs, would you like to sing any from that group."

LENORE: "No, I don't think so. I never really got to listen to any of last year's Round Dance songs because I didn't really record."

JUDY: "Do you think that next summer [1982] you'd be singing some of the Round Dance songs from this summer [which Lenore had recorded in 1981]?"

LENORE: "Probably."

JUDY: "For your own amusement, do you sometimes sing a Round Dance song when you're by yourself?"

LENORE: "Mostly War Dance songs, because that's what we mostly sing. The Round Dance, I can't really, you know, I could sometimes think of one of them—then I want to sing it, but you know, it's just that we don't have time to practice. Most of the time when we travel to powwows we don't really sing Round Dance. They usually pick the host drum to sing on that. Either that or they pick a drum group that's well known."

JUDY: "When you're here at your own powwow, do they ask you to sing a Round Dance?"

LENORE: "Every once in a while."

Chart 4 summarizes several of the points that Lenore makes about her Round Dance repertoire. The recordings in 1981 are especially important, since they were done specifically for this study and represent her Round Dance repertoire for that year—eight songs, which jibe with the number she estimates as average for any given year. Aware and proud of Shoshone traditions, Lenore borrowed a fourteen-inch hand drum for that occasion to accompany herself in the old way.[17] Ironically, of all five women only Lenore was too young to have actually seen and heard Round Dance songs performed with hand drums, or squaw drums as they were sometimes called. Before singing each song Lenore almost invariably listened to the song on tape (for a picture of the drum and of this recording session, see plate 29 following p. 266).

Although the sampling in chart 4 is not adequate to show the occasional Round Dance songs that overlap from year to year, the predominant pattern of new songs for each year is very much in evidence. The marginal existence of the Round Dance at the Shoshone powwow is clearly reflected in the 1978–80 recordings. For all three years I recorded the Big Mountain Singers

17. In 1981 Lenore wanted to buy a hand drum. "I never did find the right one I was looking for," she commented. "Some are too hard and too thin hide." By 1984 she found one to her liking and had bought it.

CHART 4
Round Dance Song Recordings of Lenore Shoyo
and the Big Mountain Singers

1977	1978	1979	1980	1981	1982	1983	1984
Private		None	None		None		
1							
2							
3							
4							
5							
6							
	Powwow						
	7**						
	Private						
	8						
				Private			
				9**			
				10****			
				11***			
				12			
				13			
				14			
						Museum	
						15	
						16**	
						17	
							Private
							18
Total 6	2	0	0	6	0	3	1

* Indicates the number of recorded performances.
The numbers in this chart are chronological and do not correspond to the song numbers
in the book.

throughout the Eastern Shoshone Indian Days and in 1979, for a community Halloween dance as well. In 1978 Lenore and her sisters sang nine War Dance songs and only one Round Dance song; in 1979, seventeen War Dance songs and no Round Dance songs; and in 1980 fifteen War Dance songs and no Round Dance songs. In addition to powwow recordings, I taped Lenore and her sisters at home in 1978. On that occasion they sang twelve War Dance and two Round Dance songs. The extent of Lenore's Round Dance repertoire in comparison with that of her War Dance songs and her much greater reliance on the tape recorder for recalling Round Dance songs indicate the infrequency of such dances at most of the powwows she and her sisters attend and the sporadic performing opportunities for the Big Mountain Singers when Round Dances occur.

JUDY: "Now all the Round Dance songs you've been singing are from different places. Do you ever sing or know some of the older Round Dance songs that might have come out of this reservation?"

LENORE: "The one that Charles Nipwater [well-known Shoshone singer] sings every Christmas [at the Shoshone holiday dances], I hear him sing it every year. I don't know where he picked up that song. That song's clear up in Canada now."

JUDY: "Do you think it's from here?"

LENORE: "I don't know. The first time I heard it was when Charles sang it. He sings it every New Year's with the rest of the Round Dance songs he's got. We usually refer to this song as Charles's song. I usually just say the one I first heard it [a song] from, you know, the drum group. And like if there's a song that they sing and I can't remember the name, well, if it was in '81, we'd say the song they sang in '81. That's the way we usually say it, you know, my sisters."

Round Dance Song no. 13

_ ya he ya ha we ha   he ai _ ya he_ ha   we ya_ hai _   ya _ hai _   yo

LENORE: "Charles does that one."

JUDY: "Is that the one he does New Year's Eve?"

LENORE: "No, that's a different one."

JUDY: "Do you like the songs that you know are older, do you tend to like them?"

LENORE: "Yeah, I think they sound pretty—some."

JUDY: "But you don't have a strong preference for the old?"

LENORE: "Well, I do. Because when you sing, when it's some of the old songs, whoever sings it, they got a different type of voice, lighter voice or heavier voice. It makes it sound different."

JUDY: "And you like that difference?"

LENORE: "Uh-huh." (Again we see focus on the variables of a performance, especially vocal timbre and quality, rather than the constants of the song itself.)

JUDY: "How about the song itself?"

LENORE: "Yeah. Like I've heard some of the old Round Dance songs that you sent us, like those tapes of the songs Logan Brown and those guys sing. I like those."

JUDY: "Now some of the old Round Dance songs used to have English words, too. Did you ever hear those?"

LENORE: "No. I've heard they did though."

Although Lenore knew of these songs, she could not sing them by herself for me. Four years before this conversation, however, she had assumed the more passive singing role as backup to her uncle; during that recording session he led off a group of older Round Dance songs, including an old favorite of many tribes, "One-Eyed Ford."[18] Singers of different ages—Lenore and her uncle—hold overlapping fields of songs. "One-Eyed Ford" is an example; a faint and early trace on the margin of Lenore's songprint, it is strongly central in her uncle's.

18. The origins of "One-Eyed Ford" go back at least forty years, at which time it had already been recorded (Powers 1986, personal communication).

Round Dance Song no. 14 ("One-Eyed Ford")

Singers: Ben, Lenore, Coleen, JoAnn, and Linda Shoyo

When Lenore and her sisters sang "One-Eyed Ford" with their uncle, they combined male and female singing roles similar to Helene's musical part when she sings at the drum with her brother. They repeated the opening solo call in unison with their uncle and then jumped up the octave to sing the lady's part.

JUDY: "In the past people tell me that the Round Dance used to be very popular here, before there were powwows, when you had your own Shoshone dances in the 1920s and '30s. Why do you think there aren't many Round Dances of an evening at your powwows now?"

LENORE: "Probably because nobody on this reservation really knows the Round Dance songs. Just the older people."

JUDY: "They didn't get passed on to the younger singers?"

LENORE: "Yeah, it's just like it's been held back."

JUDY: "When you were very young did more people do the Round Dance in couples?"

LENORE: "The way I used to see it they used to have couples all the time."

JUDY: "Would they ever have a man with a woman on each side?"

LENORE: "Yeah. They usually say a lady's choice. That's the reason why I think it's called *Waipë? Nïkëp* [Women's Dance]. When they say lady's choice, they usually mean that you can't refuse the lady if she asks you. Like if you would ask a man from this reservation to dance, he can't refuse you. Or if he refuses you he has to give you a dollar or a scarf."

JUDY: "But now it's just [danced mostly without partners] in a big circle."

LENORE: "Because it seems like they're too ashamed to be seen dancing with a guy no matter who it is. People think this way or that way about it. It's just only supposed to be a part of our doings."

JUDY: "But jealousy got in there and gossip."
LENORE: "Yeah."

In 1981 Lenore prefaced singing Round Dance song no. 15 with the following comment: "Here's an old one, 1978 or 1979, I can't remember when it came out. It was 1978 when I first heard it, anyway." According to this definition a powwow song is old after three or four years. Lenore learned Round Dance song no. 15 from her brother-in-law, a Canadian Cree singer who led off this song at a dance on the Wind River reservation. In solo performance Lenore sang it for me two times on the same occasion. After the first performance the following conversation took place:

JUDY: "You once told me that Cree Round Dance songs have something like 'la la la.' Did that [first performance of Round Dance song no. 15] have any of that in it?"

LENORE: "No, I just sang it straight, if you noticed. It's just like they [Crees] use every part of their vocal cords. I never seen anybody sing like that before. They got real pretty songs. I could sing it for you the way he [a Cree singer] sings it."

Round Dance Song no. 15

Note: Although the text setting of Round Dance song no. 15 is mostly syllabic, note that at brackets 1 and 2 the vocable on beat three carries over through beat one. This is yet another strategy for the vocal part to avoid emphasizing beat one of the three-beat grouping.

JUDY: "The only thing I could tell between the two ways [of singing the song], in this one I heard more accents in the melody."

LENORE: "And it makes it sound, the song sounds like it's got a lot of curves?"

JUDY: "Yeah, like coming out and in. You would get louder and come back. Is that the difference?"

LENORE: "Yeah, I guess that's really how it's supposed to be sang. You know, so that it will have a real nice tune to it."

JUDY: "When you're talking about curves here, you mean where it gets louder and softer real fast? Would you call those curves?"

LENORE: "Well I would."

JUDY: "Is that a more difficult style of singing?"

LENORE: "Yeah. Usually I just sing straight, you know. It's just like your tongue's just laying, just flips every once in a while but not all the time. But I noticed that when I watched the Crees, the Canadian Crees or the Rocky Boy people [Chippewa-Crees from Montana], when they sing they flick their tongue. You could see it when their mouth is open. It sounds like they're saying 'la' in their songs, like one of those Christmas carols—'fa la la la la.' But it's got 'la' in their songs and it really sounds good."

JUDY: "Was that [Round Dance song no. 15] a hard one to learn?"

LENORE: "Yeah, especially when you go 'we ha' when you bring it back, right back towards the end. It's just like you'd have to remember it goes back up. There's some just sing it straight."

At issue here is a small transition phrase (see ex. 9) between the end of the first section and the beginning of the second, similar to that which distinguished War Dance song no. 20B from 20A. Alternating two notes a minor third apart, this tiny new phrase adds curves to the song. Sensitive to the curves of a song, Lenore correctly observes that those who omit this tiny phrase "just sing it straight."

Example 9. Transition phrase from Round Dance song no. 15

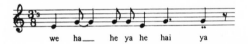

                we   ha___   he ya he   hai   ya

Today, Shoshones still usher in the New Year at 12:00 midnight with a Round Dance, a token nod to this dance's former important status. But during the powwow Round Dances are now few and far between. The reservation is not a source of new Round Dance songs, and younger singers do not know the older repertoire that Emily and Angie remember from their youth. In contrast the Round Dance remains immensely popular among the Canadian Crees and some of the Montana tribes close to the Canadian border, such as the Chippewa-Crees of Rocky Boy. Consequently they continue to maintain and generate a large stock of Round Dance songs. As Lenore notes: "The Canadian people just like to Round Dance, maybe every night, every weekend. They got really pretty songs. That's where I'd like to go, pick up some more Round Dance songs." Because there is a lack of Shoshone Round Dance songs, Lenore must look elsewhere for this genre. The Canadian Cree are a much admired and important source of such songs. Also, through her sister's marriage to a Cree, Lenore now has Cree relations. Thus, this particular song, Round Dance song no. 15, is part of her songprint, and Lenore wishes to add more of its kind: "Before my brother-in-law's brother, Daniel Fox, left [for Canada],

Plate 23. In the summer of 1979 Lenore (on the left) and Geraldine Perry (on the right) were attendants to the powwow queen Lanell Bianas. This photograph was taken at the Ft. Washakie arbor during the Eastern Shoshone Indian Days. Photograph by the author.

Plate 24. In the summer of 1980 Lenore was the powwow queen. In this photograph she leads the line of dancers, bringing them into the Ft. Washakie arbor for the Grand Entry. Photograph by the author.

Plate 25. This photograph, labeled "Group of Indian Women in Native Costume," was taken on July 4, 1938. The identification of the women in the picture (from left to right) is tentative in some cases: (?)Esther Trehero Tyler, Josie Washakie, Lily Norman Washington, (?)Deborah Kagevah Ute Trehero, and (?)Irene Bonatsie Tassitsie Barney. Photograph by Frank Fox. Courtesy of the U.S. Department of Interior, Bureau of Indian Affairs.

Plate 26. A 1983 lecture-demonstration at the Plains Indian Museum in Cody, Wyoming. Bernadine, Francine, and LaMelia Shoyo (left to right) dance to a Fancy War Dance song performance by the Big Mountain Singers. Courtesy of the Buffalo Bill Historical Center, Cody, Wyoming.

Plate 27. The Big Mountain Singers performed a Traditional War Dance song at the Plains Indian Museum at Cody, Wyoming, in 1983. LaMelia, who is dancing on the right in a buckskin dress, dances the Sioux way (see p. 238). The author is at the left. Courtesy of the Buffalo Bill Historical Center, Cody, Wyoming.

Plate 28. In a 1984 performance Lenore (center) is raising her drumstick high in preparation for a brief series of accents, while her sisters (Coleen on the left and Evalita on the right) continue with the straight, unaccented beat (see p. 252). Photograph by the author.

Plate 29. Lenore borrowed a hand drum to sing Round Dance songs for me in 1981. At home in her own trailerhouse, she sat next to her cassette recorder and listened through earphones to tapes of songs she then sang for me. The tape recorder sits on a bass drum with a rawhide head. Photograph by the author.

Plates 30A and B. The front and back of the hand drum Lenore used to sing Round Dance songs. The diameter of the drum is fourteen inches. Photograph by the author.

Plate 31. Lenore played in this Shinny game during the 1982 Eastern Shoshone Indian Days at Ft. Washakie, Wyoming. She is on the far right and rushing toward the ball. (For a description of Shinny, see pp. 52–53.) Photograph by the author.

he sang some songs and Round Dance songs on a tape. We're going up to Canada next week, and if he's up there I'm going to ask him for some more; but he's a hard guy to catch up to."

The Crees are not alone in their enthusiasm for the Round Dance. It has great popularity among tribes in Washington and Oregon. "When we went up to Pendleton, Oregon," Lenore remarks, "we thought they had their contests [for women] like ours—going around, or the traditional way. But then they had Round Dances. Then when they have time they still have Round Dances. Just nothing but Round Dances for women."

JUDY: "Is it the same step as you do here?"

LENORE: "Yeah, but they have different movements, like with their [eagle-feather] fan. They bring it up and bring it back down or do some motion."

In 1983, two years after making the above comments, Lenore observed and spoke to me about the spread of the Round Dance as a contest dance for women's Traditional Dance competitions beyond the Northwest Coast: "The Round Dance is coming out [to the powwows Lenore attends] into the Women's Traditional [contest]. They do a lot of that up in Washington. They had that for the senior citizen's contest this year [at Ft. Hall, Idaho]. As a matter of fact, me and A. and D. and I. [female members of the Snake River Singers, a Shoshone singing group from Ft. Hall] got to sing the Round Dance songs for the Senior [Ladies'] Dance.

"I know a pretty song. It's a Round Dance song we heard Ermine Treaty from Oregon, Washington—one of those places. They sang a real pretty Round Dance song. They were at Ft. Duchesne [Utah] when we recorded it."

The songs that Lenore hears and learns result from the coincidence of her own travels with that of other singers. Personal factors play a role in these occurrences. Because Lenore has Ute relatives, her family often chooses to attend the Ft. Duchesne powwow held on July Fourth. In this way she crossed paths with the Ermine Treaty 1885 Singers and Round Dance song no. 16. It was one of her favorites in 1981.

Round Dance Song no. 16

(3d and final verse)
♩. = *ca.* 76

ye___ he___ he_____ he yai___ ye___ de___ e ai___ ha

Hand drum

Lenore actually sang Round Dance song no. 16 twice in a row for me because she was very critical of the lack of dynamic shadings in her first performance. As this is not a Cree song, it is not a matter of a specific technique of tongue flicks as discussed in Round Dance song no. 15 but a part of Lenore's broader aesthetic for performance. If there were any doubt as to her use and definition of the term *curves* in relation to musical dynamics, her reiteration here clarifies it.

JUDY: "You said that you thought it seemed dead to you. You wanted to put more curves in. What did you mean by that?"

LENORE: "You know, when they started off, you know, the way the song's going it needs to go up more and come back down a little. Faster up back and forth. 'Cause it sounds like I'm just singing it straight. And it kind of sounds dead."

JUDY: "I don't know that I completely understand what you mean by curves or going up and down faster. Do you just mean something else?"

LENORE: "No, you know, going some parts louder than the other parts."

JUDY: "Oh, and that to you gives it more curves?"

LENORE: "Uh-huh."

Lenore perceives dynamic shadings in song performance as a contour, a parallel conceptualization to melodic contour. The topographical metaphor simply extends to another musical element. There is an interesting second metaphor at work here as well, one that equates straight with dead and, by implication, curves with living.

Round Dance Song no. 17

Singers: Lenore, Lottie, Coleen, JoAnn, Maxine, and Evalita Shoyo

Lenore, her sisters, and mother sang Round Dance song no. 17 in 1983 as part of our joint lecture-demonstration at the Plains Indian Museum, in Cody, Wyoming. It was the first evening program for a weekend conference on the Plains Indian woman. It seemed appropriate to end the evening and begin the conference with a Women's Dance song — Round Dance song no. 17. The audience made a large circle around the perimeter of the auditorium, and everyone danced. Like Round Dance song no. 15, Round Dance song no. 17 is a Cree song; Lenore learned it from the Chinicky Lake Singers, who sang at the 1983 Ft. Duchesne powwow.

A review of the Round Dance songs I have recorded of Lenore provides a sampler of where she gathers songs — Ft. Duchesne, Utah (Ute), Ft. Hall, Idaho (Shoshone-Bannock), Ft. Belknap, Montana (Gros Ventre, Assiniboine), Lame Deer, Montana (Northern Cheyenne), Bismarck, North Dakota (Sioux), Rocky Boy, Montana (Chippewa-Cree) — and from whom — Chinicky Lake Singers (Cree), Parker Singers (Cree), Russell Standing Rock (Cree), Ermine Treaty 1885 (? Oregon tribe), Daniel Fox (Cree), Charles Nipwater (Shoshone), Clifford Big Head (Northern Cheyenne).

Although the source of new Round Dance songs, as with new War Dance songs, is often the result of reviving old songs, this is not the only way.

JUDY: "Does anybody make up brand new songs that aren't made up from parts of old songs?"

LENORE: "Well, this guy we know, Clifford Big Head, he's a Cheyenne from Montana, he's got a lot of songs that he don't make up from old songs."

JUDY: Is that kind of unusual?"

LENORE: "No."

Round Dance song no. 8 on chart 4 was composed by Clifford Big Head, a personal friend of the family. However, as a general rule, a new song enters the stream of powwow songs without identifying tags. In the end very few people will ever know its source. Lenore simply identifies a song by the first group she heard sing it, where, and when. Her knowledge of the composer of a particular Round Dance song is an exception to the general rule. Well-known singing groups who compete in drum contests and make commercial tapes with their own songs are another exception. (See p. 235 for Lenore's comments.)

Lenore learned Round Dance song no. 18 from her mother, who grew up on the U & O Uintah reservation in Utah; Lenore's mother's mother

Round Dance Song no. 18

Singers: Lenore, Coleen, JoAnn, and Linda Shoyo

lived on the Southern Ute reservation in Colorado. Round Dance song no. 18, passed on from grandmother to mother to Lenore, is the only Southern Ute Round Dance song from Colorado that I have recorded. This alone is not significant, but that it is a Southern Plains song is. As one elderly Shoshone singer expressed it, there's a "Mason-Dixon line" that cuts across the Plains. The Northern Plains and Southern Plains each have their own distinctive musical styles and song repertoires. The Utes, who are located in Utah and Colorado, sit at the border between the north and south and have contact with both areas. Lenore states that "when the Utes sing Round Dance songs, they get their Round Dance songs from down towards Oklahoma way [i.e., the Southern Plains]. And it's just straight, you know, not like the Canada and Montana people who flick their tongue." The genre is the same; the repertoires and singing styles differ. Shoshones and other tribes on the Northern Plains look north to Montana and Canada for Round Dance songs. The Utes look south to Oklahoma for theirs. These factors, together with Lenore's personal history, account for Round Dance song no. 18, a Southern Plains song, being a part of her songprint.

JUDY: "Do you sing both kinds of Round Dance songs, the Cree and Oklahoma type?"

LENORE: "I haven't heard any from down towards Oklahoma this year. It's mostly just like the Forty-nines they have. The Forty-nine songs come from Oklahoma."

JUDY: "Do you ever sing any of those songs or listen to them?"

LENORE: "I know one or two. I listen to them, but I don't really care to learn them. Because when they have a Forty-nine [Dance], they only have the men singing them. The women sing right along, but it's just something for people to do after the dance [powwow] is through."

Forty-nine Dance Song no. 2

he ai ya he ya   he ai ya he hai__ ya   he ya ha we   ya he__

__ ya he   ya__   Oh my black-jack Dai - sy   wi ai ya   he

ya,   she got mad at   me__ be - cause I   said hel - lo   to my old - tim - er.

But that's just O   K __   with me   o ho we ya   he__   ya he   ya o

LENORE: "It's been a long time since I learned it. It's one of the old ones. I haven't really been to any Forty-nines to listen to new songs. I don't think there's really any new ones though."

JUDY: "I heard that sometimes Arapahoe [on the Wind River reservation] sometimes have a Forty-nine Dance after Sun Dance."

LENORE: "Yeah, after Sun Dance, after a dance, they usually have them across the river. Shoshones usually go down to the Arapahoe to go Fortynine. I don't really go to the Forty-nines around here. Just when I travel out of state, after dances, then we go to the Forty-nine for a while and then we go back to camp."

JUDY: "Where is it that you travel that . . ."

LENORE: "They have Forty-nines? Montana, mostly. Only once we went to Oklahoma. They have Forty-nine clear through to morning, daybreak. They got really pretty songs."

JUDY: "How are Forty-nine songs different from Round Dance songs?"

LENORE: "They got the words. They go either in English or the language of whoever's singing it. The beat's faster, way faster. Everybody usually does the slow step to it [see p. 77], 'cause they're holding onto each other."

JUDY: "With couples, or just in a circle?"

LENORE: "Well, it really doesn't matter."

JUDY: "Do the singers dance too?"

LENORE: "Sometimes they go around, sometimes they're just standing up. Some use a [single-headed] hand drum, some got the Forty-nine drum, those [two-headed] rawhide drums. It's about this size [*fourteen inches diameter*] or a little bigger.

Crow Hop Song no. 1

Singers: Lenore, Coleen, JoAnn, Maxine, and Evalito Shoyo

The Big Mountain Singers must learn songs to accompany all the types of dances called for at the powwow. Like dress fashions, these may be new or old; in either case they come into vogue. Powwow singers must stay current with these fashions. Thus, Crow Hop song no. 1 is part of Lenore's songprint.

In search of the new (here the Crow Hop Dance), powwow singers and dancers borrow and renew older traditions. There is irony in Fryett's 1971 interview with Crow singer Warren Bear Cloud, who documents what seemed at the time to be the irreversible decline of this old War Dance song genre: "This Crow Hop Dance songs, that's old time songs. The other tribes, they don't sing them songs. The Crows just use them. That's why they're called Crow Hop songs. . . . They come from Crow Indians . . . since eighteen something, around there. Old time songs. . . . They don't use it much here [on the Crow reservation anymore]" (Fryett 1977:180, 181). That which was old and passing is now current and "in." I began to notice the performance of the Crow Hop Dance at the 1982 Shoshone Crowheart powwow. In 1983 I asked Lenore whether the Crow Hop was going around at the different powwows, to which she replied: "Yeah, usually for the Women's Traditional and the Men's, they usually ask for it. Well, sometimes Fancy Dancers, they ask for it, too. This past year I noticed that at Ft.

Duchesne, on the Fourth of July powwow, they had the Crow Hop song for everybody [to dance] that went into Grand Entry."

The Big Mountain Singers performed this song in 1983 as part of our joint lecture-demonstration at the Plains Indian Museum. From a musical standpoint Crow Hop song no. 1 is indistinguishable from Round Dance songs.[19] The dance, however, is performed neither in a circle nor with partners. Lenore's three nieces danced for this performance. They moved around individually, shifting their body weight from one foot to the other every three beats. The foot no longer supporting the body remained poised on the toes with the knee bent. The supporting foot was flat on the ground with the knee straight. Shifting from foot to foot in this manner created a hopping motion. The long bone necklaces that the girls wore added a light after-beat clink to their hop-dance movement. (See plate 26 following p. 266.)

Handgame Songs

JUDY: "Did you want to sing any Handgame songs?"

LENORE: "No. I don't really know those until, unless a person I'm playing that Handgame with is singing those songs and I just sing right along with them. I haven't played much this year. I don't really pay too much attention to it. Just when I feel like I want to have something to do when they're having Handgame around here. Then I go play Handgame."

(Lenore listened to some Handgame songs on a tape.)

JUDY: "Did you find a Handgame song that you wanted to sing?"

LENORE: "I can't really know it that good, but I'll try if you want me to."

Handgame song no. 14 is one of the two Handgame songs Lenore sang for me.

Handgame Song no. 14

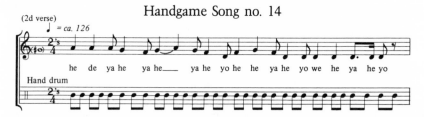

(2d verse)

♩ = ca. 126

he de ya he ya he____ ya he yo he he ya he yo we he ya he yo

Hand drum

19. Fryett included in his dissertation a transcription of Warren Bear Cloud's 1971 performance of a Crow Hop song. As preface to his transcription, he comments, "The Crow Hop Dance is a very fast war dance." The metronome marking for this performance is ♩ = 100. Fryett notates the melody in 2/4 time, and the drum accompaniment as follows: (Fryett 1977:190, 191).

Note: The bracketed connecting phrase between repetitions moves the melodic contour smoothly from lowest to highest note, creating a melodic circle well suited for the many repetitions that accompany the game.

LENORE: "I heard these down at Ft. Hall. I taped just about four of them."

JUDY: "Do you use your throat differently for the Handgame songs?"

LENORE: "Yeah, I guess it'd be much heavier, but I can't really, I don't really sing it that much."

JUDY: "Do you like the Handgame songs?"

LENORE: "I do, but then I just really don't know how to sing it that good. I just listen to them once in a while. I don't have no tapes of 'em. The only time I hear them is when we go to, if they have a Handgame tournament where we went to, you know."

Shoshone Ceremonial Songs

JUDY: "What about the Giveaway [*Nahĩnwe Nĩkĕp*, "Donating" or "Collecting Dance"]? What do you think is the meaning of giving away all those things when you're the powwow queen?"

LENORE: "That's what it's usually held for: the Eastern Shoshone Indian Days is the main time for the princess or the queen or attendants to have a Giveaway. Besides that, other people have a Giveaway if they lost a loved one. Or if somebody's on the Shoshone Entertainment Committee and they want to have a Giveaway [in honor of his or her participation], or on behalf of their daughter if she's a rodeo princess, or somebody that was maybe given an Indian name, if they want to, you know, like just give a few things away to people."

JUDY: "Is it like blessing those other people, or asking for a blessing?"

LENORE: "Well, I guess it would be asking for a blessing for everybody that's there, 'cause they usually have someone pray before. If they want to, that is. When somebody prays it's for everybody, not only one person. Like next year we'll be having LaMelia's [Lenore's niece] Giveaway. She's Crowheart Princess right now. After she gets through reigning over the year, then she'll pass it on to next year's princess. We'll have a Giveaway at Crowheart. I think Mom's friends are coming down from Montana [for it]."

JUDY: "How long in advance does the family have to start gathering things?"

LENORE: "Whenever they want to start. Like we could start right now."

JUDY: "It could take almost a year?"

LENORE: "Uh-huh, if we want to have a big Giveaway. But, you know, when you care for a person, you want something to turn out just right for them. So we just go ahead and start early. So we're going to start this month."

JUDY: "For a Giveaway you could spend hundreds of dollars?"

LENORE: "Uh-huh. Or you could make things yourself. Or if you want to help a person out because she's your best friend or you've known that person for a long time, you could help them out with their Giveaway by donating some material [fabric] or whatever you think. Besides giving material and things to people, you could also have like a little feast. Food for people to go through the line, serve them on behalf of whom you're having it for."

Lenore has had several Giveaways in her honor when she has been powwow queen or attendant. On those occasions she danced at the front of a long line of relatives and friends. All five women in this book recognize and in some sense "know" the Giveaway song. Lenore is the only one who has sung it for me. "I learned it from my dad when he sings at the drum," Lenore recalls. "I remember as a girl we used to stay at the old house where I was raised. I remember when they were singing. There's my dad, Uncle Roy, Uncle Ben, my brother Frank, and my brother Chuck. They used to practice those songs. They used to have William Wadda [Shoshone singer who knew the ceremonial songs] come over to the house, and they practiced songs with him. I think that's where he [Lenore's father] learned it from."

I have recorded Lenore singing the Giveaway song three times: twice with her sister in 1977 and once by herself in 1981. At that time I asked, "Now that one you know right off the bat. You don't have to listen to a tape. How is it that you know that one so well?" Lenore replied: "I think it's because, you know, 'round wintertime when we're having our Christmas dances, they always have that Chokecherry Dance or Giveaway song, things like that. I remember it because every time I'm at a powwow, like Shoshone Indian Days, Charles Nipwater's always singing it for the people. When I think about somebody having a Giveaway, it just comes right into my mind. Sometimes when they ask us to sing an Honor song, it always pops into my head. But then they want an Honor song [and not the Giveaway song].

We never use the Giveaway song for anything [else]. Just for our own [Shoshone] people, 'cause they got that certain dance that goes with it." (Accented beats in the second section of the Giveaway song cue dancers to turn and dance momentarily toward the center of the dancing area. Some dancers also raise their arms in front of themselves at this point. Otherwise, the Giveaway Dance is the same as the light feint, full step pattern used in the Traditional War Dance [see p. 79].)

Traditionally, men sing and drum the Giveaway song for a Giveaway Dance. Or so it was until 1978.

JUDY: "The Giveaway song is still only for men around the drum. It wouldn't be accepted if you sang it, would it?"

LENORE: "Well, we sang it last Christmas. Last year we sang it and the Chokecherry song."

JUDY: "That was pretty well accepted?"

LENORE: "Uh-huh, it was."

JUDY: "Did that surprise people?"

LENORE: "I guess so, because they think that we don't know our traditional ways, but we do." (However, as we shall see in a moment, there was not unanimous approval.)

JUDY: "What about the Chokecherry ceremony?"

LENORE: "They usually have it around towards Christmas and they boil some chokecherries and they dance for it. It's just like you would say pray for it, for when the people are going to eat it and it's just served out.

"Because when they dance [four or more costumed male dancers who perform the Chokecherry Dance], they got the—whatever they're carrying—[eagle-feather] fans. They go down like, then bring it back up. That's just like when you would respect the eagle, the feathers that we use. They say the eagle watches over us and things like that. Then they use that, and the feathers—nobody plays with them."

JUDY: "Now the Chokecherry song, that's a song that you'd recognize, but you don't really sing?"

LENORE: "No, they usually have the men sing that. The only [ceremonial] song we get to sing once in a while, if we're called upon, is the Giveaway song. Only once, I think, we were asked to sing the Gravy [Chokecherry] song.[20] Our Uncle Ben and I think when my Uncle Roy was still alive and two other younger ones danced that."

20. The Shoshone name for the Chokecherry Dance is actually *Gotsap Nïkĕp*, "Gravy Dance." Although Shoshones make a fruit gravy, or sauce, from a variety of berries, the Gravy Dance is always performed with a pot of chokecherry gravy. Most Shoshones refer to the dance in English as the Chokecherry Dance, but some will occasionally use the literal translation and call it Gravy Dance.

JUDY: "Then you girls sang that?"

LENORE: "Yeah. I can't even remember it. It's been a long time since then. I have to listen to that one [on tape]. I can't get that one [from memory]. What I'd like to do is, you know, ask my uncle to give me those songs [on tape]. That way, any time we're called upon, we'll just know those songs."

JUDY: "Did anybody make [negative] comments that you were women singing those [ceremonial] songs?"

LENORE: "Well, at first they did, but then they didn't have no other drum group. See, when we have any kind of our [Shoshone] dances going on, sometimes we end up with just one drum group, with Charles's drum group."

If, for some reason, this drum group is not able to sing, there is a vacuum. Apparently this happened, and the Big Mountain Singers helped out by singing the song at the drum. Although their singing of a ceremonial song raised some eyebrows, the ultimate result of their action could only be commended. Their performance of the Chokecherry song set the dance and ceremony in motion, just as their performance of the Giveaway song set that dance and ceremony in motion. Innovation made possible the performance of traditional dance and ceremony. This beautifully illustrates Sahlins's observation: "Every practical change is also a cultural reproduction . . . culture functions as a *synthesis* of stability and change, past and present, diachrony and synchrony" (Sahlins 1985:144).

JUDY: "Would you recognize the War Bonnet songs if you heard them?"

LENORE: "No, I was too young to even know what that War Bonnet song was. Unless they were having the War Bonnet Dance, then I would know that was [the War Bonnet songs]. But they never sing it unless they're going to have that. That's supposed to be done once a year every Christmas. But they haven't done it for quite a while."

JUDY: "Have older people taught you the meaning of that?"

LENORE: "I guess nowadays older people don't really care to talk to the younger people about it because they don't listen. They're too busy out in town or someplace else. And even if they were told about that War Bonnet, they wouldn't know how to go about it. They started to have young ones help them do that War Bonnet Dance, but then after a while it just quit all of a sudden. We never had it for I don't know how many years."

JUDY: "Did you ever sing with the women when they used to perform it?"

LENORE: "No, I was too young yet to understand what was going on at that time. 'Cause by the time I got of age to start understanding my traditional ways and respecting, you know, it just seems like they never did have it. Just my [older] sister danced with them when they wore the war bonnets. That was only once I think. That was the last time they had it."

We see a break here between Lenore and the other women in the book. Emily, Angie, Alberta, and Helene have all seen the War Bonnet Dance many times. In addition to recognizing the songs, Angie, Alberta, and Helene have sung in War Bonnet performances. In contrast Lenore was only a teenager when the last War Bonnet Dance was performed in the mid-1970s. Her memory of it is tenuous and fades with the passage of time. Such is also the fate of the *Chichuga,* Pointing Stick or Forked Stick Dance, which was last performed in 1968 when Lenore was only nine years old.

Non-Indian Music

JUDY: "Do you ever sing any of the white pop songs, the non-Indian stuff?"

LENORE: "I just listen to them and sing right along with that, sing along with the tape if I have 'em. I don't really know it without the tape."

JUDY: "So you wouldn't sing that by yourself?"

LENORE: "No, I don't think I would. I wouldn't know it by myself."

For this reason I have no recording of Lenore singing non-Indian songs. They are not an active part of her songprint.

Nevertheless, Lenore keeps current and knows all the latest singers and songs. This came out in a humorous way during our joint lecture-demonstration in 1983. On that occasion I talked about many aspects of Lenore's musical experience, including her enjoyment of non-Indian music. Using information she had given me in 1979, I listed some of her favorite singers: Waylon Jennings, Fleetwood Mac, and Jefferson Starship. Afterward Lenore came up and told me that I had made a mistake during the presentation. She was quite embarrassed by such a passé list of pop singers and made sure that I wrote down then and there her 1983 favorites: Men at Work, Don Henley, David Bowie, and Rod Stewart. Smiling, I wondered how long the new list would last.

Lenore's Musical Roles

Lenore has four musical roles on the reservation today. First and foremost she is a singer. For religious ceremonies—Sun Dance and Native American Church—she adheres to tradition, but as a powwow singer she is part of a pioneer generation that has expanded female participation by moving into

Songprint 5: Lenore Shoyo

Sample Size: 93

Naraya	0
Sun Dance	5
Peyote	♩
Round Dance	18
Forty-nine	2
Crow Hop	1
Honor	1
Flag	1
War Dance	59
Handgame	5
Giveaway	1
Chokecherry	♩
War Bonnet	0
Lullaby	0
Euro-American	♩

(only with tape)

Key: 0 does not know, does not sing

♩ sings, but not represented in sample

male musical roles. Helene's performance at the drum and her female-male singing part began the process, and Lenore and her sisters completed it, creating a female counterpart to the male drum group. On the one hand it was revolutionary to have a female drum group; on the other it was in the service of Indian music and asserted Indian identity. Receiving strong support from her family, a respected traditional family, Lenore and her sisters added a much-needed drum group to the community. These were important factors in their acceptance among the Shoshones on the reservation.

Shoshone ceremonial music is another matter. The fast rate of change, exchange, adaptation, and borrowing that are part of the powwow scene are out of place in the performance of traditional Shoshone ceremonies. It is significant, however, that Lenore and her sisters have sung the Giveaway and Chokecherry songs and that Lenore was asked to compose an Honor song. Whether these are to remain exceptions or become the beginning of new traditions in the performance of ceremonial music remains to be seen.

Lenore is a dancer, both of the Fancy Shawl and Traditional Dance. She has seen style changes, but the major innovation for women to dance to War Dance songs occurred before her time. In this area Helene's generation and that of Lenore's older sister were the experimenters, dancing in buckskin dresses to War Dance songs and even dressing in male costume and dancing the male dances. Female adaptations or versions of the Fancy and Traditional War Dances evolved from these early experiments and were already in place when Lenore started dancing.

Lenore is a teacher. Assuming Chuck's role, she has taught her sisters to sing at the drum with her. Now she teaches her nieces and nephews, the next generation of Shoyos. "I'd like to encourage younger kids to learn how to sing," Lenore states, "because that way it'd make our Shoshone dance more—more people might come out and dance because their sons or their daughters are singing. We're really encouraging our nieces and our nephews to sing. That way maybe one of these days they're going to end up maybe [our family], we'll have two drum groups, like how many years from now."

Lenore, a lead singer, is teaching both her nieces as well as her nephews to be lead singers at the drum. Thus, as a female role model she represents a new possibility for Shoshone girls on the Wind River reservation.

Singer, dancer, teacher, and, last but not least, role model—these are Lenore's four musical roles.

Conclusions

We can now layer the five songprints one on top of the other and create an archaeological slice of Shoshone music making in this century. The cumulative songprint (see pp. 288–89) will be a central reference for my historical conclusions about song genres and the participation and role of Shoshone women in music.

Let us consider genres Shoshones sing, as they appear in the cumulative songprint. The precipitous decline in *Naraya* songs and the appearance of Peyote songs (although unrepresented in the sampling itself) are, in part, an expression of the antithetical relationship between the two religions. For this and other reasons the *Naraya* religion did not survive. Likewise, there is a positive correlation between the decline of the Women's Dance or Round Dance and the rise of the War Dance. Compare Emily's sixteen Round Dance and two War Dance songs with Helene's six Round Dance and thirty-seven War Dance songs or Lenore's eighteen Round Dance and fifty-nine War Dance songs. Due to several factors within the contemporary powwow, most notably contests and large cash prizes, War Dancing is now the principal activity. In fact, powwow song is now commonly used as synonym for War Dance song.

Unlike the genres mentioned in the previous paragraph, there is no compelling pattern to Handgame songs in the cumulative songprint. Rather, it is as much a matter of personal taste as it is the vagaries of communal popularity. Emily does not care for the game; Angie does, and she remembers a former popularity of the game and even games played exclusively by women. Helene and Alberta also like Handgame, whereas Lenore is only an occasional player. Gaming and gambling are popular on the reservation; Shoshones play bingo and Squaw game, a card game, every week. Most people feel that, for whatever reasons, Handgame has been on the wane in recent years.

For ceremonial songs in the cumulative songprint, the predominating status quo is only disturbed at two points. First, the performance of the

Cumulative Songprint of Five Shoshone Women

	Sample Size	Naraya	Sun Dance	Peyote	Round Dance	Forty-nine	Crow Hop
Lenore b. 1959	93	0	5 ♪⊙ Sunrise Song ♩ Flag Song ♩ Prayer Song	♪⊙	18	2	1
Helene b. 1938	80	1	5 ♩ Sunrise Song ♩ Flag Song ♪⊙ Prayer Song	♪⊙	6 (recognizes Goodnight Sweetheart song)	♪⊙	0
Alberta b. 1929	14	0	14 ♪⊙ Sunrise Song ♪⊙ Flag Song ♪⊙ Prayer Song	♪⊙	♪⊙ sings only with tape	0	0
Angelina b. 1921	32	7	8 ♪⊙ Sunrise Song ♪⊙ Flag Song ♩ Prayer Song	♪⊙	6 ♩ Goodnight Sweetheart song, p. 71	1	0
Emily b. 1911	213	147	48 ♩ Sunrise Song ♩ Flag Song ♪⊙ Prayer Song	0	16 ♩ Goodnight Sweetheart song, p. 39	0	0

Key: 0 does not know, does not sing
⊘ knows but does not sing
♪⊙ knows, unrepresented in sample
♩ represented in sample

Honor	Flag	War Dance	Hand-game	Give-away	Choke-cherry	War Bonnet	Lul-laby	Euro-American
1	1	59	5	♩	♪	0	0	♪ sings only with tape
0	1	37	24	♪	♪	♩ (no. 3)	1	4
0	0	♪ sings only with tape	♪ sings only with team	♪	♪	♪	♪	0
0	0	3	5	♪	♪	♪	1	1
0	0	2	0	♪	♪	♪	0	0

Giveaway song by a female drum group is new. And second, because there have not been performances of the War Bonnet Dance since the mid-1970s, Lenore does not know these songs.

The genre that enjoys the greatest stability and constancy for all five songprints is the Sun Dance. It has the greatest number of shared songs between the five songprints. All five women know the Sunrise Ceremony Song, the Sun Dance Flag Song, and the Prayer Song. I have taped Emily and Helene singing the Sunrise Ceremony Song; Emily, Helene, and Lenore singing the Sun Dance Flag Song; and Angie and Lenore singing the Prayer Song. All the women would recognize the special four Morning Prayer songs performed by the Sun Dance Chiefs (without drum and without participation by the regular Sun Dance singers). In the past both Emily and Angie joined with others to sing the Fourth Morning Prayer song, which accompanied the ceremonial raising of the Sun Dance Lodge center pole. In my sampling I have Emily singing this song.

There are also crossovers between the five songprints for Sun Dance songs with no special identification. Of these Emily and Angie sang one song in common, Alberta and Angie one song, and Alberta and Helene two songs. But this sharing is but the tip of the iceberg. The Sun Dance repertoire is very large, and my sampling is not adequate to justly represent the extent of the repertoire shared by all five women. My own Sun Dance experience is useful here; I have attended the Sun Dance from 1977 to 1982 and have sung with the women since 1978. During that period I recognized thirty-seven of the eighty different Sun Dance songs recorded by the women (the largest number of my recorded songs not performed during that period are from Emily's repertoire; only nine of her forty-eight Sun Dance songs were performed). These thirty-seven Sun Dance songs could serve as a baseline estimate of Sun Dance songs shared in the cumulative songprint.

Other shared songs between the songprints are:

Naraya
    5 songs   Emily and Angie
Round Dance
    Goodnight Sweetheart   Emily and Angie
    song (pp. 39, 71)   (Helene recognized but
                                      could not sing it)
    1 song   Angie and Lenore (Lenore's
                                      uncle was lead singer for
                                      this performance)

War Dance
    4 songs   Helene and Lenore (this
                                      includes Fancy War Dance
                                      song excerpted on p. 79)

Handgame
    1 song   Helene and Lenore

The cumulative songprint reflects many cultural aspects that influence the song genres Shoshones sing. It also demonstrates the reality of strong musical involvement by twentieth-century Shoshone women, both in private and public:

1. Public singing of all songs sung by the Shoshone community, with the exception of some ceremonial songs.
2. Private singing of specifically male parts of several genres, e.g., Sun Dance songs.
3. Participation as drummers, indeed as the entire drum group.
4. Public participation in all dance genres with the exception of Sun Dance and some ceremonial dances.
5. The receiving of new songs in dreams or visions and the conscious composition of new songs.

From a historical viewpoint a clear line of differentiation traditionally separates the musical roles of Shoshone men and women. Men begin a song, first with their drumming, then by the lead singer's opening solo call and the repeated response by the rest of the male singers around the drum. Finally, women enter and sing an octave above the men. The presence or absence of pulsation in male and female vocal styles, respectively, creates another point of musical separation between Shoshone men and women. Similarly, dancing roles in the past were distinct: men did the War Dance, and women did the Women's (Round) Dance. Women danced in a circle with other women or picked a male partner; in contrast each male War Dancer danced alone. Musical differentiation underscored the separation of these dances. The underlying rhythmic organization for Women's Dance songs and the use of hand drums for accompaniment clearly set apart Women's Dance songs from War Dance songs. The different male-female roles complemented one another. The Women's Dance complemented the War Dance. In singing, Sun Dance songs offer the most striking example of this complementary relationship: males perform beginnings—drumbeat, solo lead part, group response; women perform the final ending, singing by themselves with no drum or male singers. Men punctuate the women's ending with a brief flurry of unmeasured and unsynchronized drumbeats.

In recent times the participation by women, especially young women, has increased. We see this within the ceremonial context of the War Bonnet Dance with the selection of young women to perform the third War Bonnet Dance. For the powwow we have chronicled the growing number of younger queens, the growing importance of the position itself, and the new trend of public name giving for girls. In music the differentiation based on gender discussed earlier has eroded. As a consequence women have increased their potential musical roles by moving into men's roles. Women dance the Traditional and Fancy Shawl Dance, female adaptations of the male Traditional and Fancy War Dance. They may assume any and all instrumental and singing roles around the powwow drum. Even the ceremonial Giveaway song has been affected by this change.

Sahlins states that "by encompassing the existentially unique in the conceptually familiar, the people embed their present in the past" (Sahlins 1985:146). Herein lies the nub of Shoshone perception and acceptance of changes for women in the twentieth-century musical scene. Changes in the present are but new expressions of traditional Shoshone values of the past. For example, supporting one's family is a cardinal value. Whenever Angie, Helene, and Lenore have departed from the musical norm for women, it has been to support family members: Angie sang with her father; Helene and Lenore sang and drummed with father and brothers. The circle of support moved from the women to their families, who, in turn, stood behind the women and their musical participation, both traditional and nontraditional. In this regard male support is noteworthy. In the lives of the women we have seen the importance of male role models (Chuck for Lenore), male support for exceptional instances of female musical roles (Angie's father introducing to the community the Sun Dance Prayer Song received by her mother), and male support for change in female roles (Helene's father making her a male War Dance bustle).

Each of the five women comes from an established, well-known, and respected family within the Shoshone community. Both from a biological and sociological viewpoint, this is another aspect of a present embedded in the past. Change originated at the center, not the margin of Shoshone society.

If support of one's family is a cardinal value, then its corollary is support for the Shoshone community. The musical participation by all the women has been in the service of Indian music and every communal occasion — social, religious, ceremonial — for which music plays a vital role. All five women, indeed most Shoshones, equate Indian music with Indian culture and identity. The singer — male or female — is felt to support an ever-broader series of identifications: family, Shoshone community, and Native America.

The obverse to the present being embedded in the past is also true: the past is embedded in the present. We see this in the substantial consensus by all five women about such matters as musical perception, process, judgment of song and performance, and ways of conceptualizing and talking about music. *Nüwë dïnigwëp,* "Indian songs," is the closest Shoshone translation for music; singing defines Shoshone musical experience. Therefore, it is not surprising that in their perception of music, the women are extremely sensitive to aspects of vocal performance such as voice quality, individual timbre, and where a song is pitched. These variables color song performance, imparting a sense of newness to different performances of the same song.

Old songs are prized; within the context of the Sun Dance, they have more power. However, within the context of the powwow, new songs are sought and prized. Complicating matters still further, new songs are often made out of old songs, that is, old songs pieced together or with new added parts. There is ambiguity. Is a song old or new? It depends on the age of the listener and his or her experience.

Relevant here is Shoshone sensitivity to the song itself and to different degrees of variation. Within very narrow limits variation enlivens song repetitions. At another level still small differences (but greater than those in song repetition) can establish a new song and identity. This coupled with compositional techniques just mentioned create a large number of songs, many of which are very similar. At one time or another all five women have commented on the similarity of many songs of the same genre and about the difficulties this causes for song recall.

Singing is a social process. The five women describe learning songs at the drum, at the powwow, at the Sun Dance, or at the *Naraya.* A song becomes associated with a person, with who sang it, when, and where. This becomes a song tag and helps in identifying and recalling a song. Tapes extend and complement this process.

Judgment on songs and song performances depends upon their successful function within a given context. A War Dance song or performance that arouses many dancers to dance is considered good. The same is true of a Sun Dance song or song performance. A Handgame song performance that plays its part in the successful hiding of the unmarked bones is, by definition, good.

Cooperative support, an ideal value in many realms, shapes the musical scene and its performers, the drum group. Singers help out and support, hence Lenore's comment that she is "just singing to help out" or Angie's that "I never back off when my dad is singing, 'cause we always got to support him." This is valued. On the other side of the coin, undue attention to or the spotlighting of an individual singer is frowned upon and criticized.

The women talk about songs in visual-linear terms, as if they were line drawings or landscapes. Songs have curves and dips and drop-downs. They can be straightened, smoothed out, made more curvy, and zigzagged.

"Responding to the shifting conditions of its existence . . . the cultural order reproduces itself in and as change" (Sahlins 1985:xii). The songprints and musical experience of Emily, Angie, Alberta, Helene, and Lenore document a particular sequence of Shoshone reproductions. Within the constraints of culture, age, and personality, each woman has evolved her own synthesis of stability and change, past and present. Each individual musical history has shaped and been shaped by Shoshone musical life in the daily unfolding of its history. Emily, Angie, Alberta, Helene, and Lenore make up that history. Not that they are a definitive sequence of Shoshone reproductions; rather they are one set of variations of a theme never overtly stated but that nevertheless orders the music of a particular time in a particular place.

Appendix

Shoshone Description of the Sun Dance

SHOSHONE INDIAN RELIGION
SUN DANCE
DA-GOO-WIN-NET
LYNN ST. CLAIR
PREPARED BY
HERMAN ST. CLAIR

A man was riding alone in the prairie long long ago. As he rode by a white buffalo skull he heard singing. He stopped his horse and listened, but he heard nothing. Turning his horse around he retraced his horse's tracks. Very slowly he rode, until he heard singing again, he stopped his horse and got off. The singing was coming from the white buffalo skull. He got down on his knees and looked into the buffalo skull, thru the empty eye sockets. There, inside the skull, Indians were dancing the Sun Dance. Now this Indian was told all about the Dance of Thirst and fasting. He was told all about the Sun Dance.

He was told how he must see a vision and telling him all the sacred rituals or ceremonies of the Sun Dance. How he must go without food and water for three days and nights, sometimes it was four days and four nights. The Sun Dance has been handed down from generation to generation or from father to son by lip to ear. It is like a big church for all of the Indians. All can come watch and take part. This was not so, long ago. For those taking part in the Sun Dance had many things to do, which seemed cruel today.

American Indian News 1, issue 1:5 (Aug. 3, 1977)

One of the things they did was tie a buckskin thong to the middle pole and the other end to a slit in the chest. This was to prove your strength, endurance, in the Sun Dance. If you had your skin torn, it was a sign, that

295

you had failed to meet the wishes of the Great Spirit. This was outlawed and done away with when the white man came into this part of the country.

The Sun Dance is a prayer dance to the Great Spirit, in it we try to keep alive our prayers and belief in God, who is also the "Great Spirit", "NAW, NAW, SOO-WE-GHINT", all powerful.

Now let us try and follow in detail how and who sponsors the Sun Dance.

The Medicine Man when asleep has vision, telling him to give a Sun Dance at a certain time.

He tells the TA-WAN-NEE-WUP, the crier, who in turn tells the people when, where the Sun Dance will be held and who will give the Sun Dance.

The moving day is also announced by the TA-WAN-NEE-WUP, the crier.

Now, there are four practice sessions of four nights of singing, with the Medicine Man and his assistant taking part in these rituals. The dance is done in three original parts.

1. The hunt.
2. Preparation for the "Making-the-Ground" sacred.
3. The dance of Thirst.

Going to the mountains the Medicine Man carries out the traditional ritual of the hunt. Stripping to the waist, the Medicine Man, and his helpers are painted white for purity.

Facing the east, the Medicine Man, with his helpers kneeling behind him in a semi-circle, four (songs) chants of prayers are sung, and four prayers are said.

They are given to the east, north, west, and south, because the four directions are true and square and from where all these directions have power (POAH) medicine.

A search for a large forked cottonwood tree takes the place of when once the hunt for buffalo took place long ago. The large forked cottonwood tree must be found for the center pole, for the Sun Dance lodge or hall. For the cottonwood lives after it is cut down and its new growth is a sign of ones life which goes on and on.

The pine tree is very old among all trees and promises the climb of man upwards. Twelve forked trees are cut for the circle. The number of these trees matching with the eagle tail feathers of the medicine man's vision.

Now the trees are carried down the mountains to the Shoshone Indian camp. The crier goes among the people, telling them to come and join in of "Making the Ground" sacred.

A rock is placed in the chosen site and a line drawn towards the rising sun from which the buffalo and the eagle brought their messages. In front of the center rock a tripod is set up representing the three spiritual fires will, form and energy. On this is placed eagle feathers, a bundle of willows, a sign for life and also a buffalo head facing the west. The large center forked pole has been placed some distance from the Sun Dance campgrounds. Next day a sham battle takes place. After the battle, the Medicine Man or someone who had killed an enemy would ride up to the center pole as if to kill, but only to poke it with his spear, then would tell of his adventure and then pray.

Loaded on a wagon, the center forked pole then was hauled to the Sun Dance site, with several chiefs riding in front of wagon, chanting which are migrating songs or chants. (These songs you've heard if you were paying attention.) Many braves followed the wagon, with willows bundled behind their saddles.

Then they get into camp, the people are waiting to watch and some to join the parade. All are dressed in their buckskin clothes, like you see in the 4th of July parade.

Later, the crier calls to the people to come and join in the preparation ceremonies. The large center pole is placed where the tripod stood. At each fork top a flag is tied, these are the colors of the medicine man and his helper. A bundle of willows, sweet sage, wild mint are placed and tied in the large cottonwood fork, as a sign of abundance or lots of luck, etc.

Below the fork is placed a buffalo head, its' nose filled with sweetsage representing the foul air exhaled by the buffalo in the first vision by the medicine man.

American Indian News 1, issue 2:5 (Aug. 10, 1977)

With a prayer for all the people on earth, the sickly and aging, the people in four chants. Lifting the large center pole four times and each time aloud war whoops could be heard some distance away, the center pole is raised and set in place. A large hole has been dug earlier in the day and several small ones for the small forked poles. The twelve forked poles are set about twelve places circling the center pole. The path pole is then carried in. One end is fastened to the center pole with the forked end tree toward the east. Eagle feathers are tied to its crotch. Then it becomes the first ridge pole and stands for life's path that each must follow with the choice of good or evil when you have grown to be a man or woman.

Small cottonwood trees are placed around on the outside of the Sun Dance hall. An opening is toward the east and this is the pathway. Now the days of preparation having ended the Medicine Man tells all who will take part in the Sun Dance to bathe, not only for clean body but for pure thoughts and feeling.

Now after the dancers have bathed, they are painted with much ritual or ceremony. Barefooted, stripped to the waist with different colored shawls. Each dancer has around his neck a whistle made from the hollow wing bone of the eagle a fluffy white eagle feather at the end, from his fingers hang soft, fluffy feathers of the sacred bird the eagle, BEYA QEENAH.

Now, those dancers wearing aprons are gifted or have healing powers and those with beaded breast plate around their necks on which is a white weasel hide, have special medicine or PO-AH earned by them in other Sun Dances.

When the evening star shines. The Crier, TA-WANEE-WUP, goes around the camp, telling the dancers and Medicine Man, and the people to come to the Sun Dance Hall for the "Dance of Thirst," is about to begin.

The Medicine Man (who is really the sponsor), and the dancers gather back and west of the Sun Dance lodge. In a single file, with their whistles blowing, the dancers circle the Sun Dance Hall three times. Now each time the dancer blows his whistle, he is praying for the earth to be clean and free from disease, like the air high, up where the eagle flies. The motion of the dancers is also a prayer, it is a prayer for life and action for a dead body does not move.

Separating at the entrance, the dancers take their positions or places to the west, south and north. Singers and drummers follow by the women, carrying willow batons. They seat themselves near the center pole for a prayer. A fire song is sung for the "keeper" of the sacred fire. Now the fire is lighted and the ritual that has connected the centuries together announces to the world that the "Dance of Thirst" has begun.

There are many reasons why the dancers are in this Sun Dance sometimes for family or personal health. But very often it is for special blessing, but always the dance is sacrificial. (To suffer the hardship of one's thirst and hunger for blessings.)[1] The dancers move back and forth, to the center pole with their eyes always on the buffalo head. Their whistles blowing in time with the singers and the drum.

There are special ceremonies during the entire Sun Dance. (The Sunrise Service is followed by the Fire Ritual of prayer.) Every morning before the sun rises, the dancers stand in row of two or three deep facing the east behind the center pole as the sun makes its appearance.

1. The first three sentences in this paragraph are taken from an unpublished version of St. Clair's article and do not appear in the serial publication.

When the sun comes out, the dancers blow shrill notes as the drummers chant louder. The dancers reach their hands upward and using the small white fluffy eagle feather, that is on their little finger, brush their bodies, for purity and blessing in life, for the light of the Great Spirit NAW NAW SOO WE GHINT, the all powerful has come.

Now all dancers are seated east of the center pole, around the fire. Four songs or chants are sung, with prayers by the Medicine Man.

American Indian News 1, 3:6, 7 (Aug. 7, 1977)

References

Blake, William
  1982 *The Complete Poetry and Prose of William Blake.* Edited by David V. Erdman. New York: Anchor Press/Doubleday.
Borst, Greg
  1975 "Within the Circle." *Sing Out* 24:5–10.
Brackett, Colonel Albert G.
  1879 "The Shoshonis, or Snake Indians, Their Religion, Superstitions, and Manners." In *Annual Report,* 328–33. Washington: Smithsonian Institution.
Collier, John
  1947 *Indians of the Americas.* New York: Mentor Books.
Deloria, Vine, Jr.
  1970 *Custer Died for Your Sins.* New York: Avon Books.
Densmore, Frances
  1918 *Teton Sioux Music.* Bureau of American Ethnology Bulletin, 61. Washington: Smithsonian Institution.
  1951 "Songs of the Sioux." Record notes for AFS L23. Washington: Library of Congress.
  1968 *Frances Densmore and American Indian Music.* Edited by Charles Hofmann. New York: Museum of the American Indian, Heye Foundation.
DeRiso, Michelle
  1968 "Female Activism among the Wind River Shoshone, 1966." Master's thesis, Department of Anthropology, University of Illinois.
Donne, John
  1952 *The Complete Poetry and Selected Prose of John Donne.* Edited by Charles M. Coffin. New York: Random House.
Farrer, Claire R.
  1980 "Singing for Life: The Mescalero Apache Girls' Puberty Ceremony." In *Southwestern Indian Ritual Drama,* edited by Charlotte J. Frisbie, 125–59. Albuquerque: University of New Mexico Press.
Feder, Norman
  1964 "Origin of the Oklahoma Forty-nine Dance." *Ethnomusicology* 8:290–94.
Fletcher, Alice C., and Francis LaFlesche
  [1905–6] 1972 *The Omaha Tribe.* Reprint. Lincoln: University of Nebraska Press.

Fryett, Thomas Jere
1977 "The Musical Culture of the Crow Indians in Montana." Ph.D. diss., Department of Music, University of Colorado.

Guild of the Holy Saints John and Audrey Ward, comps.
1973 "1883-1973 Shoshone (Episcopal Mission)." Ft. Washakie, Wyo.

Hatton, Thomas O. (1986 publication was under the name Orin T. Hatton)
1974 "Performance Practices of Northern Plains Pow-wow Singing Groups." *Yearbook for Inter-American Musical Research* 10:123-37.

1986 "In the Tradition: Grass Dance Musical Style and Female Pow-wow Singers." *Ethnomusicology* 30:197-222.

Hebard, Grace Raymond
1930 *Washakie.* Cleveland: Arthur H. Clark Co.

Herzog, George
1935a "Plains Ghost Dance and Great Basin Music." *American Anthropologist,* n.s. 37:403-19.

1935b "Special Song Types in North American Indian Music." *Zeitschrift für vergleichende Musikwissenschaft* 3:23-33.

Hinton, Leanne
1980 "Vocables in Havasupai Song." In *Southwestern Indian Ritual Drama,* edited by Charlotte J. Frisbie, 275-305. Albuquerque: University of New Mexico Press.

Hoebel, E. Adamson
1938 "Bands and Distributions of the Eastern Shoshone." *American Anthropologist,* n.s. 40:410-13.

Johnson, Thomas H.
1968 "The Wind River Shoshone Sun Dance: 1966 and 1967." Master's thesis, Department of Anthropology, University of Illinois.

1975 "The Enos Family and Wind River Shoshone Society: A Historical Analysis." Ph.D. diss., Department of Anthropology, University of Illinois.

Jorgensen, Joseph G.
1972 *The Sun Dance Religion.* Chicago: University of Chicago Press.

Koskoff, Ellen, ed.
1987 *Women and Music in Cross Cultural Perspective.* Contributions in Women's Studies, no. 79. New York: Greenwood Press.

Lakoff, George, and Mark Johnson
1980 *Metaphors We Live By.* Chicago: University of Chicago Press.

Laubin, Reginald, and Gladys Laubin
1977 *Indian Dances of North America.* Norman: University of Oklahoma Press.

Lord, Albert B.
1974 *The Singer of Tales.* New York: Atheneum.

Lowie, Robert H.
1909 "The Northern Shoshone." *Anthropological Papers of the American Museum of Natural History* 2, pt. 2:165-307.

1913 "Military Societies of the Crow Indians." *Anthropological Papers of the American Museum of Natural History* 11, pt. 3:143-217.

1915 "Dances and Societies of the Plains Shoshone." *Anthropological Papers of the American Museum of Natural History* 11:803–35.

1919 "The Sun Dance of the Wind River Shoshoni and Ute." *Anthropological Papers of the American Museum of Natural History* 16:387–410.

Lurie, Nancy Oestreich

1972 "Indian Women: A Legacy of Freedom." In *Look to the Mountaintop,* edited by Charles Jones, 29–36. San Jose: Gousha Publications.

McAllester, David P.

1949 *Peyote Music.* Viking Fund Publications in Anthropology, no. 13. New York: Viking Fund.

1984 "North America/Native America." In *Worlds of Music: An Introduction to the Music of the World's Peoples,* edited by Jeff Todd Titon, 12–63. New York: Schirmer Books.

Merriam, Alan P.

1967 *Ethnomusicology of the Flathead Indians.* Viking Fund Publications in Anthropology, no. 44. Chicago: Aldine Publishing Co.

Mooney, James

[1896] 1965 *The Ghost-Dance Religion and the Sioux Outbreak of 1890.* Reprint. Chicago: University of Chicago Press.

Murie, James R.

1914 "Pawnee Indian Societies." *Anthropological Papers of the American Museum of Natural History* 11, pt. 7:545–644.

Murray, Larry, ed.

n.d. "The Wind River Reservation Yesterday and Today."

Nettl, Bruno

1954 *North American Indian Musical Styles.* Philadelphia: American Folklore Society.

1967 "Studies in Blackfoot Indian Musical Culture," pt. 2. *Ethnomusicology* 11:293–309.

1983 *The Study of Ethnomusicology: Twenty-nine Issues and Concepts.* Urbana: University of Illinois Press.

Pantaleoni, Hewitt

1987 "One of Densmore's Dakota Rhythms Reconsidered." *Ethnomusicology* 31:35–55.

Peterson, Harold, ed.

1976 *I Wear the Morning Star: An Exhibition of American Indian Ghost Dance Objects.* Minneapolis: Minneapolis Institute of Arts.

Powers, Marla N.

1980 "Menstruation and Reproduction: An Oglala Case." In *Women: Sex and Sexuality,* edited by Catharine R. Stimpson and Ethel Spector Person, 117–28. Chicago: University of Chicago Press.

1986 *Oglala Women: Myth, Ritual and Reality.* Chicago: University of Chicago Press.

Powers, William

1961a "The Social Dances." *American Indian Tradition* 7, no. 3:97–104.

1961b "War Dance Songs." *American Indian Tradition* 7, no. 4:128–34.

1961c "The Contemporary Music and Dance of the Western Sioux." *American Indian Tradition* 7, no. 5:158–65.

1962 "Sneak-Up Dance, Drum Dance, Flag Dance." *American Indian Tradition* 8, no. 4:166–71.

1968 "Contemporary Oglala Music and Dance: Pan-Indianism versus Pan-Tetonism." *Ethnomusicology* 12:352–72.

1973 *Indians of the North Plains.* New York: G. P. Putnam's Sons.

1978 "Male Competition and Female Sexual Selection: An Ethnoethological Perspective on Dance." Paper presented at the meeting of the Society of Ethnomusicology held in St. Louis.

1979 "Structure and Function of the Vocable." Paper presented at the meeting of the Society for Ethnomusicology held in Montreal.

1980a "Oglala Song Terminology." In *Selected Reports in Ethnomusicology* 3, no. 2, edited by Charlotte Heth, 23–41. Los Angeles: Department of Music, University of California.

1980b "Plains Indian Music and Dance." In *Anthropology on the Great Plains,* edited by W. Raymond Wood and Margot Liberty, 212–29. Lincoln: University of Nebraska Press.

1982 *Yuwipi.* Lincoln: University of Nebraska Press.

1984 "Responses to Feld and Roseman." *Ethnomusicology* 28:458–61.

Robertson, Carol E.

1979 " 'Pulling the Ancestors': Performance Practice and Praxis in Mapuche Ordering." *Ethnomusicology* 23:395–416.

Sahlins, Marshall

1985 *Islands of History.* Chicago: University of Chicago Press.

St. Clair, Herman, and Lynn St. Clair

1977 "Shoshone Indian Religion." *American Indian News* 1, issues 1:5, 2:5, 3:6, 7. Ft. Washakie, Wyo.

Shimkin, D. B.

1938 "Psychological Aspects of the Wind River Shoshone Family." Ms.

1940 "Shoshone-Comanche Origins and Migrations." In *Proceedings of the Sixth Pacific Science Congress of the Pacific Science Association* 4:17–25. Berkeley: University of California Press.

1942 "Dynamics of Recent Wind River Shoshone History." *American Anthropologist,* n.s. 44:451–62.

1947a "Wind River Shoshone Ethnogeography." *Anthropological Records* 5, no. 4:245–88.

1947b "Childhood and Development among the Wind River Shoshone." *Anthropological Records* 5, no. 5:289–325.

1947c "Wind River Shoshone Literary Forms: An Introduction." *Journal of the Washington Academy of Sciences* 37, no. 10:320–52.

1949a "Shoshone, I: Linguistic Sketch and Text." *International Journal of American Linguistics* 15, no. 3:175–88.

1949b "Shoshone, II: Morpheme List." *International Journal of American Linguistics* 15, no. 4:203–12.

1953 "The Wind River Shoshone Sun Dance." *Anthropological Papers*

41:397–491. Bureau of American Ethnology Bulletin, 151. Washington: Smithsonian Institution.

1986   "Eastern Shoshone." In *Handbook of North American Indians,* edited by William C. Sturtevant. Vol. 11, *Great Basin,* edited by Warren L. D'Azevedo, 308–35. Washington: Smithsonian Institution.

Stenberg, Molly Peacock
1946   "The Peyote Culture among Wyoming Indians." *University of Wyoming Publications* 12, no. 4:89–156.

Tidzump, Malinda
1970   *Shoshone Thesaurus.* Grand Forks: Summer Institute of Linguistics, University of North Dakota.

Titon, Jeff Todd, general ed.
1984   *Worlds of Music: An Introduction to the Music of the World's Peoples.* New York: Schirmer Books.

Vander, Judith
1978   "A View of Wind River Shoshone Music through Four Ceremonies." Master's thesis, Department of Musicology-Ethnomusicology, University of Michigan.

1982   "The Song Repertoire of Four Shoshone Women: A Reflection of Cultural Movements and Sex Roles." *Ethnomusicology* 26:73–83.

1986   *Ghost Dance Songs and Religion of a Wind River Shoshone Woman.* Monograph Series in Ethnomusicology, no. 4. Los Angeles: University of California.

Vennum, Thomas, Jr.
1980   "A History of Ojibwa Song Form." In *Selected Reports in Ethnomusicology* 3, no. 2:42–75, edited by Charlotte Heth. Los Angeles: Department of Music, University of California.

1982   *The Ojibwa Dance Drum.* Smithsonian Folklife Studies, no. 2. Washington: Smithsonian Institution.

1986   "Music." In *Handbook of North American Indians,* edited by William C. Sturtevant. Vol. 11, *Great Basin,* edited by Warren L. D'Azevedo, 682–702. Washington: Smithsonian Institution.

Voget, Fred
1948   "Individual Motivation in the Diffusion of the Wind River Shoshone Sundance to the Crow Indians." *American Anthropologist,* n.s. 50:634–46.

1953   "Current Trends in the Wind River Shoshone Sun Dance." *Anthropological Papers* 42:485–99. Bureau of American Ethnology Bulletin, 151. Washington: Smithsonian Institution.

1984   *The Shoshoni-Crow Sun Dance.* Norman: University of Oklahoma Press.

Weeks, Rupert
1981   *Pachee Goyo.* Laramie, Wyo.: Jelm Mountain Press.

Wilson, Gilbert L.
1914   "Reports, Hidatsa-Mandan 1914 Gilbert Wilson Papers." Division of the Archives and Manuscripts, 16. Minnesota Historical Society. In Vennum 1982:55.

Wissler, Clark

1912a "Ceremonial Bundles of the Blackfoot Indians." *Anthropological Papers of the American Museum of Natural History* 7, pt. 2:65–298.

1912b "Societies and Ceremonial Associations in the Oglala Division of the Teton-Dakota." *Anthropological Papers of the American Museum of Natural History* 11, pt. 1:3–99.

1913 "Societies and Dance Associations of the Blackfoot Indians." *Anthropological Papers of the American Museum of Natural History* 11, pt. 4:361–474.

1916 "General Discussion of Shamanistic and Dancing Societies." *Anthropological Papers of the American Museum of Natural History* 11:853–76.

Young, Gloria Alese

1981 "Powwow Power: Perspectives on Historic and Contemporary Intertribalism." Ph.D. diss., Department of Anthropology, Indiana University.

Index

male musical roles in, 40, 43; meaning of, 46–47, 126, 143. *See also* Grass Dance; War Dance

Wolf Dance songs: dissemination of, 43; drum accents in, 42; drum-vocal relationship, 42; form and melodic range of, 42; half step intervals in, 42; male musical roles in, 40, 48; meaning of, 46; recordings of, 43; rhythmic organization of, 41–42; tempo of, 43. *See also* War Dance songs
— transcriptions of: no. 1, 40–41; no. 2, 42–43

Women and the Native American Church, 109–10

Women's All-Indian Basketball Tournament, 198

Women's Dance, 46 (6–7); dissemination of, 36; history and description of, 35–37, 71, 113, 171–74; lady's choice for, 263–64; male payment for, 76, 114, 172; musical roles for men and women, 36, 43. *See also* Round Dance

Women's Dance songs: drum-vocal relationship, 38, 39; form of, 38; hand drum for, 37, 175–77; history of, 35–37; learning and dissemination of, 36–37; rhythmic organization of, 38, 39. *See also* Round Dance songs
— transcriptions of: no. 1, 37; no. 2 (Goodnight Sweetheart), 39; no. 3, 40; no. 4 (Goodnight Sweetheart), 71

Women's dress, 97, 113–14, 173, 174

Women's Handgame songs, 83

Women's Handgames, 95

Women's musical role models, 123, 124, 203. *See also* Musical role models

Women's musical roles, 49–50, 90–91, 117–18, 193–94, 283–85; for Chokecherry and Giveaway ceremonies, 87; as complement to men's, xvi, 65, 291; dream of Sun Dance song, 104; as drummers, 125; female drum group, 207; "finishing" songs, 163; for Fourth Morning Prayer song, 290; gossip as inhibit-

ing factor of, 78; group context of, 98; in Handgame songs, 186; of Helene Furlong, 124; the "lady's" part, 86, 207, 209, 235–36; of Lenore Shoyo, 195; male-female singing roles, 161–63, 194, 263; new, xvi, 125, 226, 281, 282, 283–84; in nineteenth-century dances, 44; at old communal dances, 171–72; for older women, 49; in Omaha or Grass Dance, 45; partners for Round Dance, 76; and Peyote song taboos, 140; in private, 10, 34, 140, 163, 291; in public, 32, 57, 65, 98, 125, 291; in the Round Dance, 71, 81; in Round Dance songs, 73; singing at powwow, 77–78; in the Sun Dance, 101, 102, 107, 107n, 137, 138, 213; in Sun Dance ensemble, 30, 31, 32, 33; taboos and, 81; in transition, 221; in twentieth century, 291–92; in War Bonnet ceremony, 86, 87, 117, 188–89; in the War Dance, 48–49, 116, 122; in War Dance songs, 81, 124, 161–62, 235; War Dancing pioneer in, 196; for younger women, 49, 291–92. *See also individual song genres*

Women's powwow dress, 113

Women's role models, Euro-American, 124

Women's roles: Angelina Wagon's understanding of, 54–55; increase of for young, 223–24, 291–92; Lenore Shoyo's understanding of, 202; in marriage, 55; in Native American Church, 109–10; postreservation, 4; prereservation, 3, 7; in Sun Dance, 65. *See also* Gender roles; learning

Women's song (Handgame song no. 1), 83

Women's Traditional Dance contest, 97

Women's ululation, 65

Women's war whoop, 136

Work ethic, Shoshone, 54, 200

Wyoming Indian High School, 122, 197, 199

Yellow Bangs Society, 44, 131, 189

Yoriki, 179

Note on the Recording

I have prepared a one-hour cassette recording of a selection of songs discussed in *Songprints*. Because this tape represents only a fraction of the music in the book, I have deposited a complete tape at the Library of Congress and the Archives of Traditional Music of Indiana University for those who wish to hear all the songs.

As with all field tapes, the musical recordings I have made of the women include some extraneous sounds of the recording environment — such things as movement near the mike, birds, people talking, a clock, electric appliances, and so on. All performances are complete with the exception of Forty-nine Dance song no. 2. To fit this final song on to the tape, it was necessary to omit the first two verses. Thus, what appears as verse 2 is actually verse 4, transcribed on pp. 274–75. Despite these minor imperfections, I believe the accompanying tape richly testifies to the vibrant singing and musical personalities of the women. The following songs are included on the tape:

SIDE 1

Song	Transcription	Singer(s)	Recording Date
Naraya no. 2	p. 17	Emily and Dorothy	8/8/1977
Naraya no. 5	pp. 19–20	Emily	7/12/1978
Naraya no. 10	p. 25	Emily and Dorothy	8/8/1977
Naraya no. 11	p. 26	Emily and Dorothy	8/8/1977
Women's Dance no. 1	p. 37	Emily	8/8/1977
Women's Dance no. 2	p. 39	Emily	7/8/1978
Wolf Dance no. 1	pp. 40–41	Emily	6/29/1979
Naraya no. 13	p. 63	Angie	9/18/1981
Round Dance no. 8	p. 75	Angie	9/22/1981
War Dance no. 5	pp. 81–82	Angie	9/22/1981
Handgame no. 1	p. 83	Angie	9/22/1981
Miss Ross's Hymn	p. 88	Angie	9/18/1981
Flag Song no. 1	pp. 148–49	Helene and Wayland	8/17/1977

SIDE 2

Song	Transcription	Singer(s)	Recording Date
War Dance no. 7	pp. 154–55	Helene and Wayland	7/10/1978
War Dance no. 8	pp. 158–61	Helene and Wayland	8/24/1981
War Dance no. 9	pp. 166–68	Helene and Wayland	8/26/1981
Round Dance no. 11	pp. 174–75	Helene and Wayland	8/17/1977
Handgame no. 10	p. 181	Helene	8/24/1981
Handgame no. 12	p. 183	Helene	8/24/1981
"Humpty-Dumpty Heart"	p. 191	Helene	8/24/1981
Honor Song for Bird Woman	pp. 224–25	Lenore	9/19/1981
War Dance no. 12	pp. 236–37	Lenore	9/16/1981
War Dance no. 18	pp. 250–51	Lenore, Coleen, JoAnn, and Linda Shoyo	7/11/1978
Round Dance no. 16	pp. 267–68	Lenore	9/23/1981
Round Dance no. 17	pp. 269–70	Lenore, Lottie, Coleen, JoAnn, Maxine, and Evalita Shoyo	10/7/1983
Forty-nine Dance no. 2 (verses 3–5)	pp. 274–75	Lenore	9/23/1981

Books in the Series Music in American Life

Resources of American Music History: A Directory of Source Materials
from Colonial Times to World War II
D. W. Krummel, Jean Geil, Doris J. Dyen, and Deane L. Root

Tenement Songs: The Popular Music of the Jewish Immigrants
Mark Slobin

Ozark Folksongs
Vance Randolph; edited and abridged by Norm Cohen

Oscar Sonneck and American Music
Edited by William Lichtenwanger

Bluegrass Breakdown: The Making of the Old Southern Sound
Robert Cantwell

Bluegrass: A History
Neil V. Rosenberg

Music at the White House: A History of the American Spirit
Elise K. Kirk

Red River Blues: The Blues Tradition in the Southeast
Bruce Bastin

Good Friends and Bad Enemies: Robert Winslow Gordon and
the Study of American Folksong
Debora Kodish

Fiddlin' Georgia Crazy: Fiddlin' John Carson, His Real World,
and the World of His Songs
Gene Wiggins

America's Music: From the Pilgrims to the Present (Revised Third Edition)
Gilbert Chase

Secular Music in Colonial Annapolis: The Tuesday Club, 1745–56
John Barry Talley

Bibliographical Handbook of American Music
D. W. Krummel

Goin' to Kansas City
Nathan W. Pearson, Jr.

"Susanna," "Jeanie," and "The Old Folks at Home": The Songs of Stephen
C. Foster from His Time to Ours (Second Edition)
William W. Austin

Songprints: The Musical Experience of Five Shoshone Women
Judith Vander

"Happy in the Service of the Lord": Afro-American Gospel Quartets
in Memphis
Kip Lornell

Paul Hindemith in the United States
Luther Noss

"My Song Is My Weapon": People's Songs, American Communism, and
the Politics of Culture, 1930–50
Robbie Lieberman

Chosen Voices: The Story of the American Cantorate
Mark Slobin

Theodore Thomas: America's Conductor and Builder of Orchestras,
1835–1905
Ezra Schabas

"The Whorehouse Bells Were Ringing" and Other Songs Cowboys Sing
Guy Logsdon

Crazeology: The Autobiography of a Chicago Jazzman
Bud Freeman, as Told to Robert Wolf

Discoursing Sweet Music: Brass Bands and Community Life in
Turn-of-the-Century Pennsylvania
Kenneth Kreitner

Mormonism and Music: A History
Michael Hicks

Voices of the Jazz Age: Profiles of Eight Vintage Jazzmen
Chip Deffaa

Pickin' on Peachtree: A History of Country Music in Atlanta, Georgia
Wayne W. Daniel

Bitter Music: Collected Journals, Essays, Introductions, and Librettos
Harry Partch; edited by Thomas McGeary

Ethnic Music on Records: A Discography of Ethnic Recordings Produced in
the United States, 1893 to 1942
Richard K. Spottswood

Downhome Blues Lyrics: An Anthology from the Post–World War II Era
Jeff Todd Titon

Ellington: The Early Years
Mark Tucker

Chicago Soul
Robert Pruter

That Half-Barbaric Twang: The Banjo in American Popular Culture
Karen Linn

Hot Man: The Life of Art Hodes
Art Hodes and Chadwick Hansen

The Erotic Muse: American Bawdy Songs (Second Edition)
Ed Cray

Barrio Rhythm: Mexican American Music in Los Angeles
Steven Loza